Transnational Communities in the Smartphone Age

Korean Communities across the World

Series Editor: Joong-Hwan Oh, Hunter College, CUNY

Korean Communities across the World publishes works that address aspects of (a) the Korean American community, (b) Korean society, (c) the Korean communities in other foreign lands, or (d) transnational Korean communities. In the field of (a) the Korean American community, this series welcomes contributions involving concepts such as Americanization, pluralism, social mobility, migration/immigration, social networks, social institutions, social capital, racism/discrimination, settlement, identity, or politics, as well as a specific topic related to family/marriage, gender roles, generations, work, education, culture, citizenship, health, ethnic community, housing, ethnic identity, racial relations, social justice, social policy, and political views, among others. In the field of (b) Korean society, this series embraces scholarship on current issues such as gender roles, age/aging, low fertility, immigration, urbanization, gentrification, economic inequality, high youth unemployment, sexuality, democracy, political power, social injustice, the nation's educational problems, social welfare, capitalism, consumerism, labor, health, housing, crime, environmental degradation, and the social life in the digital age and its impacts, among others. Contributors in the field of (c) Korean communities in other foreign lands are encouraged to submit works that expand our understanding about the formation, vicissitudes, and major issues of an ethnic Korean community outside of South Korea and the Unites States, such as cultural or linguistic retention, ethnic identity, assimilation, settlement patterns, citizenship, economic activities, family relations, social mobility, and racism/discrimination. Lastly, contributions relating to (d) transnational Korean communities may touch upon transnational connectivity in family, economy/finance, politics, culture, technology, social institutions, and people.

Transnational Communities in the Smartphone Age: The Korean Community in the Nation's Capital, by Dae Young Kim

Transnational Communities in the Smartphone Age

The Korean Community in the Nation's Capital

Dae Young Kim

LEXINGTON BOOKS
Lanham • Boulder • New York • London

Published by Lexington Books
An imprint of The Rowman & Littlefield Publishing Group, Inc.
4501 Forbes Boulevard, Suite 200, Lanham, Maryland 20706
www.rowman.com

Unit A, Whitacre Mews, 26-34 Stannary Street, London SE11 4AB

British Library Cataloguing in Publication Information Available

Library of Congress Cataloging-in-Publication Data Available

ISBN 978-1-4985-4175-6 (cloth: alk. paper)
ISBN 978-1-4985-4176-3 (electronic)

∞™ The paper used in this publication meets the minimum requirements of American National Standard for Information Sciences—Permanence of Paper for Printed Library Materials, ANSI/NISO Z39.48-1992.

Printed in the United States of America

Contents

Acknowledgments

This book, like any other scholarly endeavor, is the result of innumerable debts owed to colleagues, friends, family, and research participants. While I cannot list everyone who has provided some help during the course of the project, I want to acknowledge a number of people who have been critical in making this book possible. First, many thanks go to our Saturday Washington-Baltimore study group. We first formed this group with Dr. Okyun Kwon and several Korean graduate students (who are all doctorates now) in late 2000, including Chang Won Lee, Jihyun Kim, Jee Hye Kang, Young A. Jung, and Gyu Tag Lee. Dr. Young Bae from Sung Sil University in South Korea also joined our group when he was at George Mason University's Korean studies as a visiting scholar. We met either monthly or bi-monthly at a Korean bakery in Rockville (Shilla Bakery) or in Centreville (Jireh Bakery), discussing for hours the research question, the theoretical and empirical literature, the interview guide, and data analysis, among others. What is unique about this study group is that it was all a voluntary effort from everyone who saw much need for a scholarly study of the Korean community in the Washington-Baltimore metropolitan area. Without their time and effort, including in-depth interviews with community leaders and long-time residents, this project would have not seen the light of day and also would have lacked the qualitative component of the data that was used for examining the transnational activities of Korean Americans. I thank them all not only for the help they provided in each step of the research process, but more importantly, for the collegiality that was formed from numerous discussions over coffee and Korean bakery. Though several of the members have returned to Korea after completing their PhD, we recently started an email and Kakao Talk group discussion which I hope will help us stay connected, sustaining our transnational ties for years to come. In addition, I want to thank the interviewees who took time from their busy schedules to meet with us, providing us with a wealth of information about their experiences in the Washington-Baltimore region.

Finally, I am grateful to Sarah Craig, associate acquisitions editor at Lexington Books, for her help, guidance, and patience throughout the course of the publication process, making sure at the same time I was keeping up with the deadlines. I would like to acknowledge and thank Dr. Joong-Hwan Oh for starting a new series on Korean Communities across the World with Lexington Books, accepting my title as the first monograph in the series, which will bring together under one roof timely research studies of Korean communities across the world as well as studies focusing on Korean society. My colleague Rutledge Dennis deserves special recognition for kindly reading several drafts of the chapters and offering helpful comments. Last but not least, I want to thank Hyun Mee Chae and my two children, Ryan and Brandon, for their support and patience as I endeavored to complete the manuscript.

Introduction

Transnational Ties and Their Impact on the Korean Community

In 1972, a three-minute long-distance telephone call to Korea was roughly $12 (Min 1998, 108); today the same land line call costs less than ten cents per minute, while calls using calling cards are as little as two to three cents per minute.[1] Trans-pacific flights connecting Gimpo Airport with major cities in the United States, including the Los Angeles International Airport (LAX), first started in 1972 via Korean Air (KAFGW 2009, 35), were also scarce and irregular.[2] Today, not only are there daily, nonstop flights to Korea from Los Angeles, but also in metropolitan areas with sizable Korean populations, including New York, Washington, D.C., Atlanta, Dallas, and Seattle, new routes have sharply expanded the number of flights between the two nations.[3]

Prior to the late 1990s, ethnic programming from South Korea (hereafter Korea), namely Korean television soap operas (hereafter Korean dramas), variety shows, and news, took weeks to arrive for restless immigrants seeking a small taste of home. Brought by enterprising co-ethnic merchants in video shops, television programming from Korean networks (MBC, KBS, SBS) were copied in bulk into VHS and rented for a small fee. Fast forward to 2017, local cable television providers such as Comcast or Cox, or satellite providers such as Dish Network have in most cases displaced video rental shops of the past and are now broadcasting the latest programming from Korea, which airs not only daily Korean news (in real time via satellite), dramas, and television shows, but also local Korean community news. Another major development is free or subscription-based websites (Kiwidisk.com, Joovideo.com, or OndemandKorea.com) that allow users to download or stream Korean programming within hours after being aired in Korea.[4]

During the early phase of Korean immigration in the 1960s and 1970s when there were only a handful of Korean groceries or restaurants in key immigrant destinations, many families struggled to find essential ingredients for preparing Korean meals or eating out in a familiar ethnic setting.[5] For example, according to an old-timer, key ingredients for making *kimchi* such as Nappa cabbage and ground red pepper were hard to find, having to either grow the cabbage locally or order them in bulk from farms in California. Since the explosion of the Korean population in the 1980s and 1990s in old and new immigration gateways such as Los Angeles, New York, and Washington, D.C., mega Korean supermarkets such as H-Mart, Lotte, Grand Mart, and Fresh World have mushroomed throughout the Washington-Baltimore region (and elsewhere), offering every conceivable consumer item sold in the home country, including frozen fish, dried vegetables, *ramyun* (*ramen*) noodles, and ice cream, to name a few. Even live fish used for sushi and sashimi are flown in weekly to co-ethnic customers seeking the latest Korean food craze. Familiar food products, ranging from Korean pears, grapes, ginseng, and dates to dumplings, are also imported, adding to a growing list of staple consumer items sold in Korean supermarkets. Moreover, seeking to capture new markets and customers, provinces in Korea (*Gyeongsang, Jeolla, Gangwon*) regularly showcase and promote regional food products during various food festivals held in many mega Korean supermarkets.[6] And to the delight of many Koreans in small towns and cities without international supermarkets, brick and mortar retailers such as Costco and Internet giants such as Amazon have begun to offer a wide variety of Korean consumer goods, including Korean *ramyun* noodles, *kimchi*, and even frozen mackerel (from CJ corporation).[7]

Globalization and changing technology, in particular huge advances in transportation and communication, have indeed made the world a smaller and connected place, as global integration through trade and investment enables growing numbers of people to visit, call, and consume products from the homeland more cheaply, quickly, and abundantly. Globalization, namely the increasing interconnectedness and interdependence of the world (Chanda 2007; Dickens 2011; Steger 2009), is allowing more people around the world, but particularly immigrants, to sustain deeper ties and engage more actively with the homeland. But as many commentators on globalization and transnationalism observe, these long-lasting contacts and ties with the home country by migrants have always existed, albeit in a different form and speed, among immigrants of the past, including letters to their loved ones, home visits via steamships, and participation in homeland politics (Baily 1999; Foner 1997, 2005; Portes 2001; Portes and Rumbaut 2014; Vertovec 2007; Waldinger 1997). What is different and striking about today's transnational connections, however, is the *speed*, *ease*, and *volume* with which these activities are conducted by immigrants from all walks of life (Chanda 2007; Foner 2005; Ritzer 2012; Vertovec 2007). Not only is it cheaper to fly and call home than before, but also key innovations in communication, particularly the Internet and smartphones, are enabling migrants to also email, text message (via mobile phones and apps such as Kakao Talk, Line, and WhatsApp), and video chat (Skype, Facetime, MS messenger, Kakao Talk) with family members and friends in real time, resulting in an unprecedented compression of space and time that makes dual lives more *possible*, *accessible*, and *regular*.[8]

For instance, consider visits to the homeland. Up until recently home country visits were, for the most part, a bi-annual or even less frequent affair due to steep costs in airfare and time commitment. Today, with daily nonstop flights and inexpensive air travel, visiting the home country can be possible at a fraction of the cost and at regular intervals even for countries thousands of miles away from the United States. While cost is still a major consideration in the frequency of travels to countries separated by twelve to fourteen hours of jet travel, the sheer number of flights means that one can *theoretically* work in the homeland and visit family members back "home" over the weekend. For example, if one can afford the $1600–2000 round-trip ticket and bear the twelve-hour trans-pacific flight from Los Angeles or San Francisco, or the grueling fourteen-hour flight from New York or Washington, D.C., middle- and upper-class Korean families can presumably have the fathers hold on to their professional careers in Korea, while the wives raise and send children to school in the American suburbs on the opposite end of the globe.[9] In this real-life scenario of the *girogi* or "wild-geese" families, Korean fathers fly home to the United States on weekends to spend precious family time with wives and children and return to their daily grind, albeit traveling thousands of miles, to their jobs in Korea on weekdays.[10]

Another distinguishing feature of Korean Americans' transnational activities and ties with the home country in an increasingly connected world, although this is equally true for other immigrant communities, is access to and increased consumption of homeland media products and consumer goods, such as Korean news, dramas, variety shows, food products, and housewares, in real time or close to it. First and foremost, many consumer items purchased and consumed daily by thousands of families in Korea can be equally consumed by Korean immigrants living in America. Through the auspices of enterprising co-ethnic merchants and Korean conglomerates, numerous consumer goods from Korea can be acquired at similar or at slightly higher prices in Korean supermarkets. It is probably due to this feature of contemporary life that many in the Korean community express the often-heard cliché of immigrating to America, expecting culture shock, but finding that their lives remain unchanged despite moving to a new country. Imagine, for instance, a Korean American living in any of the three largest Korean communities in the country: Los Angeles, New York, or Washington, D.C. This individual may drive a Hyundai Sonata to work, listen to *Gangnam Style* (or the latest K-Pop sensation) while driving, come home and tune in to Korean

Broadcasting System (KBS) for news, variety shows, and dramas on their Samsung LCD TV, talk to their Korean American friends using LG smartphones, call or text message via Kakao Talk to family members and friends in Korea, attend an all Korean American Presbyterian congregation on Sunday, shop for *Shin Ramyun*, CJ frozen mackerel, Orion choco pies, Maxim coffee mix at H-Mart, cook rice on their Cuckoo rice cooker purchased from Best Buy, meet friends for dinner at *Vitgoeul Soondubu* (Korean Tofu restaurant) in Centreville, VA, drink *Jinro soju* (national alcoholic beverage), OB beer, and *Pochun makoli* (Korean rice wine) and head out for even more fun at the Korean *noraebang* (singing room). The next day, after coming home from school, in the hopes of enhancing their academic competitiveness, children are promptly dropped off to C-2 Academy (Korean-owned *hagwon* or cram school) for more intensive Korean-style education.

In this increasing incursion of ethnicity and transnationalism into the lives of immigrants as revolutions in transportation and information and communication technologies (ICT) expand the scope and speed of transnational engagement, it is ever more possible to simultaneously participate and share in the norms and practices of their counterparts in the home country through the consumption of homeland cultural products and consumer goods.[11] As a result, in light of the far-reaching consequences of the Internet and smartphones on human communication and behavior, questions arise as to how extensively immigrants like Koreans actually *engage* in transnational activities with the home country. Is changing technology indeed shrinking the constraints of time and space for immigrants separated by vast distances? And how is such globalization and rising transnational ties impacting the Korean community of old-timers in the Washington-Baltimore region as well as in other Korean communities across the nation?

This book examines the history and evolution of the Korean community in the greater Washington-Baltimore metropolitan region through the lens of globalization and transnationalism. These two concepts have been buzz words in the scholarly community, generating a vast theoretical and empirical literature on the topic. While there has been extensive research on migrant transnationalism, it has focused mostly on the economic and political transnational activities of Latino immigrants. Few have examined the transnational practices of middle-class Asian immigrants, especially their cultural transnational activities (Min 2012). Second, while the Korean community has been the subject of much scholarly attention, in particular Korean immigrant entrepreneurship and Korean-black conflicts, and important monographs covering Korean communities in major immigration gateways such as Los Angeles, New York, and Chicago exist, there is, to date, no major study of the Korean community in the greater Washington, D.C. region despite its status as the third largest Korean community in the country. Furthermore, few studies have focused on the transnational activities and ties of Korean immigrants, especially in light of changing technology and transnational media which enable increased social and cultural engagement with the homeland. In this book, I consider the impact of growing transnational activities and ties with the home country made possible by changing technology, particularly the Internet, smartphones, and television, on the lives of long-time and more recent immigrants in the Washington-Baltimore region.

As I will explain later, this approach offers a unique view on the particular transition confronting the immigrant community of old-timers, as generational and cohort changes and a radical shrinking of space and time in the digital age are bringing substantial transformations to the Korean community. For instance, the community established by long-time, first-generation members is experiencing dramatic demographic shifts as many members of that cohort have either retired or are in the process of doing so. In their place, 1.5 and second-generation adult children of the 1960s and 1970s cohort are coming of age and establishing their own families, many of them raising and sending their 2.5- and 3.0-generation children to school.[12] Further contributing to this demographic shift heightening Korean Americans' transnational ties with the home country is the influx of new cohorts of Korean immigrants who began to enter and join the community since the late 1990s. Although immigration from Korea began to slow down after the peak periods in the 1970–1979 and 1980–1989 decades, Koreans have continued to immigrate throughout the 1990–1999 and 2000–2009 periods. For example, according to the 2015 Department of Homeland Security (DHS) immigration statistics, while only 27,048 Koreans obtained lawful permanent resident (LPR) status during the 1960–1969 period, 241,192 and 322,808 Koreans obtained LPR status during the 1970–1979 and 1980–1989 periods respectively, jumping roughly tenfold since the 1960–1969 period.[13]

For this new cohort, a transnational orientation is not only a normative feature of their lives but also one which carries added significance given their pursuit of flexible or instrumental citizenship (Ong 1999). To this cohort shift must also be added the globalization of the Korean economy since the 1990s, which has spurred a new trend in temporary migrations to the United States, including tourists, foreign students, business travelers, *girogi* families, and undocumented immigrants.

In short, a major goal of this book is to make sense of the changes unfolding in the community through the lens of transnationalism, globalization, and new ICT and also to fill an important gap in the study of migrant transnationalism by investigating the evolution and transition of a middle-class immigrant community in an understudied new immigration gateway. This will be accomplished by drawing on the most current demographic and socioeconomic information from the latest U.S. Census and other publically available

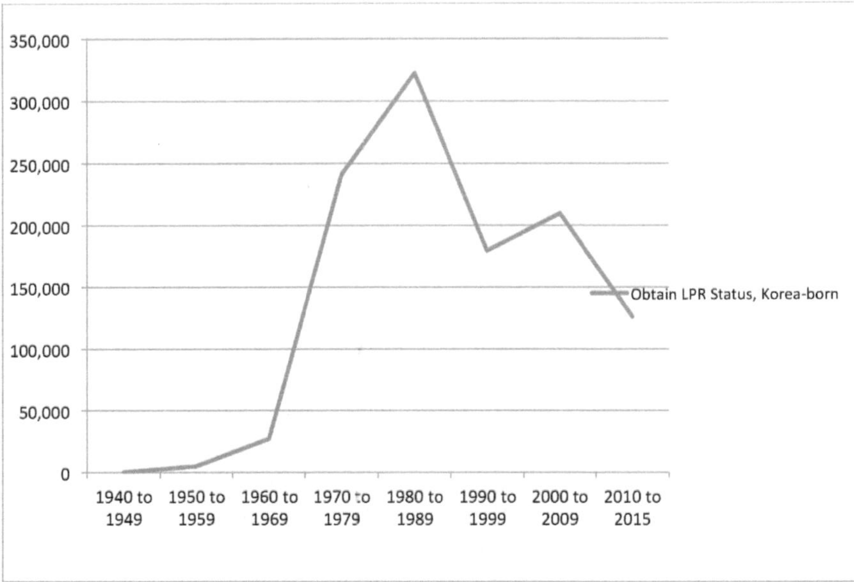

Figure 0.1 Persons obtaining lawful permanent resident status, Korea-born, 1940–2015, Department of Homeland Security. *Source*: Department of Homeland Security, Excel Files on LPR.

data sets, secondary data sources, and synthesis of scholarly literature on transnationalism, ICT, and transnational media/television.

SCHOLARSHIP ON TRANSNATIONALISM

In past scholarly studies of immigration and assimilation, research were driven mostly by questions of newcomers' adaptation and integration into the host society. Immigrants were essentially viewed as uprooting themselves from the home country in order to establish lasting roots in the receiving country (Baily 1999; Foner 1997, 2005; Vertovec 2007). New scholarship on transnationalism, examining in particular post-1960s immigrants' transnational ties, however, began to challenge many of the old assimilationist assumptions of immigration and integration by noting the enduring ties of migrants with the home country. Theorizing migration from a transnational perspective, Basch, Glick Schiller, and Szanton Blanc (1994; 6), one of the first scholars to observe and conceptualize these transnational connections, came to define transnationalism as the "process by which immigrants forge and sustain multistranded social relations that link together their societies of origin and settlement." They add that those who maintain active links and construct social fields constitute transmigrants, namely those that "develop and maintain multiple relations—familial, economic, social, organizational, religious, and political—that span borders" (Glick Schiller et al. 1992, 1).

Following this seminal study, scholars from diverse fields and disciplines began to document and reinterpret the myriad transnational activities of contemporary and past immigrants (Duany 2011; Foner 2005; Hsu 2000; Kyle 2000; Levitt 2001b; Smith 2006; Vertovec 2007). Historians, for example, began to refocus their attention on migrant connections with the home country, including home visits, letters, remittances, gifts, and return migration, bringing to light the mutual influences of the receiving and sending country in the lives of migrants. Anthropological studies such as Levitt's (2001b) study of the Dominican community in Boston drove this point home by showing how Dominican migrants maintained regular and durable contacts with the home country through the exchange of goods, news, and information. According to Levitt (2001b, 6–8), such active engagements of Dominican Americans with the home country gave rise to "transmigrants," or those who regularly engaged in cross-border activities, creating a transnational social field that linked sending countries with receiving countries. In the process, social remittances were generated as migrants and nonmigrants came to mutually influence each other via the continuous circulation of ideas, behavior, and social capital.

But why do immigrants, instead of focusing their energies on the receiving society, seek to activate and sustain these ties with the home country? Among others, the globalization of production and consumption, in particular the acceleration, intensification, and expansion of cross-border flows of goods, ideas, capital, and people, has resulted in uneven economic development, producing both opportunities and insecurities and hardship for millions of people around the world (Chanda 2008; Dicken 1998; Steger 2009). In response to these uncertainties, migrants have pursued transnationalism from below, or cross-border activities at the grassroots level to offset downward mobility (Guarnizo and Smith 1998, 5; Wong and Satzewich 2006). But the globalizing actions of states seeking to extend state authority and influence over its emigrants, on the one hand, and MNCs seeking to expand production and consumption globally, on the other, namely transnationalism from above, have also encouraged migrant transnationalism (Sklair 2001; Vertovec 2007). For example, as many sending governments have come to recognize the value of emigrants' economic, social, and political contributions to the home country, they have sought to strengthen homeland ties by granting dual citizenship, by extending the franchise, and by offering other benefits (Foner 2005, 74–75; Portes and Rumbaut 2014, 174; Waldinger 2015).

Similarly, receiving countries are also facilitating a transnational turn among migrants as governments abandon strict assimilationist policies (Americanization) of the past, which forced immigrants to cut off ties with the home country and focus on acculturation and assimilation into the host culture. Instead, with increased recognition of and support for multiculturalism and diversity in host societies, immigrants today seek to maintain their ethnic distinctiveness and ties with the home country (Foner 2005; Levitt 2001b; Smith 2006, 9; Wong and Satzewich 2006), enabling them to participate in the economic, political, social, and cultural affairs of their home country as members of that state, even though they have been dispersed or "deterritorialized" (Basch et al. 1994). In short, as Wong and Satzewich (2006, 8) observe, immigrants' ties to the homeland, whether regular, intermittent, or none, depend in part on whether the host society punishes, promotes, or tolerates transnational ties with the home country. For example, the internment and deportation of Japanese Americans during World War II, according to Wong and Satzewich (2006, 8), was in part an effort to discourage transnational ties and communities for fear of threats to national security. Yet, as Faist (2000, 219) observes, despite public fears of immigrant betrayal, dual loyalties were usually not a problem except during wars.

In a world becoming ever smaller as a result of communication and transportation revolutions, complete assimilation may not be desirable nor possible for contemporary immigrants. From a transnational perspective, as globalization renders single national attachments outmoded and immigrants become less confined to the nation-state (Basch et al. 1994), it is no surprise that migrants wish to pursue opportunities both at home and abroad. In their effort to maximize opportunities in multiple places, immigrants retain fluid identities, allegiances, and social networks. These transformations, however, affect groups and generations differently, with the immigrant generation continuing to participate materially and emotionally with their country of origin, while the second generation, whose attachments generally lie with the host society, become less oriented and more disconnected from their parents' country of origin. What remains to be seen is why and under what conditions later generations of immigrants come to reactivate their homeland ties, and whether sense of home, belonging, and identity is seriously impacted by renewed transnationalism.

DEBATES ON TRANSNATIONALISM

The widespread scholarly interest and research on transnationalism has generated a lively debate on the novelty and pervasiveness of the phenomenon (Basch et al. 1994; Foner 1997, 2005; Jones-Correa 1998; Levitt 2001b; Portes et al. 1999; Vertovec 2007; Waldinger 1997). Duany (2011, 17) notes that "persistent problems plague the field of transnationalism, including the operational definition of the concept; the classification of various types; the explanation of its causes and consequences; its alleged novelty; its relationship with assimilation; and its future beyond the first generation of immigrants." For many critics, the concept of transnationalism fails to represent or depict a new reality, or provide new insights, since immigrants of the past had also engaged in a variety of transnational activities (Foner 1997, 2005; Portes et al. 2002, 281; Vertovec 2007; Waldinger 2007). For instance, immigrants at the turn of the twentieth century were actively involved in the economic and political affairs of the home country. Not only did they maintain close ties with family, relatives, and friends through letters, telegrams, gifts, remittances, and occasional visits to the home country, but many of them also did eventually return home after a period of sojourn in the receiving country (Baily 1999; Foner 1997, 2005). Nonetheless, as Portes et al. (2002) are quick to recognize, due to unparalleled innovations in transportation and telecommunication, the *scope* and *intensity* of contemporary transnationalism have indeed changed, producing a qualitatively different transnational experience compared to those of past immigrants. Furthermore, a transnational perspective of migration is still useful for drawing attention to long-lasting linkages of immigrants with the home country since the speed, frequency, and volume with which capital, commodities, information, and people travel across national borders has triggered transnationalism from below as well as from above (Portes et al. 1999; Smith and Guarnizo 1998).

Another major criticism from those skeptical of transnationalism is migrants' actual participation in homeland activities. According to critics, few immigrants actually engage in sustained and regular transnational ties with the home country (Jones-Correa 1998; Waldinger 1997, 2015; Waldinger and Fitzgerald 2004). Instead, most immigrants seek to quickly adapt and assimilate into the host country, reducing their connections with the homeland over time (Waldinger 2007, 2015). For example, as assimilation theory predicts, the longer immigrants reside and assimilate into the host country, the less they are likely to retain long-term ties with the home country; only newer and more recent immigrants remain actively involved in home country affairs. Thus, contrary to those who underscore the increasing transnational connections among immigrants, skeptics point out that only a handful of the immigrant population is regularly involved with the homeland and such activities decline the longer they remain in the host country. In short, as Portes et al. (2002, 288) observe, the reason why scholars saw the phenomenon to be everywhere was because ethnographic studies on transnationalism had drawn their sample from the dependent variable, namely case studies of migrants involved in transnational behavior, which led to viewing the phenomenon as being more pervasive than it actually was.[14] Still, the fact that sending governments have noticed these durable connections and networks of immigrants and seek to court and influence their emigrants abroad suggests that dormant links and identities can gain greater significance as soon as states activate and sustain them (Levitt 2001b; Portes et al. 1999).

Operationalizing Transnationalism

Compounding the novelty and usefulness of the concept has also been the question of how to best operationalize and demarcate practices deemed as transnational (Itzigsohn et al. 1999, 321; Levitt 2001b; Portes et al. 2002). Some scholars have taken an expansive approach (Basch et al. 1994), while others have defined and operationalized transnationalism more narrowly. Portes et al. (2002, 6) take a stricter approach and define transnationalism as a "distinct set of immigrants who *routinely* carry on transnational activities for economic survival, and who rely upon it as an alternative mode of economic adaptation." Along these lines, they define transnational entrepreneurs as those who visit the home country at least twice per year and depend on regular contact for survival (Portes et al. 2002, 284). Furthermore, given the ubiquity of occasional transnationalism, such as sending remittances or visiting the home country among most immigrants, Portes et al. (2002, 284) argue that it is necessary to delimit the scope of transnational activities to ensure conceptual and analytical precision.

By contrast, Itzigsohn et al. (1999, 317) operationalize immigrant transnational ties and activities more loosely along a continuum—narrow and broad (see also core/expanded, Guarnizo 2000). Such an approach helps to capture variations in forms and degrees of transnational involvement from immigrants which a stricter approach is likely to miss or deem as less important. For example, although informal activities such as bringing goods to sell them in the home village during short visits to the home country (and vice versa, packing suitcases filled with home country goods for sale in the immigrant community) are irregular and involve low degree of institutionalization, they can still evolve to become a regular fixtures of immigrant transnationalism (Itzigsohn et al. 1999, 326). In short, the sum total of regular transnational activities engaged by a select group of immigrants, combined with occasional transnational participation by most, as Portes et al. (2002) are quick to recognize, can result in significant impacts for the home village and the home country. Thus, instead of dismissing them as insignificant, taking both of these practices into account helps to arrive at a more balanced view of the impact of regular and occasional transnational activities.

In this book, I use the approach adopted by Itzigsohn et al. (1999, 323) who define transnationalism along the narrow-broad continuum. Following their definition, narrow transnational participation is defined as "those people involved in economic, political, social, or cultural practices that involve a *regular* movement within the geographic transnational field, a *high* level of institutionalization, or *constant* personal involvement" (Itzigsohn et al. 1999, 323). Broad or occasional transnational engagement, by contrast, is defined as "a series of material and symbolic practices in which people engage that involve only *sporadic* physical movement between the two countries, a *low* level of institutionalization, or just *occasional* personal involvement, but nevertheless includes both countries as reference points."

Itzigsohn et al. (1999) also break down the forms of transnational participation into four main types: political, economic, civil-societal, and cultural. In the political arena, narrow political transnationalism emerges when home country political parties establish branches in American cities, while a broad political transnationalism takes shape when immigrants participate in home country elections. In the economic realm, a narrow economic transnationalism develops when immigrants launch transnational businesses, while a broad economic transnationalism arises when immigrants bring goods for sale during sporadic visits to the homeland. In civil-societal level, we can speak of narrow civil-societal transnationalism when immigrants link up with home village or home town associations, while a broad civil-societal transnationalism surfaces when they participate in immigrant sports leagues and religious organizations. In the cultural realm, a narrow cultural transnationalism forms when immigrants gain access to and utilize home country newspapers, cable television, and radio stations (Itzigsohn et al. 1999, 333). Itzigsohn et al. (1999) also view academic centers such as the Dominican Studies Center in New York as constituting a narrow cultural transnationalism since they are institutionalized and serve as places of cultural production and faculty exchanges. By contrast, listening and dancing to home country music constitutes broad cultural transnationalism.

In this book I use Itzigsohn et al.'s (1999) four typologies to examine the forms and scope of transnational involvement among Korean immigrants in the Washington-Baltimore metropolitan area, focusing particularly on their cultural transnational activities.

EMPIRICAL FINDINGS ON MIGRANT TRANSNATIONALISM

Recent survey data find that regular or narrow transnationalism is indeed less common for most immigrants. In fact, only a handful of the immigrant population is actively engaged in narrow transnationalism, while most practice broad or occasional transnationalism. For instance, Portes et al. (2002, 286) found that only 5% of migrants in their CIEP survey study fit the definition of regular transmigrants. Yet, among immigrant entrepreneurs in their sample, more than half (58%) were regularly involved in transnational economic activities.

Similarly, in his analysis of the Pew Hispanic Center's 2006 National Survey of Latinos, Waldinger (2007, 16) found that only 9% of Latino immigrants met the description of transmigrants, namely those who regularly sent remittances, called weekly, and visited the home country frequently. Close to two-thirds (63%) of Latino immigrants were moderately involved with their country of origin, whereas 28% were not at all engaged transnationally (Waldinger 2007, 1). Thus, survey findings suggest that only a small proportion of the immigrant population is actively involved in and regularly maintain ties with the home country.

But which demographic, socioeconomic, and migration-related factors affect transnational participation? And why are some groups more transnational than others? In their CIEP study, Portes et al. (2002, 289) found that long-term residence in the United States increased the probability of engaging in transnational enterprise since economic stability and resources were conducive to transnational participation for immigrant entrepreneurs. As Portes et al. (2002, 290) explain, "It is the better qualified, more experienced, and more secure immigrants who are overrepresented in these economic activities." Moreover, transnational involvement had a substantial economic payoff on entrepreneurs' monthly incomes (Portes et al. 2002). Yet, the findings were less conclusive on children's prospects for remaining in their parents' line of work, or even using these transnational networks and resources as a stepping stone to occupations in the mainstream economy.[15]

By contrast, based on the 2006 National Survey of Latinos, Waldinger (2007) found that attachment to the home country was stronger among recent immigrants and among those who migrated as adults rather than among those with moderate residence in the United States. Waldinger (2007, 16) observes, "Cross-border connections are a natural byproduct of any migratory situation, as many migrants arrive with uncertain settlement plans that change only gradually. Consequently, the high volume of contemporary migration makes for extensive back-and-forth flows of many types that tend to decline with years of residence in the U.S." Furthermore, age of immigration and generational status had an effect on levels of transnational engagement, with the 1.5 generation being less likely to be transmigrants than the immigrant generation. Having a child in the home country also increased the chances of being a transmigrant by more than two times compared to the average immigrant (Waldinger 2007).

In their survey study of recent immigrants in Vancouver, Canada, Hiebert and Ley (2006) found that while most immigrants maintained extensive informal social ties with family, relatives, and friends in the home country, transnational economic activities tended to decline in intensity over time. Unlike Portes's (2003) study, which linked education, longer residence, and higher occupational status with increased transnationalism among immigrants, Hiebert and Ley (2006) found that socioeconomic status was not associated with transnational activities. They also found that recent immigrants were more likely to activate transnational ties because of difficulties integrating economically and socially in Vancouver. Among Asian groups, East Asians were more transnational, with the Taiwanese being more transnational than the Chinese from Hong Kong.

Among Latino immigrants, Portes et al. (2002) found that Salvadorans were more likely than Dominicans to be transnational, while Colombians were the least likely. Waldinger (2007) also found that Colombians and Dominicans had more active transnational involvement than Mexicans, while Cubans had the least. These differences appear on the surface to be meaningful, yet multivariate analysis found that after controlling for citizenship, work, and education, national differences in transnational participation began to disappear (Waldinger 2007, 19). However, due to their unique political situation, Cubans were the least likely to be transnational, while Colombians were the most likely, even after controlling for these factors.

Thus, empirical studies on the intensity of immigrant transnational engagement and the motivations behind them suggest that only a fraction of the immigrant population are transmigrants and that most curb their transnational participation with time in the host country. Yet, a decline in remittance sending, weekly phone calls, or home country visits, while capturing the scope and intensity of transnational engagement, may not give a fuller picture of other forms of transnational participation that may influence immigrants' sense of home and identity, such as cultural transnational practices. It is to these forms of transnational activities at the cultural level that this book examines in order to assess their impact on Korean immigrants' orientation and identity toward the home country.

FROM SOJOURNERS TO PERMANENT SETTLERS TO TRANSNATIONAL CONNECTIONS

Korean Americans have been in the United States for over one hundred years. During the early phase of Korean and Asian immigration, transnationalism was indeed a prominent feature of their migration (Abelmann and Lie 1995, 49). For instance, as early as 1852 Chinese merchants were exporting gold and silver to China, while they were also importing rice, tea, and silk to the immigrant community from the homeland (Yoon 1997, 42).[16] Among the more than 7,000 Koreans who came to Hawaii between 1903 and 1905 as sugar cane plantation workers, their goals were to quickly amass fortune in America and return back to the homeland (Patterson 1988).[17] But after Japan's annexation of Korea in 1910 and subsequent colonization of the country for thirty-five years, the hopes of returning home after temporary sojourn were dashed. In its place, a more permanent immigrant community began to form in Hawaii with the arrival of one thousand picture brides during the 1910–1924 period, transforming the nascent community of sojourning men as families were started and the second generation was born. Still, Korean Americans during this period never wavered in their support for the homeland, becoming involved in political transnational activities by donating money and participating in the movement for the independence of Korea through church and political organizations (Abelmann and Lie 1995, 55). Many families also retained and sought to transmit transnational identities to their American-born/raised children, stressing learning the Korean language and imbuing a sense of loyalty to a homeland afflicted by colonial rule (Abelmann and Lie 1995, 55). When Japan was finally defeated in the Pacific War, bringing independence to Korea in 1945, transnational ties came to the fore again, especially among Korean students and political refugees who were among the first to return to the homeland to participate in the rebuilding of the country (Min 1996, 27).

Starting in the 1950s and onto the early 1960s, transnational connections with the home country became more muted as few Koreans were able to immigrate under the 1952 Immigration and Nationality Act (also known as the McCarran-Walter Act), which, while removing racial restrictions, still placed significant quotas against Asian entry into the United States (Gjelten 2016). However, due to U.S. involvement in the Korean War and military presence in Korea thereafter, 28,000 Korean women married to U.S. servicemen, along with 45,000 Korean adoptees during the 1962–1983 period, immigrated to the United States, helping to spur transnational activities among the women who sent letters, gifts, and more importantly, remittances to parents and siblings in the home country (Abelmann and Lie 1995, 57; Kim 1987, 330–331).[18]

Following the passage of the landmark Immigration and Nationality Act in 1965 (also known as the Hart-Celler Act), which finally abolished the national-origins quota, the number of Korean immigrants began to soar from a low of 11,000 in 1960 to 864,000 in 2000 (Gjelten 2016, 90). From the perspective of Koreans seeking to immigrate to the United States during this period, Korea was still an impoverished nation ravaged by memories of the Korean War but undergoing brisk industrialization under authoritarian rule, which brought economic and political instability to the urban and middle classes (Kim 1981). In this context, the opportunity to immigrate as families to the United States was seen as one of a permanent break from the homeland

(Park 2009). Even up until the mid-1980s, when South Korea was in the midst of joining the ranks of successful newly industrialized countries (NICs) into the global economy, many continued to hold on to this view of immigration as permanent and irreversible, prompting the liquidation of properties, assets, and other valuables and shelving any ideas of returning back to the home country (Park 2009).

To be sure, this did not mean that this 1960–1980 cohort cut off all ties with the home country since many of them continued to keep in touch with loved ones by writing letters, calling home, or visiting the homeland. In fact, many went on business trips to Korea, imported clothes, and visited the home country to shop for Korean goods (Park 1997, 98). Firms handling gifts, remittances, and care packages to the home country also appeared in the immigrant community, since customary of practices in Korea monetary gifts had to be sent during holidays, birthdays, weddings, deaths, or illnesses (Park 1997, 99, 102). Homeland connections were also instrumental in establishing Korean immigrant businesses such as the import-export of wigs, which served as stepping stones into other businesses, creating important niches for importers, wholesalers, and retailers in the immigrant community (Chin et al. 1996; Kim 1981, 121–143; Yoon 1997, 41–42). And in Los Angeles and other Koreatowns, Korean immigrants sought to recreate the trends and lifestyles of the home country by importing the latest Korean furniture and decorations, underscoring the significance of transnational connections (Abelmann and Lie 1995, 85).

Beginning in the late 1980s and early 1990s, however, due in part to the pursuit of globalization by the Korean state and Korean conglomerates and also huge advances in transportation and communication technologies, new cohorts from Korea were no longer viewing immigration as permanent and irreversible as previous waves. Instead, for many of them, transnationalism and instrumental citizenship, which were attempts to advance their class goals of providing greater educational, occupational, and citizenship opportunities for the children, have become part and parcel of their goals of migration (Abelmann and Lie 1995; Finch and Kim 2012; Jung 2015; Park and Abelmann 2004). This is reflected among both permanent immigrants to America and temporary visitors such as the *girogi* or "wild-geese" families migrating for the sole purpose of boosting the children's education and English language abilities (Jung 2015; Kang 2012; Finch and Kim 2012). Reminiscent of, but quite different from, past Asian American split households when immigration restrictions and obligations to parents in the homeland forced laborers, brought in to work as cheap labor, to leave their wives and children behind in the home country (Glenn 1986), the *girogi* split households are sending the wives and the children to the United States (or other English-speaking countries such as Canada, the United Kingdom, Australia, and the Philippines), while the fathers remain in Korea to pursue their professional careers and support the family abroad (Finch and Kim 2012).

In conjunction with a transnational orientation to immigration from recent cohorts, another contributing factor comes from transnationalism from above, namely the policies and activities promoted by the Korean state. For example, the Korean state has been actively courting emigrants abroad to expand its authority and influence in the overseas community by granting voting rights in the Korean parliamentary and presidential elections, by extending health insurance coverage to seniors, by offering investment and work opportunities, by funding Korean studies and Korean language education, and/or by intervening in community affairs (Min 2012).

The pursuit of globalization from the Korean state and Korean conglomerates (*chaebols*), following increasing integration of South Korea into the world economy, is also producing new groups of migrants or temporary visitors who take part in ever more frequent cross-border movements, including students, professors on sabbatical, H1B workers, *jujaewons* (Korean corporate subsidiary workers), wild-geese families, diplomats, and tourists.[19] For example, according to the DHS, the number of temporary visitors (I-94) from Korea jumped from 230,000 in 1991 to 841,863 in 2001, 1,460,972 in 2011, and 1,946,887 in 2015. For this new group of temporary visitors who intend to stay temporarily in the United States, although for H1B workers and students their sojourn can extend for several years with entire families joining them in America, engaging transnationally with the home country by reading Korean newspapers online, listening to live Korean radio, or viewing streamed Korean television programming, as well as regularly keeping in touch with family members, relatives, and friends back home, is a familiar and taken-for-granted feature of their sojourn abroad.

The influx of new cohorts of immigrants, temporary visitors, and/or undocumented migrants, whose goals involve immigration, education, work, or travel, is introducing and infusing the latest home country cultural norms, practices, and identities onto the community of long-time residents as regular communication and closer ties are maintained with the home country. This mixing of the old with the new, invariably through interactions as neighbors, church members, and parents of school-age children, may encourage and transmit transnational practices and identities which support ethnic renewal and identification with the homeland in the immigrant community. As Levitt (2001b) notes, ethnic renewal or persistence may be activated and sustained from new immigrant flows (and temporary visitors), which continue unabated, rather than through ethnic transmission across generations. Thus, efforts by the Korean state, along with globalization from Korean multinationals and transnationalism from below, are enabling larger numbers of Korean Americans to create and maintain more durable ties with the homeland.

In addition, as mentioned earlier in the chapter, two key revolutions in ICT—the Internet and smartphones—are also establishing the foundation for increased prospects for transnationalism in years to come. The digital age of cheap Internet telephone calls, email, video chats, and text messaging via mobile instant messenger apps is radically altering the way we communicate with each other since people with smartphones can be reached at all times and in all places (Chen 2011; Madianou 2014, 667; Yoon 2015, 7). In particular, the evolution and morphing of mobile phones into smartphones is bringing profound changes to human communication, including transnational communication (Madianou 2014, 667). As a device that enables an "always on lifestyle" (Boyd 2012) for users, where being online is the "default position" (Chen 2011; Madianou 2014, 678), it is invariably at the forefront of technological convergence, earning the apt label of the "Swiss army knife of the 21st century" (Madianou 2014, 669–670). Thus, inexpensive and instantaneous communication is qualitatively changing the barriers of space and time (Dicken 1998; Harvey 1989), making transnational activities and ties a far more realistic goal for immigrants.

Another is the consumption of transnational media, particularly Korean television, which is again being facilitated and speeded up by ICT. Though past Korean immigrants may have equally sought transnational media as soon they appeared within the community, the difference today is that ICT such as the Internet, cable and satellite television, and smartphones enable an easier and faster consumption of homeland media irrespective of immigrants' desires to watch, listen to, or read transnational television, radio, and news. Thus, the prospects for increased cultural transnationalism have risen significantly as the barriers of space and time have been appreciably reduced.

In sum, considering the changes in new immigrants' orientations toward immigration, the explosion of temporary visitors, active interventions from the Korean state, globalization of Korean food and cultural industries, and vast leaps in ICT that have dramatically lowered the costs and speed of such activities, this book seeks to examine the following questions: What is the scope and nature of the transnational activities and ties being established by members of the Korean community in the Washington-Baltimore metropolitan area? Which ones are most salient for Korean Americans? Why? And how do these transnational activities and ties affect their sense of home and identity? Ultimately the book is less interested in measuring the exact scope and intensity of transnational participation among immigrants than in understanding the forms these take, the reasons for engaging in them, and their impact on Korean Americans' sense of home, identity, and belonging.

THE KOREAN COMMUNITY IN THE WASHINGTON-BALTIMORE REGION

The history of Koreans in the Washington-Baltimore region goes as far back as 1880s when a handful of Joseon envoys arrived to the United States in 1883 following the Treaty of Peace, Amity, and Trade with the United States in May 1882.[20] This first ten-member Joseon envoy arrived to Washington, D.C. on September 15, 1883, and returned back to Joseon on May 31, 1884 after a ten-month stay in the United States (Choy 1979, 69; KAFGW 2009, 1, 8).[21] Nonetheless, it is during this period of early diplomatic relations between Joseon and the United States that several official envoys to Washington, D.C., including Penn Su, Kwang Beom Suh, and Philip Jaisohn (Suh Jaepil), decide to remain in America and become pioneers of Korean immigration to the United States, especially to the Washington, D.C. area.

As one of the original ten envoys who came to Washington D.C. and stayed behind to pursue additional education in the United States rather than returning home, Penn Su (Byun Su) was the first Korean to graduate from an American college, namely the Agricultural College of Maryland in 1891 (later the University of Maryland at College Park) (KAFGW 2009, 4). After graduating from college and attaining U.S. citizenship, he obtained a position within the Department of Agriculture, but his new life in America came to a tragic end when a moving train hit him and took his life at the prime age of thirty in October of 1891.

Another original member of the Korean legation who also remained in the United States and enrolled with Penn Su in the Agricultural College was Kwang Beom Suh. Unlike Penn Su, however, Suh was never able to complete his degree because he was called back by Joseon to serve as minister of justice and minister of education. But during his reappointment as the Korean Envoy Extraordinary and Minister Plenipotentiary to the United States (KAFGW 2009, 5), instead of returning to Korea as ordered by the Joseon government, Suh decided to remain in the area and settle down. But like Penn Su, he also met an early death in August 1896 after becoming ill at the age of thirty-eight.

The third notable pioneer of Korean immigration history during this period was Philip Jaisohn (the famed Suh Jae Pil). Also a member of the official Korean legation in 1888, Jaisohn was the first Korean to graduate from an American medical school (KAFGW 2009, 5). According to KAFGW (2009, 6), Jaisohn attended the Hillman Academy through the auspices of John Wells Hollen Beck, and after graduation, found a well-paying job as a translator for the Army Medical Corps, which enabled him to attend the Corcoran School of Science and the Arts of Columbian University (later George Washington University) where he earned his medical degree in 1892 from the Columbia Medical School (KAFGW 2009, 6). Later, he became an important figure in the Reformation Movement as well as a major contributor to the Korean independence and democratic movements (Choy 1979).

Because of Washington, D.C.'s location as the nation's capital and political center, prominent Koreans from Hawaii, notably Syngman Rhee, also came to the area to engage in political transnational activities, particularly to lobby for Korea's independence to the American government (Choy 1979; KAFGW 2009, 6). According to KAFGW (2009), Syngman Rhee first came to the United States in 1904 to plead with the American government to halt Japan's colonization of Korea. But after failing in his lobbying efforts, Rhee decided to remain in the Washington, D.C. area and study at the Columbian School at George Washington University in 1905 (KAFGW 2009, 7). When a major uprising for independence in Korea broke out on March 1, 1919, a provisional government was established in Shanghai on April 17 and Syngman Rhee assumed the position of the Premiership and later the presidency of the provisional government. Seeking to gain official recognition of the provisional government and perform diplomatic duties, Rhee opened an office in the Continental Building on 14th and H Streets in Washington, D.C. to begin lobbying activities toward the U.S. government. But contrary to his objectives, President Woodrow Wilson refused to recognize Rhee's provisional government for fear of causing diplomatic strain on relations with Japan (KAFGW 2009, 7). These set of events, including the inability to influence U.S. foreign policy toward Korea and the charge that Syngman Rhee had assumed the presidency of the provisional government without obtaining formal approval from the cabinet counsel and leaders of the independence movement (Ahn Chang Ho and Park Yong Man), led to his impeachment on March 25, 1925, and with it, the end of the American Committee for the Korean Independence Movement (KAFGW 2009, 7).[22]

Hence, during the 1910–1945 period of Japanese colonial rule, the history of the Korean community in Washington, D.C. was closely intertwined with transnational struggles for the independence of the home country as Korean Americans in the area worked together with Rhee's Washington branch of the provisional Korean government to influence U.S. foreign policy.

Following the outbreak of the Korean War in 1950, the number of Koreans immigrating to the United States, and in particular to Washington, D.C. was miniscule, registering a paltry twenty-two, comprising mostly of students and embassy staff (KAFGW 2009, 16). Even in 1960, the Korean population in the area was a mere five hundred, composed of mostly students pursuing studies in various academic fields (KAFGW 2009).[23] Beginning in the 1970s, however, the Korean population in the Washington-Baltimore region shot up from a low of 3,000 in 1970 to 20,000 in 1975, jumping almost sevenfold in five years (KAFGW 2009). Soon after, more Koreans began to arrive to the Washington-Baltimore region, recording 35,000 (28,000) in 1980, 50,000 in 1985, 80,000 (61,400) in 1990, and 130,000–150,000 in 2003.[24] The latest statistics from the American Community Survey (2009–2011) finds that more than 104,322 Koreans (Korean alone) reside in the region, making the Washington-Baltimore area the third largest Korean community after Los Angeles (301,534) and New York (203,020), with the three communities accounting for approximately one-half (43.3%) of the total Korean population in the United States.[25]

Settlement Patterns

Like other immigrants, many Koreans have chosen the Washington-Baltimore metropolitan region because the area offers economic stability from jobs in the federal government and defense-related industries (Abbott 1999; Gjelten 2016, 135; Manning 1998). The region also combines the amenities of a large metropolitan area (Washington, D.C.), including cultural centers, extensive public transportation networks, low crime, and quality schools in the surrounding affluent suburbs (Gjelten 2016; KAFGW 2009, 41; Repak 1995). In fact, according to *Newsweek*'s 100 best high schools in the United States, the area's fourteen schools, including George Mason, Wood Run, Woodson, York Town, Wootten, Churchill, and Woodmont, were among the top-ranked high schools in the country. As the region with the highest proportion of PhDs and counties boasting one of the highest median household incomes in the nation (Fairfax, Loudoun, Arlington, Montgomery, and Howard counties top off the list), well-paying high-tech and professional jobs have drawn Korean immigrants and natives alike to the region (Gjelten 2016; KAFGW 2009, 41).

Residentially, the Washington-Baltimore metropolitan area departs from traditional urban ethnic enclaves of the past, that is, involuntary residential clustering of immigrant groups in urban centers (Gjelten 2016, 137; Singer et al. 2008). Instead, following the model of new immigration gateways and settlement in the suburbs, most immigrants in the region reside in areas of high immigrant concentration, creating visible ethnic communities (Gjelten 2016, 137; Singer et al. 2008). In fact, this exodus to the suburbs has produced what Wei Li (2009) has coined "ethnoburbs," or suburban ethnic communities where increasing numbers of Korean and Asian Americans cluster and rub shoulders as neighbors in what used to be predominantly white suburban communities. For instance, in the two census tracts in Centreville, VA, a visible ethnoburb in the Washington-Baltimore region, the proportion Asian was 53% in one and 33% in the other according to the 2010 *New York Times* census map.

A number of places have emerged as key areas of immigrant settlement and concentration such as Langley Park, MD (Salvadorans), Seven Corners (Vietnamese businesses), and Centreville (Singer et al. 2008). Korean Americans typically reside in the inner suburbs of Northern Virginia such as Fairfax, Loudoun, and Prince William counties and Montgomery and Howard counties in Maryland. The major areas of residence in Northern Virginia are Centreville, Burke, Fairfax, Chantilly (Fairfax County), Ashburn (Loudoun County), Manassas (Prince William County), while in the Maryland suburbs, which include both Montgomery, Howard, and Prince George's counties, the principal areas of settlement are Rockville, Gaithersburg, Silver Spring, Wheaton (Montgomery County), Ellicott City, and Columbia (Howard County).[26]

Demographically, whites, at over one-half (53.2%), constitute the largest group in the region, followed by blacks, Latinos, and Asians respectively.[27] Blacks, whose presence in the region traces back for centuries, comprise more than a quarter (27.6%) of the region's population, while new immigrant groups such as Latinos (11.0%) and Asians/Pacific Islanders (8.2%) compose the rest. A noteworthy feature of the Asian population in the Washington, D.C. metropolitan area is that their share in the region, at 8.2%, is twice their figures nationally (4%), and this proportion is comparable to the proportion of Latinos in the area.

Among Asian groups in the metropolitan region, Korean Americans constitute the third largest group after Asian Indians and Chinese. In Northern Virginia, Korean immigrants (51,498) are the second largest after Asian Indians (76,256), followed by the Vietnamese (41,637) and Chinese (36,803) respectively. Interestingly, although Chinese Americans are more numerous than Koreans in the Washington-Baltimore region, they trail behind Koreans in Northern Virginia and even lag behind the Vietnamese.

Another notable trend of the Korean settlement in Northern Virginia is that more than three-fourths (78%) reside in Fairfax County, which contrasts sharply with their settlement in Maryland where Koreans are much more evenly distributed between Montgomery and Howard counties. The choice of Fairfax County as the preferred place of residence, however, is not unique to Koreans, as the county, with a populuation of 1.13 million, is not only the largest county in the Washington-Baltimore region, but is also home to most Asian groups in Northern Virginia. The only exception to this trend is Asian Indians, who, although twice as many of them reside in Fairfax County compared to Loudoun, have made Loudoun County the second largest area of Asian Indian concentration in Northern Virginia.

In Maryland, Koreans (43,455) constitute the third largest group after Asian Indians (70,619) and Chinese (65,448). Most Koreans reside in Montgomery (38%), Howard (27%), and Baltimore (14%) counties. An interesting residential pattern among the Chinese in Montgomery County is that, despite their size relative to Asian Indians, the Chinese outnumber them there. Moreover, while most Asian groups, including Filipinos, reside in Montgomery, Howard, and Baltimore County counties, Filipinos are the only group that also has sizable numbers in Prince George's County.

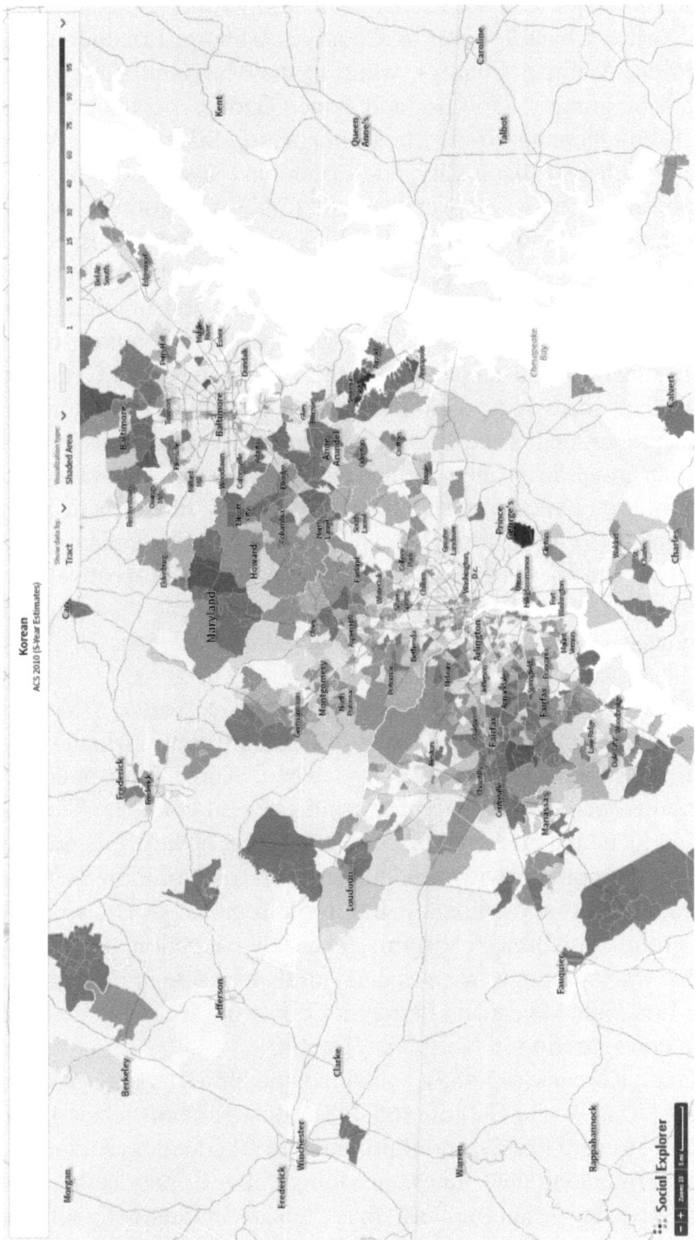

Figure 0.2 Map of Korean Americans in the Washington-Baltimore region, ACS 2010, five-year estimates. *Source*: Social Explorer (https://www.socialexplorer.com/).

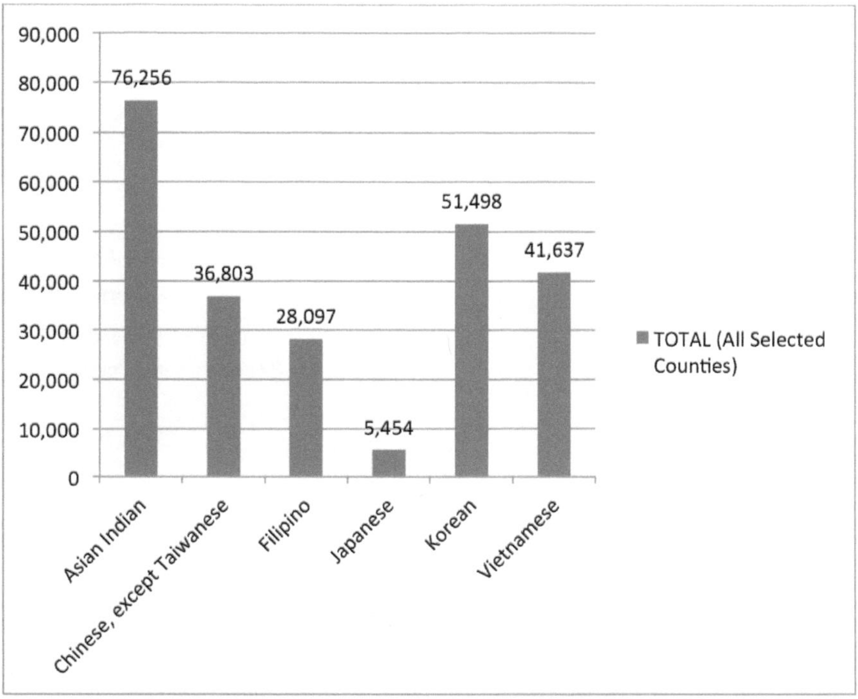

Figure 0.3 Select Asian groups in Northern Virginia counties (Arlington, Fairfax, Loudoun, Prince William), ACS 2013, five-year estimates. *Source*: Social Explorer (https://www.socialexplorer.com/).

In terms of top census-designated places (CDP) for Koreans in the region, they are overwhelmingly concentrated in the Centreville CDP (7,832), outpacing the combined two biggest Korean CDPs in Fairfax County—Fair Oaks CDP (3,097) and Burke CDP (2,346). As a result of such clustering, Koreans represent 40.9% of the total Asian population (19,130) in Centreville, closely resembling an ethnoburb. In Maryland, there are no comparable CDPs where Korean Americans cluster like in Centreville, VA although Ellicott City, MD, with a population of 4,789 Koreans, is by far the largest Korean CDP in Maryland, followed by Columbia CDP (2,850) and Baltimore City (2,419) as the second and third largest CDPs for Korean Americans.

DATA SOURCES

This study is based on various data sources, including the 2009–2011 American Community Survey (hereafter the ACS 2009–2011) and the 2003

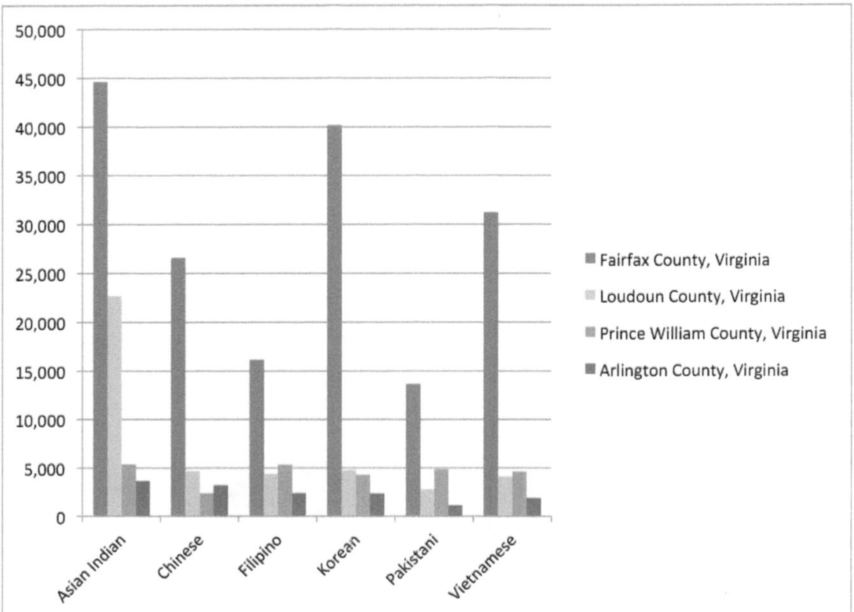

Figure 0.4 Distribution of select Asian groups in Northern Virginia counties, ACS 2013, five-year estimates. *Source*: Social Explorer (https://www.socialexplorer.com/).

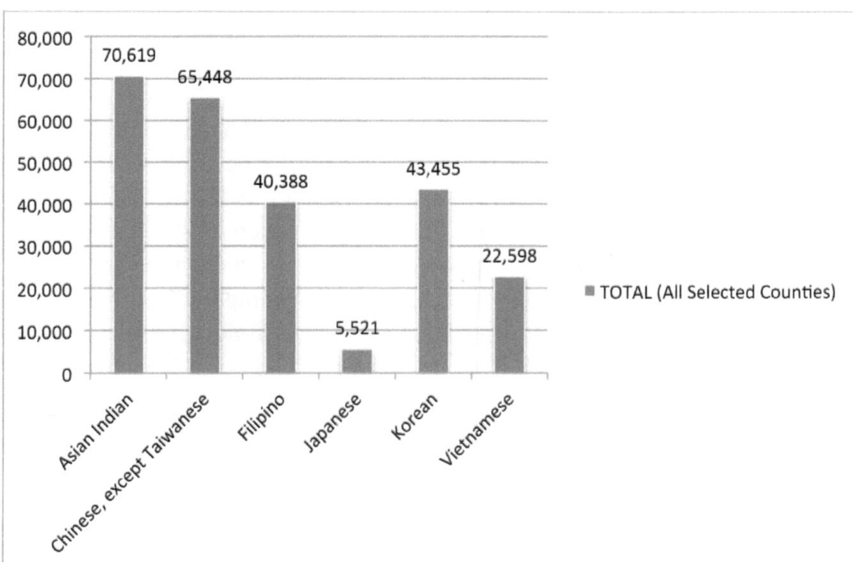

Figure 0.5 Distribution of Koreans in Maryland counties, ACS 2013, five-year estimates. *Source*: Social Explorer (https://www.socialexplorer.com/).

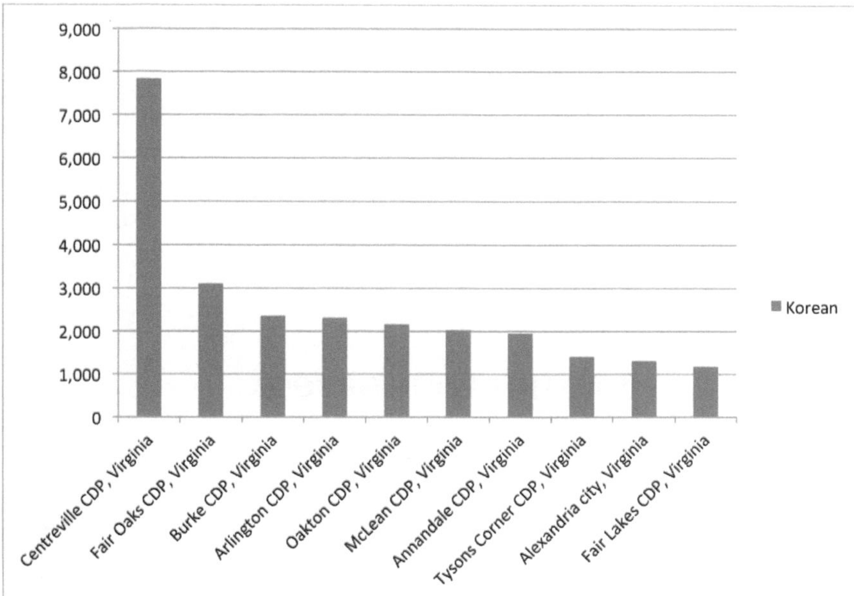

Figure 0.6 Top ten Korean CDP, city, place in Northern Virginia, 2013, five-year estimates. *Source*: Social Explorer (https://www.socialexplorer.com/).

Washington-Baltimore Korean Community survey (hereafter the 2003 D.C. Korean community survey). The 2003 D.C. Korean community survey (N=303) was a project commissioned by the Centennial Committee of the Korean Immigration to the United States, a joint effort between the Washington, D.C. committee (Okyun Kwon and Youngchang Chae) and the *Korea Times*, D.C. In order to commemorate one hundred years of Korean immigration to the United States, the committee charged Dr. Kwon to conduct a survey of the Korean community in the Washington-Baltimore metropolitan area in 2003. After completing his data analysis for the Centennial Committee, Dr. Kwon kindly made the dataset available to me, which I have used to examine the forms and degree of transnational activities among Korean immigrants in the greater Washington, D.C. region. I have also drawn on historical materials from the *History of the Korean-Americans in the Washington Metropolitan Area*, 1883–2005, a monograph commissioned by the Korean American Foundation-Greater Washington, as well as analysis of the 2014 Washington, D.C. Giant Korean Business Directory.

In addition, in order to examine the evolution of the Korean community in the nation's capital and the impact of transnational ties on the community of old-timers, we conducted twenty-three in-depth interviews with Korean community leaders in business, politics, education, social service, and religion as well as long-time residents in the greater Washington, D.C. region in 2011.[28] We used a snowball sampling strategy to contact community leaders and long-time residents, building on these referrals (as well as our own networks) to find and conduct additional interviews. The interviews, usually lasting from one to two hours, were conducted primarily in the interviewees' homes, digitally recorded, and later transcribed. Since the community leaders are public figures, they consented to the use of their real names. Pseudonyms, however, are used for long-time residents and for those preferring to remain anonymous.

ORGANIZATION OF BOOK

Chapter 1 provides the latest demographic and socioeconomic profile of Korean Americans in the Washington-Baltimore metropolitan area on the 2009–2011 American Community Survey (ACS) and the 2003 D.C. based Korean community survey. Key demographic and socioeconomic characteristics of Korean Americans are discussed by presenting substantive profiles of Korean immigrants in the region as well as their prospects for transnationalism. Chapter 2 provides a theoretical and empirical discussion of ICT and transnational media and their impact on migrants and transnational families. Chapter 3 considers both the regular and occasional transnational practices of Korean Americans, focusing on transnational communication with family and friends, economic and political transnational activities, including remittances and participation in homeland politics, and home country visits. Chapter 4 examines the cultural transnational activities of Korean immigrants, focusing on the consumption of transnational Korean media. This chapter also examines the role of the *Hallyu* or the Korean Wave, namely Korean dramas, films, and K-Pop, in Korean American and mainstream interest in transnational media. Chapter 5 examines questions of identity and the sense of home in light of increased transnational activities and ties by Korean Americans. Chapter 6 considers the compatibility of assimilation with ethnic preservation and transnationalism, examining the views of community leaders and long-time residents on the community's prospects for assimilation and integration. Chapter 7 concludes with a discussion of the future of transnational activities and connections and their implications on Korean Americans' orientation and identity toward the home country and the host society.

NOTES

1. With the cost of local and international telephone calls falling continuously, the changes mentioned above simply reflect the costs at the time of the writing of the book.

2. Before a new, state of the art airport was completed in Incheon, Korea, about forty-five minutes away from downtown Seoul, all international flights to Seoul were routed through Gimpo Airport on the outskirts of Seoul. It was not until the 1960s that commercial air flights first began to operate between the two nations. During this time period, flights connecting Seoul to major U.S. cities, which were served by Korean Air and other international airlines, were limited and required several connections and stopovers.

3. The *Korea Times* (11/19/12) reported that in 2012 Korean Air operated ninety-six U.S. flights per week from ten major metropolitan areas. The Incheon-Los Angeles route operated twenty-four flights per week, while the Incheon-New York route had fourteen flights. Asiana Airlines, the second largest Korean carrier, operated two daily flights for the Incheon-Los Angeles route, fourteen flights per week for the Incheon-New York route, and daily flights for the Incheon-San Francisco and Incheon-Honolulu routes. The carrier was also planning to add new daily flights for the Incheon-Chicago and Incheon-Seattle routes in 2013 (see Asiana website). Following the new visa waiver program, the number of Korean visitors to the United States rose sharply. According to boarding records for Korean Air, there were 1,033,006 visitors to the United States (excluding Hawaii) in 2009, 1,169,799 in 2010, and 1,132,880 in 2011, which shows a sharp rise in the number of temporary visitors from Korea.

4. In an attempt to stem the illegal downloading of television shows and movies, a new legal streaming service called NTV, among others, offers video on demand for a monthly subscription fee, which includes programming from the three major Korean networks: the Korean Broadcasting System (KBS), the Moonwha Broadcasting Company (MBC), and the Seoul Broadcasting System (SBS). Recently, Apple TV has also added new Korean channels or apps (some free and some paid apps) to its service, enabling Korean television programs to be streamed both live and on demand.

5. According to KAFGW (2009, 44), the only Asian grocery store carrying essential ingredients such as rice, soybean sauce, salted radish, noodles, and chopsticks in Washington, D.C. during the 1950s and 1960s was a Japanese grocery named Hanawoomi. Another grocery store in Chinatown called Maywharung sold tofu and bean sprouts.

6. Agricultural and regional products from these Korean provinces are usually marketed as domestically grown products to contrast them from Chinese-grown farm products. Usually, they fetch a higher price for being locally grown and having been produced without the use of pesticides and chemical fertilizers. Min (2012) also finds in his content analysis of cultural transnational activities among Korean New Yorkers that these provinces have partnered with Korean community organizations to promote their products during traditional Korean holidays and food festivals, selling them at reduced prices to attendees.

7. CJ is a South Korean conglomerate specializing in food and entertainment and media products. Originally a branch of Samsung, it broke off the conglomerate in the 1990s.

8. Kakao Talk is a free social networking service (SNS) from Korea, available in both Android and iOS versions for smartphones and tablets. It is the equivalent of WhatsApp, an SNS which was recently purchased by Facebook for $19 billion (Covert 2014). See also chapter 2.

9. With price fluctuations in global oil prices and airline competition, the cost of airplane tickets can vary time to time. But at the time of the writing, off-peak fares from Dulles Airport, Washington, D.C. averaged $1600–2000.

10. There is a similar version of a transnational family among the "astronaut" Taiwanese families whose fathers hold on to jobs in Taiwan, while the wives and children reside in middle-class suburbs in the United States (Chee 2003; Chiang 2008; Waters 2002; Wong 1998). Obviously, due to the cost and time required for travel between Asia and America, few families, in practice, will be able to make weekly trips between the two countries as I have noted in this hypothetical scenario above.

11. Globalization is enabling a similar penetration of global consumer and cultural goods into the home country, with citizens in Korea enjoying a wide variety of cultural and consumer products from all over the world.

12. The first generation is defined as those who were born abroad but immigrated to the United States by the age of eighteen and older; the 1.5 generation is defined as those who were born abroad with at least one foreign-born parent and who arrived to America by the age of twelve and younger; the second generation is defined as those who are born in the United States with at least one foreign-born parent.

13. I have compiled tables and graphs on lawful permanent resident status, persons naturalized, and nonimmigrant admissions using data (excel files) from the Yearbook of Immigration Statistics from the Department of Homeland Security.

14. To address the problem of sampling from the dependent variable, which has been the case with most ethnographic case studies, Portes et al. (2002) conducted a survey of transnational entrepreneurs to examine whether transnationalism was indeed extensive among immigrants.

15. Waldinger (1997) points out that due to sampling issues with Portes et al.'s (2002) CIEP survey study, the conclusions derived may have been biased toward entrepreneurs.

16. Japanese immigrants were also importing cooking ingredients from Japan (Chan 1991, 40–41).

17. During this period, diplomats, ginseng merchants as well as 900 political exiles and 541 students also came to the United States, reinforcing the community's orientation toward the homeland (Patterson 1988, 9–10; Yoon 1997, 53; Yu 1983, 23).

18. During the 1950–1970 period, Korean wives of U.S. servicemen also played key roles in the chain migration of Koreans to the United States as many of them sponsored parents and siblings to immigrate after becoming U.S. citizens. After 1965, the occupational preference and family reunification provisions of the 1965 Immigration Act set off the migration of highly educated and skilled Koreans, especially doctors and nurses, as well as the migration of family members. In addition, sizable numbers of Korean Vietnam War veterans immigrated to the United States after the conclusion of the Vietnam War, contributing to the brisk increase of the Korean population during this fifty-year period (Abelmann and Lie 1995, 65).

19. Among temporary visitors who enter with tourist visas, some overstay their visas and remain in the country "illegally" but find ways to legalize their stay. A number of these tourists-turned-migrants maintain a transnational orientation toward the homeland since many of them, if they are unable to legalize their status, have to return home after years of residing and working abroad.

20. Joseon or also Choson refers to the Joseon dynasty in Korea which ruled the Korean peninsula from 1397 to 1897.

21. The exchange of official envoys with the United States was short lived, however, because China put pressure on Joseon to halt diplomatic exchanges. But no sooner had Joseon resumed its diplomatic exchanges with the United States, sending Jeong Yang Park (Juk Chun) as its Minister Plenipotentiary to the United States in January 1888 (KAFGW 2009, 2), Japan's defeat of Russia in the 1905 Russo-Japanese War, followed by imperial expansion to and encroachment of Korea, brought for a second time an end to diplomatic exchanges with the United States, which concluded the eighteen-year Joseon legation to Washington, D.C. (Choy 1979; KAFGW 2009, 3).

22. But when Japan launched an attack against the United States at Pearl Harbor in 1941, the ensuing Pacific War against Japan helped to revive Syngman Rhee's control and leadership of the provisional government, and with it the reestablishment of the Korean Commission in Washington, D.C. (KAFGW 2009, 8). Rhee began to intensify his lobbying activities toward the White House, the Congress, and the State Department and also encouraged fellow Koreans in Hawaii and elsewhere to join the United States in the war effort and donate funds for the independence of Korea. When Japan surrendered on August 15, 1945, Koreans in the Washington, D.C. area gathered at Syngman Rhee's residence to celebrate the defeat of Japan (KAFGW 2009, 13).

23. A Korean student directory published in 1959–1960 listed 174 students, eighteen Embassy staff members, three Library of Congress employees, eight employees of the Voice of America, and sixteen nonstudents in Washington, D.C. (KAFGW 2009, 21). The sex ratio of the student body was overwhelmingly male, with a ratio of twenty males to one female, while the class background of those who came between 1941 and 1950 was predominantly landed elites or individuals working for the Korean government (KAFGW 2009, 34). Most resided in the Mount Pleasant area (near 16th Street and Park Road) and held various odd jobs to support themselves since the Rhee government placed limits on the amount of money that could be sent abroad (KAFGW 2009). One of the favored places of employment was D.C. Public Libraries. Some also found work as cab drivers, while a few worked for the Voice of America, a news agency founded in New York by the American government in 1942, but which relocated to Washington D.C. in 1954 (KAFGW 2009, 31). After completing their studies and obtaining their degrees, which were mostly at the doctoral level, several students returned to Korea, landing positions as high ranking diplomats in the Korean government. Others, however, found that their advanced degrees limited their employment options in the home country, forcing them to seek jobs in the United States as economic uncertainties in Korea discouraged many from going back (KAFGW 2009, 23). Among the many challenges Korean students and residents faced during this period were finding, among other things, appropriate ingredients to prepare Korean meals and maintaining Korean cultural traditions (KAFGW 2009). Still, Korean residents like Walter K. Park managed to make *kimchi* for their Korean guests by purchasing Asian cabbage from Hanawoomi located on 15th Street, the only Japanese and Asian grocery store in the area (KAFGW 2009, 18). The early community was also highly fragmented, and it was not until the Korean War that the immigrant community came together to exchange information and news about the homeland devastated by

the war. This gathering of mostly students, which began to meet every Saturdays at Byung Cheol Koh's house, became known as the Korean social group. Later, as more Korean immigrants settled in the area in the 1970s and 1980s, the student-based group (the Washington Student Association) gave way to the Korean residents in Washington in 1986, becoming over time the Korean Association of the Greater Washington area, a major organization representing the Korean community in the region today (KAFGW 2009, 17, 24).

24. The figures in parentheses are decennial census figures, which are often disputed by the Korean press and the Korean Association who estimate the Korean Washingtonian population to be between 130,000 and 150,000 (in 2003) compared to 86,396 according to the 2000 Census, because the former includes those who may be undocumented (KAFGW 2009, 34). Regardless, the region has experienced rapid increasesin the immigrant populations since the 1970s, including those of Korean immigrants, bringing in the process of swift demographic transformations to the Washington-Baltimore metropolitan region.

25. In the ACS 2009–2011, I use the variable "metarea" to combine the Washington, D.C./MD/VA and Baltimore metropolitan areas into the Washington-Baltimore region. The Los Angeles metropolitan area refers to the Los Angeles-Long Beach, CA area, while the New York area is comprised of New York-Northeastern New Jersey. The top four, five, six, and seven places of residence for Korean Americans are tthe Chicago-Naperville-Michigan City IL-IN-WI consolidated statistical area (CSA), the San Jose-San Francisco-Oakland, CA CSA, the Atlanta-Sandy Springs-Gainesville, GA-AL CSA, and the Seattle-Tacoma-Olympia, WA CSA (ACS 2009–2011). Among the new places of settlement for Korean immigrants, the Atlanta metropolitan area and the Dallas-Fort Worth region have emerged as one of the fastest areas of Korean growth.

26. According to KAFGW (2009, 43) and old-timers, when Korean immigrants first began to arrive to the area in the 1970s, many initially rented apartments in Kent Village in Landover, Maryland (Prince George's County). It is estimated that as many as five hundred Koreans resided in Kent Village at one time. Most of the residents were single, skilled Korean Vietnam War veterans who had experience with the U.S. military prior to immigration (KAFGW 2009, 57). The story is that an immigration agent named Ms. Dolly Cohen in Baltimore recruited skilled Korean immigrants who had experience in Vietnam to come to work in auto repair jobs in Landover, MD (KAFGW 2009, 57). Many of these skilled veterans also found work in welding, air conditioning, and heavy equipment operation (KAFGW 2009, 45). Underscoring the large concentration of Koreans in Kent Village, two media outlets in spring of 1976, the *Chosun Ilbo* ("Kent Village for Skilled Korean Immigrants") and a KBS program called "Human Triumph," gave media coverage of the place, documenting the struggles and triumphs of these early immigrants (KAFGW 2009, 57). By the mid-1980s, however, many Koreans began to leave the area after purchasing their first homes in parts of Prince George's county, including Upper Marlboro, Lanham, and Greenbelt (KAFGW 2009, 58). During this time Koreans also began to rent apartments in Rock Creek Terrace Apartments in Montgomery County (KAFGW 2009, 59). Concerned about schools, crime, and home values, those with financial means began to move

to Potomac, Rockville, and Gaithersburg in Maryland. Others also chose to reside in Northern Virginia, settling initially in Arlington and Alexandria and moving later to Fairfax, Burke, Springfield, and Oakton. In Virginia, there were no comparable apartment complexes like those in Kent Village where early Koreans had clustered. Instead, most of them were scattered into various apartment complexes in Arlington, Alexandria, and Falls Church, where rent was low and the commute to Washington, D.C. was shorter (KAFGW 2009, 59). With rapid growth of the Korean population in Virginia in the 1990s, the Korean community in Northern Virginia began to outpace those in Maryland, thereby making Virginia the largest place of residence among Korean immigrants in the region (KAFGW 2009, 57).

27. The three racial groups (whites, blacks, and Asians) exclude Hispanic whites, Hispanic blacks, and Hispanic Asians. They have been collapsed in the Latino category instead. Six Asian American groups, including Korean Americans, constitute the largest Asian groups in the nation, although in the D.C. region, Japanese Americans represent a tiny share of the Asian American population. Also unlike the national trend where Chinese Americans usually outnumber other Asian groups, in the Greater Washington area, it is Asian Indians who constitute the biggest group (28.1%), followed by Chinese (22.7%), Koreans (19.6%), Filipinos (15.0%), and Vietnamese (12.1%).

28. Although I have written the bulk of the chapters for this book, the project was a truly collaborative effort, which involved a number of graduate students (now all doctorates) from the start to the data collection and analysis phase of the research (see Acknowledgment section).

Chapter 1

Demographic and Socioeconomic Characteristics of Korean Immigrants in the Washington-Baltimore Area

The Korean community in the Washington-Baltimore region, like its counterparts in Los Angeles and New York, is experiencing important cohort and generational changes which will shape their transnational activities and ties in years to come. In this chapter, I examine key demographic and socioeconomic characteristics of Korean Americans in the greater Washington, D.C. area to provide a portrait of the community as well as to identify the factors that may drive them to engage in transnational practices with the home country.

PLACE OF BIRTH AND GENERATION

Transnational engagement, whether regular or occasional, is less likely to arise among later generations of immigrants than among recent immigrants (Foner 2005, 85; Levitt 2001b; Portes et al. 2002; Portes and Rumbaut 2014, 183; Waldinger 2007, 2015). Whether an immigrant group is composed primarily of first-, second-, or later- generations will affect the scope and intensity of transnationalism practiced by the group, given that acculturation and assimilation will diminish a group's orientation toward the home country. As a general rule, first-generation immigrants are more likely to be oriented toward and seek to maintain ties with the home country than their second-generation counterparts (Foner 2005; Portes 2001; Waldinger 2007, 2008).

Korean Americans in the Washington-Baltimore metropolitan area, similar to other Asian Americans in the region, were disproportionately composed of the foreign-born. Over three-fourths (76.7%) (all ages) were foreign-born, while 23.3% were U.S.-born (ACS 2009–2011). Korean Americans ranked first in the proportion of the foreign-born among the region's six select Asian American groups (Chinese, Filipinos, Asian Indians, Japanese, and

Vietnamese). Japanese Americans, a group which has seen dramatic reductions in immigration from Japan since the 1960s, and as a result, were disproportionately U.S.-born at the national level, were largely foreign-born in the Washington, D.C. region.[1]

The proportion of foreign-born among Latinos (57%) was also much lower than among Asian Americans in the region. A slightly higher proportion of Asian women were foreign-born relative to men, and Korean Americans had the highest proportion of the foreign-born of all Asian American women. There was also little to no difference in the proportion of foreign-born among the three Korean communities as they all hovered around 76%.

The proportion of foreign-born, however, does not take into account the share of the first generation vis-à-vis the U.S.-raised generations, that is, the 1.5 generation and U.S.-born, as U.S.-raised Korean Americans will be culturally and linguistically more acculturated than the first generation.[2] For instance, first-generation Koreans accounted for almost one-half (48.9%) of the Korean American population, while U.S.-raised Koreans comprised the other half (43.9%) (ACS 2009–2011). Relative to other Asian Americans, Korean Americans had the lowest percentage of U.S.-born (23.5%) of all Asians, although the share of the first generation was actually the second lowest (48.9%) after the Vietnamese (47.2%). The share of the 1.5 generation, however, was the highest (20.4%) of all Asian Americans, raising appreciably the proportion of Korean Americans raised and schooled in America.[3]

Compared to Korean communities in Los Angeles (53.8%) and New York (52.1%), the proportion of the first generation was slightly lower among Korean Washingtonians (48.9%), but the share of the 1.5 generation was a little higher. These small differences suggest that in all three communities transnational ties will persist among the first generation and will be more resilient and pervasive in the Los Angeles Korean community in light of its proximity to Korea, the size of the Korean population there (as well as the size of the first generation), and a long-standing Koreatown.[4]

SEX

Research on transnationalism has found that transnational practices vary considerably between men and women, with immigrant men entertaining more seriously the thought of returning back to the home country, while women seek to establish more permanent roots in the host society (Foner 2005; Goldring 2002). This was also the case among Korean immigrants studied by Park (1997, 97) in the 1980s, who found that women were more likely to become naturalized and to sponsor family members, establishing a more permanent foothold in the place of settlement, whereas men were more likely to return to the homeland.

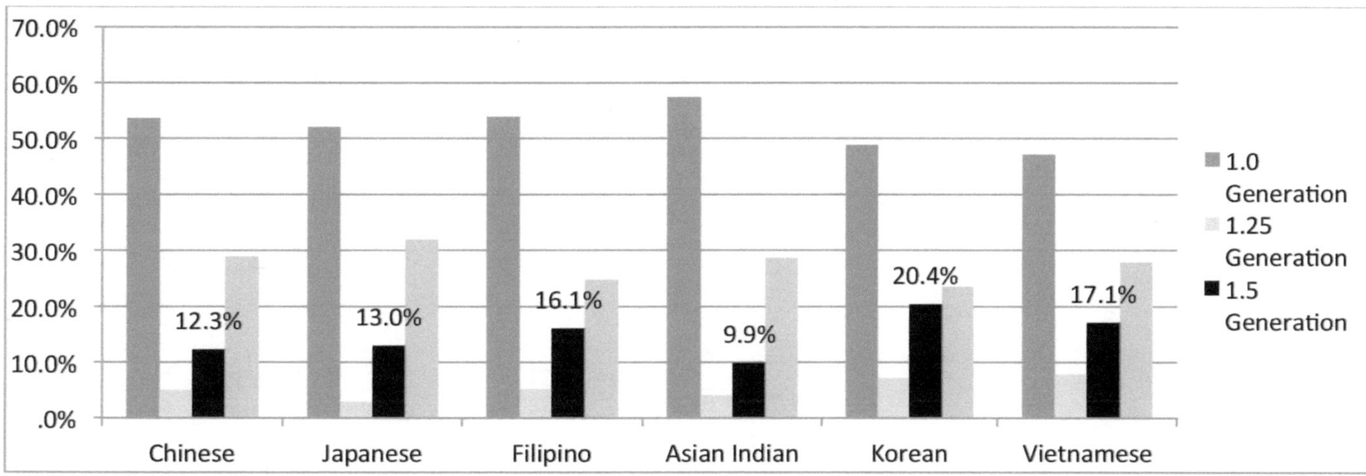

Figure 1.1 Generation by select Asian groups, ACS 2009–2011, Washington-Baltimore region. *Note*: Chinese (N=116,072); Japanese (N=14,785); Filipino (N=79,560); Asian Indian (N=157,569); Korean (N=103,501). Graphic courtesy of the author.

The Korean community today, both nationally and regionally, is no longer marked by extreme gender imbalances of early Asian bachelor societies of the past (Matthaei and Amott 1990). Because Korean immigrants have been immigrating as families and women now also come on their own, censuses since the 1970s have documented a slightly higher ratio of women relative to men. In the Washington-Baltimore area, Korean American women (54.9%) somewhat outnumbered their male counterparts, which was true of all groups except for Asian Indians (49.8%).[5] Cross-metropolitan comparisons find that Korean women slightly outnumbered men in the three biggest Korean communities, suggesting a more stable orientation toward the host society in all of these communities.

MARITAL STATUS

Another important demographic information to consider may be marital status. Compared to men (and women) who migrate alone for the purpose of sending remittances to family members in the home country, immigrants who arrive with their wives and children, or who establish families via marriage in the United States, will have weaker transnational attachments since there are no separated family members or split households, enabling more long-term investments in the host society. Among Korean Washingtonians the proportion married (fifteen and older) was 58.3%, a figure on par with the region's Asian Americans as a whole (62.7%), but still the lowest of all Asian groups in the region.[6]

Approximately a third (31.4%) of Koreans in the greater Washington, D.C. region were never married/single, the highest figure of all Asian American groups in the region, but still far lower than figures for blacks and Latinos, two groups with the lowest and second lowest marriage rates of all groups. Korean Americans in the greater Washington, D.C. area also had slightly higher proportion married than Koreans in Los Angeles (56.6%) and New York (53.8%). The proportion of never married/single was also higher for Korean Washingtonians than in the latter Korean communities.

Even without examining the marital status differences by generation and sex, the figures above suggest that Latinos will be more transnational than Asian Americans because of their relatively low marriage rates. Cross-tabulations of marriage by sex indicate that Latino men have higher proportion of never married, suggesting that many of them migrate as target earners and remain transnational since their family members, particularly parents and siblings, continue to reside in the home country and may be dependent on remittances. The higher proportion of the married among Koreans, on the other hand, suggest that Korean families will become more established in the

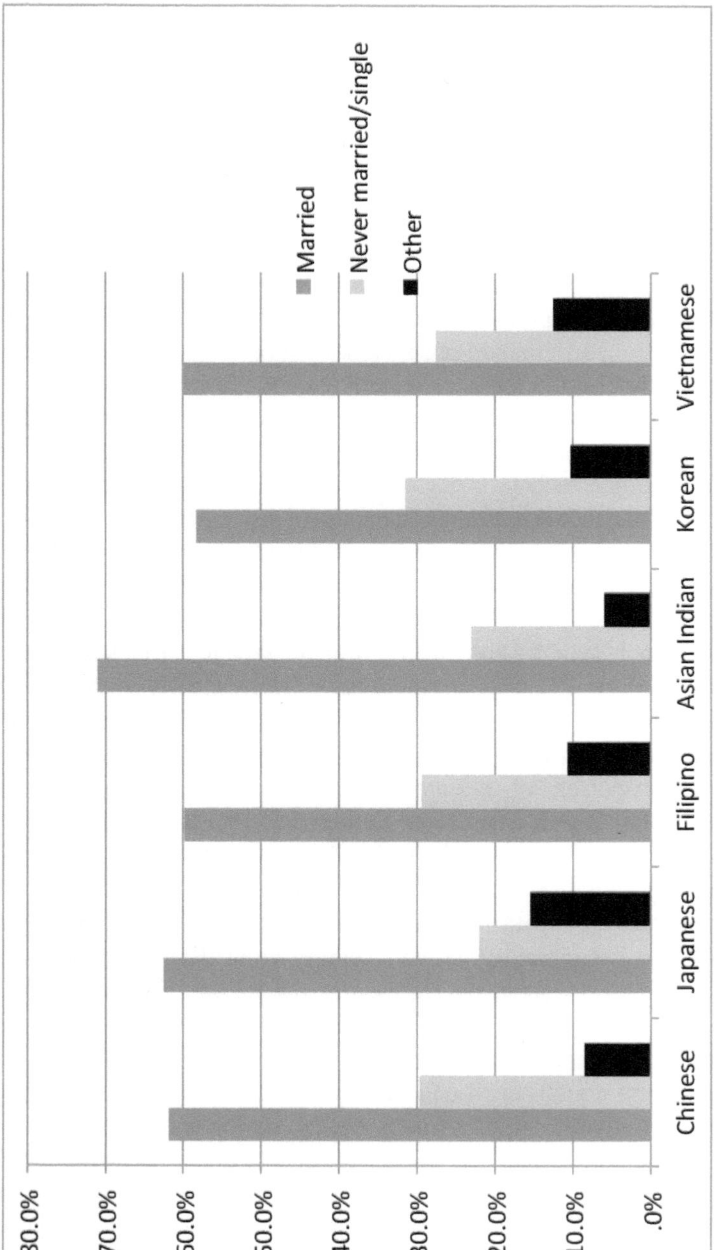

Figure 1.2 Marital status by select Asian groups, fifteen and older, ACS 2009–2011, Washington-Baltimore region. *Note*: Chinese (N=96,729); Japanese (N=12.868); Filipino (N=66.857); Asian Indian (N=124,116); Korean (N=88,240); Vietnamese (N=53,414); Total (N=442,224). Graphic courtesy of the author.

host country since many of them no longer have dependent parents or siblings for remittance obligations (see chapter 3), enabling long-term investments, both financial and psychological, in the country of settlement.

EDUCATION

Educational attainment has generally been found to have an impact on levels and forms of migrant transnational engagement (Hiebert and Ley 2006; Portes et al. 2002). While Portes et al. (2002; Portes and Rumbaut 2014) find that the more educated and financially stable engage in transnational activities as they are more economically secure, others find the reverse to be true, where transnational participation occurs among those with limited opportunities for upward mobility in the host society.

Korean Americans in the Washington, D.C. area (twenty-five and older, not in school), like their national counterparts, were well educated, with more than half (51.6%) holding a bachelor's degree or higher. This figure is comparable to whites (51.5%) in the region but lower than those of Asian Americans (60.9%). In fact, among Asian Americans, they were second last to the Vietnamese (30.5%) in the proportion of college graduates, while Asian Indians had the highest proportion of college graduates (79.8%), followed by Chinese Americans (70.3%).

Although higher than figures from national averages, Black Americans (26.0%) and Latinos (22.0%) in the region were clearly disadvantaged educationally, relative to other groups, as they had the lowest proportion of college graduates of all groups.[7] Except for Filipino American men in the region, higher proportion of Asian men had college and beyond education than women. Relative to Korean New Yorkers (57.1%) and Korean Angelenos (53.5%), Korean Washingtonians (51.6%) also had slightly lower rates of college completion.

The high levels of education among Koreans were corroborated from the 2003 D.C. Korean community survey, which, while dated, represents one of the few surveys conducted on Koreans in the region. The survey found that 59.7% (24 and older) of Korean Washingtonians were college graduates, a proportion comparable to the 2009–11 Census data figures. Women in the sample were equally well educated, with 59.8% of women holding a college degree relative to 60.7% of men, but the caveat is that fewer women responded to the 2003 mail survey, cautioning against drawing reliable conclusions from the small sample size. Similarly, the 2012 Pew Research Center's Asian American survey (2) confirmed the selective nature of Korean immigration to the United States, with a quarter (27%) of South Koreans aged between twenty-five and sixty-four holding a bachelor's degree or more, while nearly 70% of Korean Americans had a bachelor's degree or more.

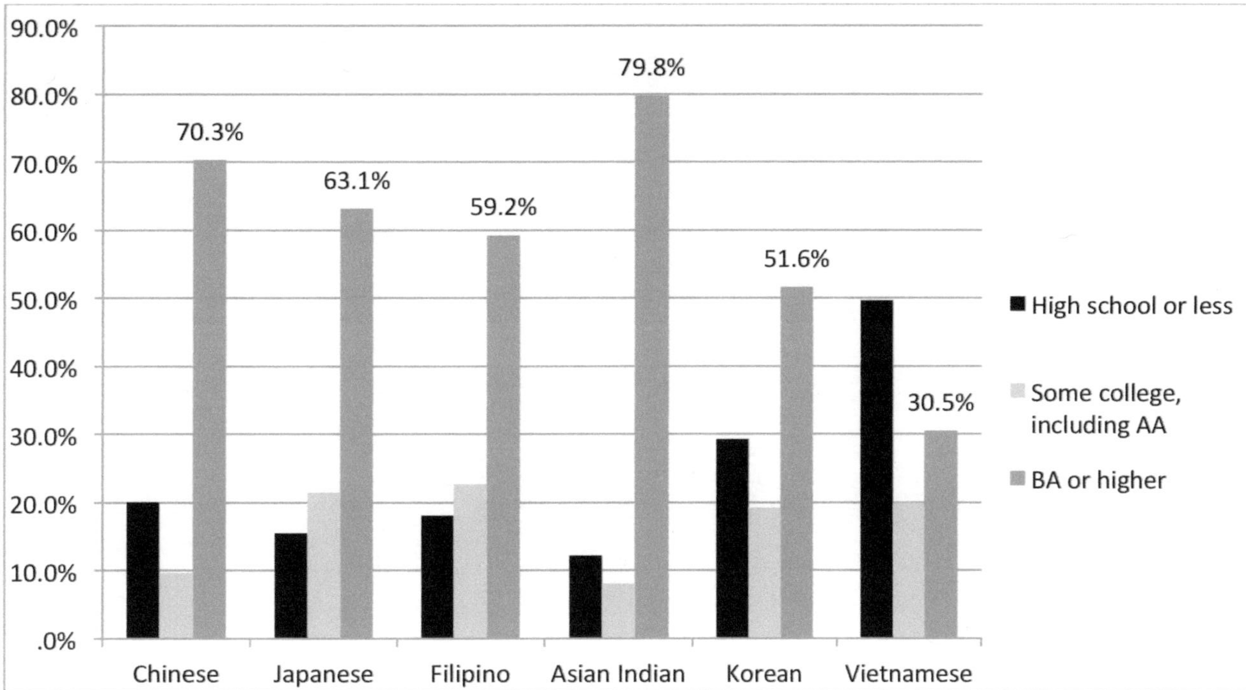

Figure 1.3 Educational attainment, select Asian groups, twenty-five and older, NIS, ACS 2009–2011, Washington-Baltimore region. *Note*: Chinese (N=76,073); Japanese (N=11,064); Filipino (N=53,803); Asian Indian (N=100,922); Korean (N=66,697); Vietnamese (N=42,448); Total (N=351,007). Graphic courtesy of the author.

LABOR FORCE PARTICIPATION

Rates of participation in the labor force provide important clues about the economic strength of the immigrant community and their prospects for transnational engagement. Relative to whites (72.4%), Korean Americans (70.5%) in the Washington, D.C. region had lower rates of labor force participation (sixteen and older, not in school) (ACS 2009–2011). In fact, they had the lowest rate of labor force participation of all Asian Americans, while Asian Indians had the highest labor force participation (79.0%), followed by Chinese and Vietnamese. Latinos (83.5%) had the highest rate of labor force participation of all groups, followed by Asians, whites, and blacks.

One possible reason for Korean Americans' low labor force participation is that Korean American women (60.4%) had the second lowest rate of labor force participation of all Asian Americans after Japanese American women (54.2%). Considering the small number of Japanese Americans in the region and their status as high-income earners as Japanese subsidiary managers, Korean American women's participation rate could well be the lowest of all groups. This has a number of implications, including Korean American women's impact on family/household income, which was also the lowest of all Asian Americans, as well as the role of self-employment in masking the contributions of Korean women (as unpaid family labor) to the family business. Furthermore, even when the generational status is taken into account, although 1.5 and second-generation Korean women generally outpaced first-generation Korean women (51.5%) in labor force participation, U.S.-raised Korean Americans still had the lowest rate of labor force participation among their Asian American counterparts.[8]

Cross-city comparisons indicate that Korean Washingtonians' (70.5%) labor force participation was comparable to that of Korean New Yorkers (70.1%), while Korean Angelenos (64.0%) had slightly lower rates of labor force participation.

SELF-EMPLOYMENT

In their survey study of Latino immigrants, Portes et al. (2002) observe that transmigrants are more likely to be found among immigrant entrepreneurs. Chin et al. (1996) also observe that transnational linkages with South Korea during its period of light industrialization were pivotal in establishing Korean immigrant businesses such as import-export of wigs, which helped to set the stage for entry into other businesses as well as securing important niches for importers, wholesalers, and retailers (Kim 1981, 121–143; Yoon 1997, 41–42). These studies suggest the significance of transnational connections in establishing small businesses both in the receiving country and in pursuing entrepreneurial opportunities in the sending country.

Korean Americans nationally but also in the greater Washington, D.C. region are disproportionately involved in entrepreneurship, which, for better or worse, has come to define first-generation Koreans (Abelmann and Lie 1995; Bates 1997; Kim 1981; Light and Bonacich 1988; Min 1996, 2011; Park 1997; Yoon 1997). Korean Washingtonians were no exception to this trend, registering the highest self-employment rate (sixteen and older, working, and not in school) of all groups, including other Asian Americans: 22.9%. Black Americans had the lowest self-employment rate at 5.5%, while among Asians, Filipinos had the lowest self-employment rate (3.7%).

Korean American women, like their male counterparts, were also highly involved in entrepreneurship, exhibiting higher rates of self-employment than women of other ethnic groups in the region. While Korean Washingtonians' (22.9%) self-employment rates stood midway between those of Korean Angelenos (24.7%) and Korean New Yorkers (20.7%), they were high nonetheless, underscoring the significance of self-employment for Korean Americans regionally and nationally.

Number and Types of Korean-Owned Businesses

Like their counterparts in traditional immigration gateways in New York and Los Angeles, Korean immigrants in the area operate many small businesses serving majority, minority, and co-ethnic clientele.[9] For instance, the KAFGW (2009) reports that there were 11,000 Korean-owned businesses in the Washington, D.C. area in 1997, with an average annual sales or revenue of $257,000. There were 5,169 businesses with total sales receipts of $972 million in Virginia, 5,831 businesses with a total sales receipt of $1.2 billion in Maryland, and 972 businesses with average sales of $257,000 in Washington, D.C. (KAFGW 2009, 48).

Typical of Korean-owned businesses in other major urban centers, liquor stores and convenience stores catering to black customers in inner cities in Washington, D.C. and Baltimore were prominent among Korean Washingtonians. For instance, one-half of liquor stores in Washington, D.C. were Korean owned, and Koreans also controlled most of Washington, D.C.'s lottery sales despite the fact that few of them actually lived in the district (Gjelten 2016, 158). Before ordinances reducing hours for selling liquor were implemented, the share of Korean-owned businesses in black neighborhoods, especially in Washington, D.C., reached a high of 65% of all small businesses in the district (KAFGW 2009, 47). Korean Washingtonians, like their counterparts in New York City, have also been highly visible in dry cleaning

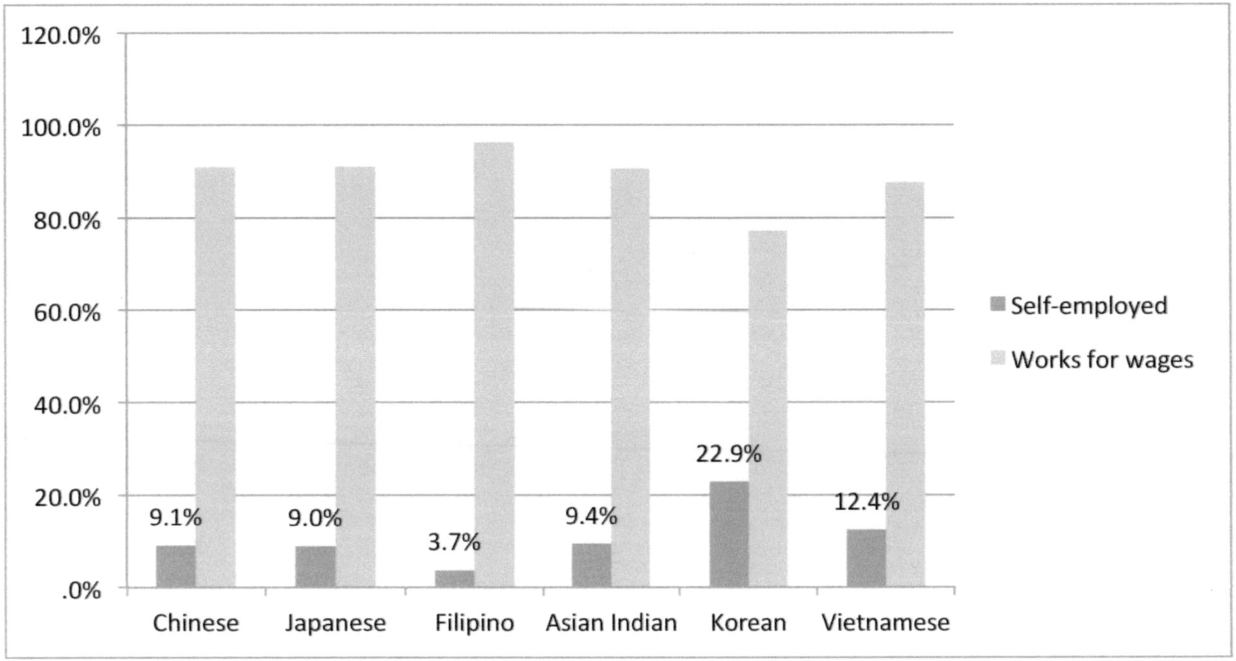

Figure 1.4 Self-Employment rates, select Asian groups, sixteen and older, NIS, working, ACS 2009–2011, Washington-Baltimore region. *Note*: Chinese (N=60,367); Japanese (N=7,064); Filipino (N=40,354); Asian Indian (N=74,450); Korean (N=42,018); Vietnamese (N=32,155); Total (N=256,408); NIS (Not in School). Graphic courtesy of the author.

and delis. In 2000, there were approximately 2,000 Korean dry cleaners in the area, out of which a whopping 90% were Korean owned (KAFGW 2009, 45). By 2012, this pattern of Korean dominance persisted, with nine out of ten dry cleaners in the Washington-Baltimore metropolitan area being Korean owned (Gjelten 2016, 215).

To examine the number and type of Korean-owned businesses in the metropolitan Washington-Baltimore area, I conducted an analysis of small business listings published by the Giant directory.[10] Though the Giant business directory is limited to businesses catering to a co-ethnic clientele, it still provides a glimpse into the size and scope of Korean-owned businesses since the 1980s. According to the 1985 Giant directory, auto repair (47) and real estate (42) were the most numerous businesses within the Korean community. What is worth noting is that the number of businesses (2,507), reflecting the size of the Korean population in the 1980s, was quite small. However, by 1994, real estate businesses (227) began to overtake auto repair (145) to claim the top spot, jumping more than five times from the previous decade. While auto repair (205) and other businesses held steady in 2004, real estate businesses doubled in number in 2004 to 447, reflecting the real estate boom of the 2001–2007 period in the region as well as in other major metropolitan areas. In other words, the growth in the number and type of area businesses begins around 1994 with the expansion of the Korean population in the area.[11] By 2004, there is additional increase, but with the exception of real estate and industries related to that sector, the numbers remain relatively constant. Interestingly, by year 2014, real estate businesses jump twofold to 856, while auto repair businesses (222) experience little to no growth.[12]

A major caveat with real estate, however, is that though it is a stable growth sector, many real estate agents obtain their licenses but do not practice, putting their numbers to about one-half of what is listed on the directory (Lee 2014a). The number of construction and construction-related businesses (330), niches that Koreans have carved out in the construction industry in the Washington-Baltimore metropolitan area, has also multiplied significantly since 2004 (85), highlighting again growth areas for the region.[13] This is, in fact, corroborated by my 2009–2011 ACS analysis of top ten industries/occupations for Koreans in the area, which shows construction to be a top industry among Korean Washingtonians (and also Korean Angelenos) but not for Korean New Yorkers.

In sum, it is clear from the analysis of the Giant business directories that with the growth of the Korean population in the region, numerous businesses have appeared to meet the needs of a flourishing community. Not only have their numbers increased over the thirty-year period, but also they have diversified into new industries and sectors. While some of them relied on business ties with the home country, most of them seem to have been the product of the

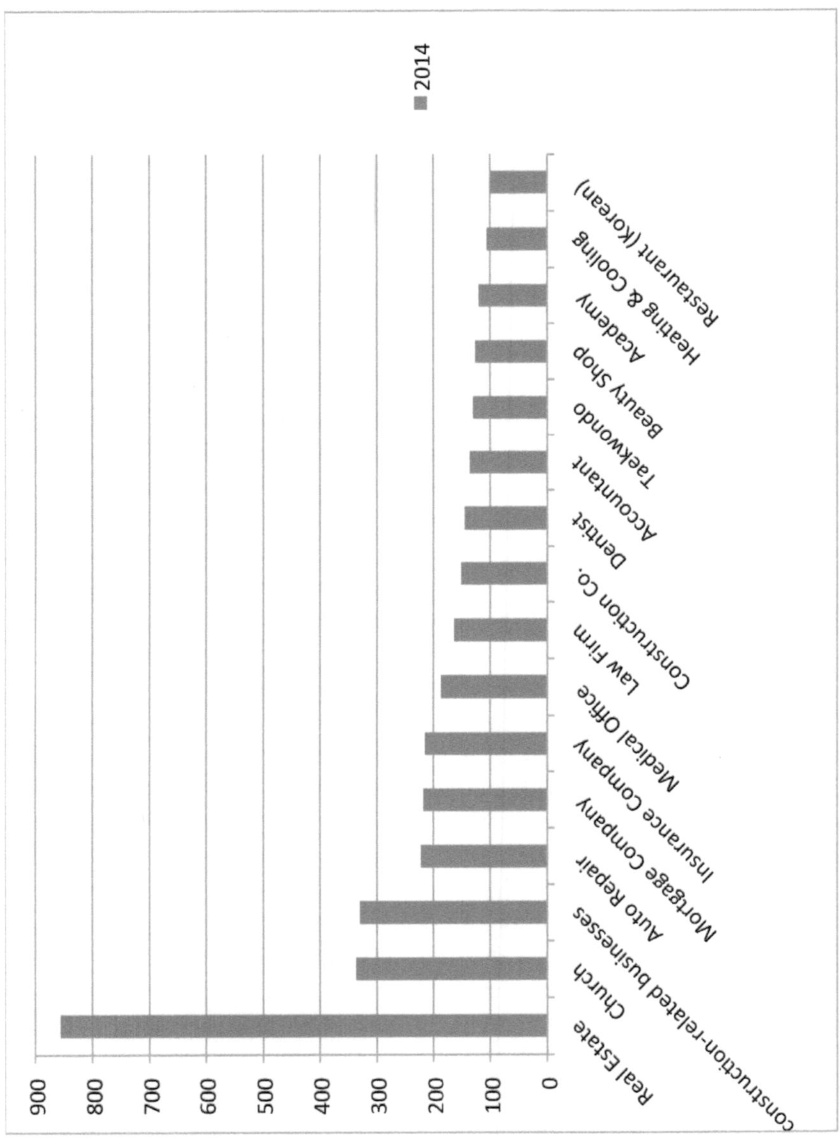

Figure 1.5 Korean-Owned business, Washington-Baltimore region, 2014 Giant Business Directory. Graphic courtesy of the author.

opportunity structure of the metropolitan region such as the real estate boom and niches in the construction industry.

Koreatowns in Annandale, Virginia, and Centreville, Virginia

The previous section underscored the development of the ethnic enclave with the sharp rise in the Korean population in the area. Because ethnic enclave businesses clustering in specific geographic areas and serving a co-ethnic clientele, namely Koreatown businesses, are most prone to transnational influences, in this section I describe the evolution of two key Koreatowns that serve as conduits for ethnic preservation and transnational activities and ties.

Among locals and the Korean community, Annandale, Virginia, in Northern Virginia is referred to as the region's Koreatown (Seminara 2011). Stretching 13.8 square miles inside the beltway, Annandale has a population of 41,008 according to the 2010 U.S. Census. In 1970, Annandale was 98.3% white, but by 2000, the white population declined precipitously to 57.2%. Today, the racial composition of Annandale is 27.6% Latino, 24.6% Asian, 5.7% Black, and 50.4% white (2010 Census). The number of Koreans in Annandale Census Designated Place (CDP) also grew from 724 in 1980 to 2,107 in 1990, 3,651 in 2000, but began to slide to 3,256 in 2010 and to 1,949 in 2013.

Korean-owned businesses were initially attracted to Annandale for its low rents and close proximity to D.C., given its easy access to the beltway (495) and Interstate 395 (KAFGW 2009, 60). In the late 1980s Annandale began to assume the formal title of Koreatown as many Koreans started purchasing properties there, especially small commercial buildings (KAFGW 2009, 61, 63). It is reported that 70% of businesses in Annandale are Korean owned (KAFGW 2009, 61), and approximately 300 Korean companies do business there. But as indicated earlier, few Koreans actually live there, making up only 5.2% of the Annandale population in 2015.[14]

Since 2000, a second Koreatown has appeared in Centreville, Virginia, that has also been witness to a growing Korean population (Lee 2014b, 2015).[15] Centreville, Virginia, has a total population of 71,135 (2010 Census) and covers 12.04 square miles. Whites constitute more than one-half (57%) of the area population, followed by 25.7% of Asians, 7.5% of blacks and 13.4% of Hispanics. The median household income was $101,537 (2008–2012 ACS). In 1990 there were 378 Koreans in Centreville, but by 2000, their numbers rose to 2,028, and by 2009–2011, to 7,832, representing 11% of the CDP's population, but 40.9% of the total Asian population in Centreville (Lee 2014b). It is indeed the most numerous Korean CDP in the region, nearly three times bigger than the second largest CDP in Northern Virginia (Fair Oaks CDP), and almost twice as big as the largest Korean CDP in Maryland, Ellicott City.

Centreville became an attractive place to settle and raise a family because affordable, new detached, and townhome constructions appeared for young families priced out from places like Burke, Springfield, and Fairfax (KAFGW 2009, 65; Lee 2014b). In fact, Centreville's location at the far western end of Fairfax County was not ideal for commuting to Washington, D.C. since it took forty to fifty minutes by car to the district. But with the heating up of the real estate market in Northern Virginia beginning in 2000 and the ability to purchase new, relatively inexpensive homes, many young Korean families chose Centreville despite the long commute (Lee 2014b). Moreover, the fact that both Centreville and Chantilly were also in Fairfax County appealed to many Korean families looking to send their children to good schools. With the opening of Grand Mart in 2002 (which has been replaced by Lotte Plaza today), Centreville became even more attractive for Korean Washingtonians, hastening the growth of the Korean population there, and in turn, causing an influx of Korean businesses to serve an expanding co-ethnic clientele.[16]

Unlike Annandale, Centreville is both a major place of Korean residence and business activity (Lee 2015a). In practical terms, this means that while Koreans residing in the metropolitan Washington, D.C. can drive to Annandale, Virginia, to experience Koreatown (K-Town), Korean residents in Centreville can meet all of their ethnic needs such as food, shopping, and social life there, enabling them to avoid the notorious route 66 and 495 traffic. Though Annandale Koreatown is where Korean businesses serving a Korean clientele are located but few Koreans actually reside, Centreville has emerged as a new suburban Koreatown where both residences and businesses coexist and ethnic institutional completeness flourishes with Korean restaurants, spas, supermarkets, churches, and bakeries, to name a few. Another key difference between Centreville and Annandale is that few businesses in Centreville center on nightlife, illustrating the residential and family orientation of the ethnoburb (Lee 2015a).[17] As a new epicenter of the Korean business and social life in the exurb, Centreville has not only attracted Korean residents residing in nearby Prince William County, including Manassas, Gainesville, and Haymarket, which is further west from Centreville, to dine and shop, but has also spurred more Koreans to move further out into these areas as it is a short driving distance from Centreville (Lee 2014b).

There were 274 Korean-owned businesses in Centreville in 2014, ranging from realtors (forty-two), construction firms (fourteen), heating and cooling (ten), beauty and hair salons (seven) to insurance agents (seventeen), restaurants (nineteen), chiropractors (eleven), dentists (sixteen), acupuncturists (eight), bakeries (four), and cram schools (twenty) (Lee 2014b). This is a dramatic change from fifteen years ago when there were no Korean restaurants in the area, but today close to twenty Korean restaurants operate in Centreville. Lee (2014b) notes that there were three main business areas of Korean concentration in Centreville: Grand Plaza strip mall where Spa World and H-Mart are located; Centrelee Business Park where Dunkin Donuts is located; and Centreville Crest Shopping Center where Lotte Plaza is housed. The biggest among the three is Grand Plaza strip mall, a seventeen-acre commercial lot that houses not only H-Mart and Spa World, but also Woori America Bank, Tous Les Jours bakery, Jang Won Korean-Chinese restaurant, and Honey Pig restaurant, to name a few. Up until early 2000, this strip mall had been a desolate place during weekends, but after Min Sik Kang, president of Grand Mart, purchased it for $24 million in 2004 and Korean-owned businesses began to lease and open new businesses there, the strip mall has breathed new life, becoming the principal area of Korean business activity in Centreville (Lee 2014b).[18]

OCCUPATION

Although scores of Korean Americans are self-employed, given that more than half are also college graduates, many of them find employment in the professional sectors of the mainstream American economy. Due to the unique opportunity structure of the Washington-Baltimore region, namely, the vast network of jobs in the civilian and military sector in the federal agencies as well as in the private sector connected to defense-related government contracts, many are employed as professionals in federal agencies and in defense-related and high-tech companies.

A breakdown of occupations among Korean Washingtonians using the ACS 2009–2011 reveals that roughly a third (29.8%) of Korean Americans held professional and related occupations (sixteen and older, not in school, and working) compared to 32.9% of whites, 21.1% of blacks, 39.6% of Asians, and 11.7% of Latinos. This figure was slightly below those of the region's whites, and the second lowest of all Asian groups in the region. Asian Indians had the highest proportion working in professional and related occupations: 51.1%. What is worth noting about the relationship between education and occupation, which are generally associated, is that despite their higher rates of college graduates in comparison to the Vietnamese, Korean Americans trailed slightly behind the Vietnamese (27.1%) in the proportion in professional and related occupations.

The proportion of Korean Americans in management, business, and financial operations occupations (sixteen and older, not in school, and working) was 19.3% compared to 25.4% of whites, 17.4% of blacks, 19.2% of Asians, 10.1% of Latinos. Asian Indians (23.6%) had the highest proportion of employment in management occupations among Asians, followed by Japanese Americans (23.0%). The Vietnamese (11.4%), reflecting their lower proportion of college graduates than Koreans, had the lowest proportion in management occupations of all Asians.

These occupational distributions suggest that despite significant educational attainments by Asian Americans, returns to education for Asian Americans in the region, including Korean Americans, are lower relative to whites, particularly in management, business, and financial operations positions. Even when age is taken into account, given that whites on an average are older (among twenty-five- to sixty-four-year-olds), only Japanese Americans seem to somewhat surpass whites in the proportion in management occupations, while the rest of Asian Americans in the region trail behind whites.

Cross-metropolitan comparisons indicate that Korean Washingtonians (30.8%) fared somewhat better than Korean Angelenos (24.3%) and Korean New Yorkers (24.0%) in the proportion in professional and related occupations. The proportion in management, business, and financial operations occupations, on the other hand, favored Koreans in Los Angeles (23.0%), whose population was older and as a result, more established.

Using the ACS occupation and industry codes in the ACS 2009–2011, I also examined the top ten occupations and industries among Korean Americans (sixteen and older, NIS, working). While carpentry was a top occupation in the greater Washington, D.C. area, it did not make the top ten occupations in Los Angeles and New York. What is notable in cross-metropolitan comparisons of top industries is the opportunity structure of each region in their occupational specialization despite many similarities in the industries Korean Americans tend to cluster.[19] For example, national security and international affairs was in the top ten industry category among Korean Washingtonians, reflecting the role of the federal government for Korean and other Washingtonians alike. Restaurants and other food services, construction, dry cleaning and laundry services, and grocery services were also the top service and manual work industries.

By contrast, securities, commodities, funds, trusts, and other financial investments was in the top ten industry category among Korean New Yorkers, reflecting the role played by Wall Street in the employment of residents of New York City. Nail salons, the top industry among Korean New Yorkers but absent in Los Angeles and Washington, D.C., was invariably a New York phenomenon as the industry in the Greater Washington, D.C. area was dominated by the Vietnamese (Kang 2010). Probably reflecting the larger Korean population in Los Angeles, real estate and religious organizations industries, while not making the list in Washington, D.C. and New York, were the top ten industries among Korean Angelenos.

INCOME

Disposable income, whether from personal or household incomes, will impact one's ability to engage in transnational activities such as sending remittances,

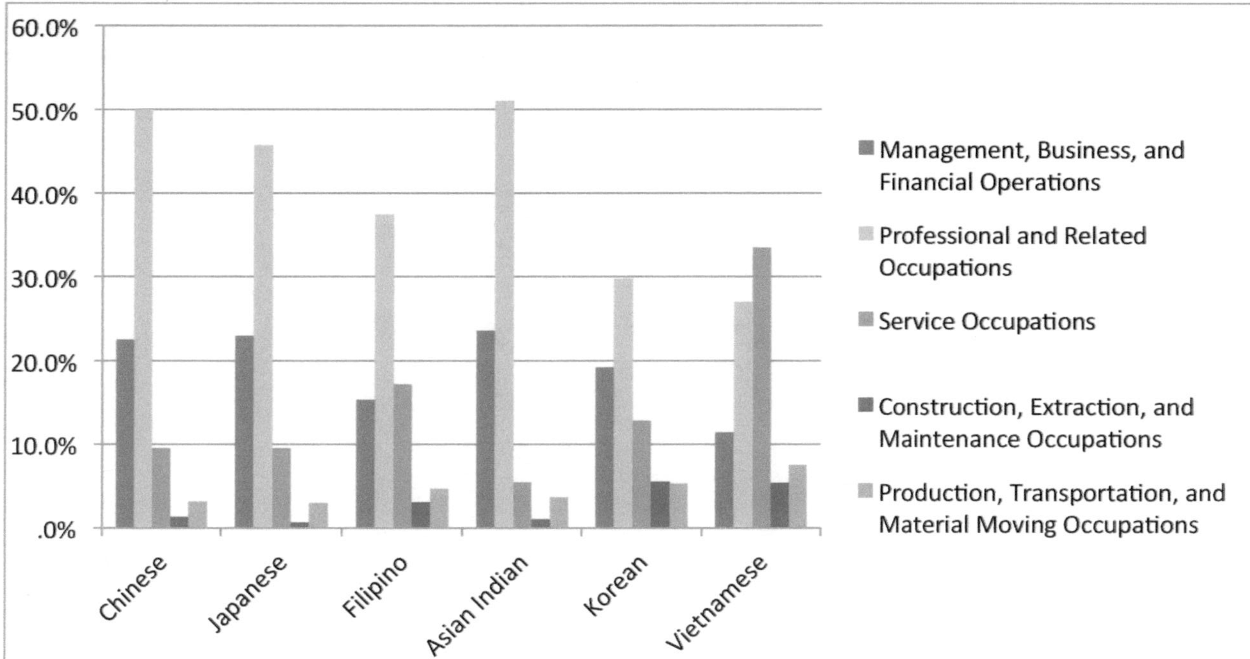

Figure 1.6 Occupation, select Asian groups, sixteen and older, NIS, working, ACS 2009–2011, Washington-Baltimore region. *Note*: Chinese (N=57,704); Japanese (N= 7,198); Filipino (N=41,870); Asian Indian (N=77,884); Korean (45,880); Vietnamese (N=31,863); Total (N= 262,399); NIS (Not in School). Graphic courtesy of the author.

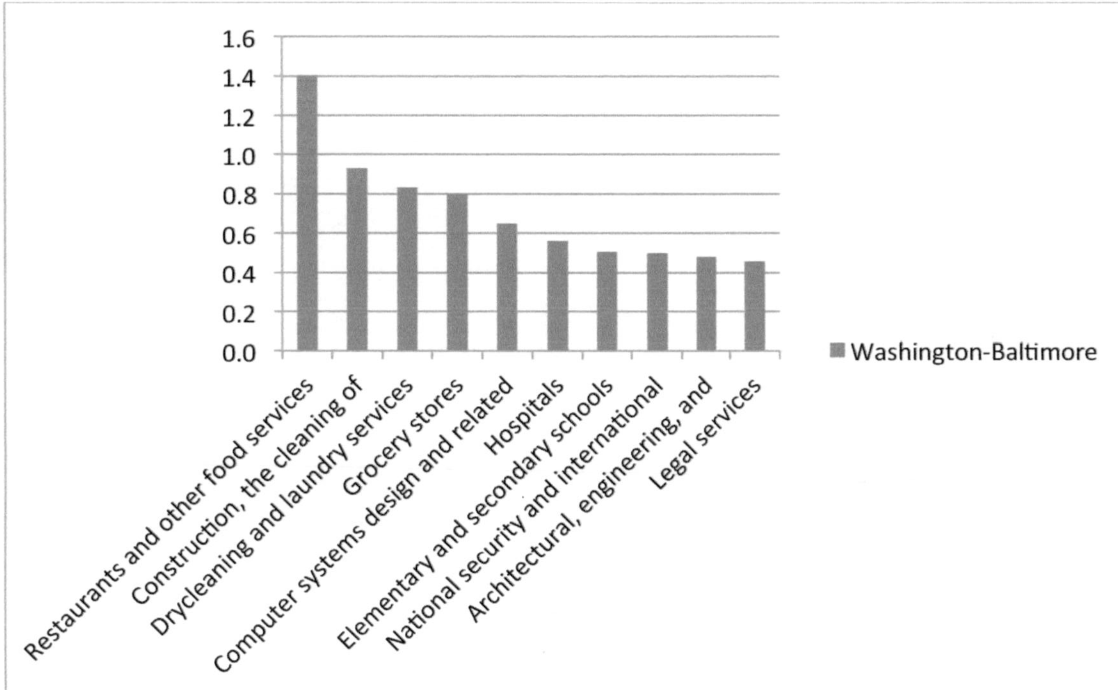

Figure 1.7 Top ten industries for Koreans in the Washington-Baltimore region, sixteen and older, not in school, working, ACS 2009–2011.
Note: Chinese (N=110,135); Japanese (N=14,379); Filipino (N=75,632); Asian Indian (N=144,294); Korean (N=99,783); Vietnamese (N=63,113); Total (N=507,336). Graphic courtesy of the author.

making investments, or visiting the home country. Korean American households ($92,841) had much lower median household income (eighteen to sixty-four, not in school and working) than whites ($122,700) and Asian Americans ($116,886), but somewhat higher median income than blacks ($80,296) and Latinos ($77,367).[20] Korean Americans in the region had the lowest household income of all Asian Americans, slightly below Vietnamese households ($104,085).[21] Asian Indians ($136,666), followed by Chinese ($125,000), had the highest and second highest household incomes of all Asian Americans. Interestingly, despite having the lowest median household and family incomes of all Asian Americans in the region, the median home values of Korean Americans were the third highest, slightly above those of Japanese, Vietnamese, Filipino, and also white households/families. Korean households in Washington, D.C. ($92,841) were a bit better off than Korean households in New York ($86,651) but far above those in Los Angeles ($76,800).

HEALTH COVERAGE

Anecdotal evidence suggests that many immigrants often visit the home country for health reasons, especially to undergo dental treatments, surgeries, or screenings for cancer or other illnesses. For instance, in his content analysis of postings on MissyUSA, the largest Korean women's online community in the United States and Canada, with a membership of 13,000 in 2002, Oh (2016, 2235, 2237) found that questions regarding medical, especially dental, services and costs were often asked, prompting the following responses:

> As soon as I visit Korea, I am going to have plastic surgery. . . . Can you recommend one of its clinics or hospitals that have already gained great reputations in the field? (February 20, 2012).
>
> I need to have one of my teeth crowned. Here, its cost amounts to almost $1,000 without endodontic treatment. This summer, I am going to Korea. Is it a good idea that I put the crown of my tooth in Korea? (February 19, 2012)
> Six responses to the inquiry:
>
> Its cost may be almost over $300 in Korea. Do it there. (Respondent 1)
>
> Its full crown costs $500 in Korea. (Respondent 2)
>
> I did it in Korea last fall by paying for $300. Of course, you can put a crown valued at $500. (Respondent 3)
>
> Here I paid for almost $1,000 to replace my broken crown without endodontic treatment. . . . If I were in your place, I would do it in Korea. (Respondent 4)

Can you believe that it costs $3,600 in Manhattan? (Respondent 5)

> American dentists recommend a porcelain crown, not a gold one. When you smile, a gold crown looks awkward. If you want to wear a porcelain crown here, its cost will not be as expensive as you thought. (Respondent 6) (Quoted in Oh 2016, 2237)

Additionally, the Korean state has granted health coverage to Korean American seniors who reside in Korea for more than six months, prompting return migration. Newspaper advertisements often feature and promote homeland medical tour packages, especially comprehensive health screenings for colon and stomach cancers.

Korean Americans in the Washington, D.C. region (27.1%), due to their high self-employment rate, had the lowest health insurance coverage of all Asian Americans (14.1%), and these figures were only surpassed by Latinos (32.2%) who had the lowest health insurance coverage of all groups.[22] The lack of health insurance coverage for Korean Americans, for example, was more than twice that of Vietnamese (12.9%) and four times that of Filipinos (7.6%) and three times that of Asian Indians (8.9%). The three biggest Korean communities also suffered from limited health coverage, with a third (33.2%) of Korean Angelenos and 28.1% of Korean New Yorkers lacking health insurance coverage.

ENGLISH PROFICIENCY

English proficiency, or the lack thereof, along with difficulties in transferring foreign education credentials, has been one of the primary reasons for undertaking self-employment among Korean Americans (Kim 1991; Min 1996; Yoon 1997). Levels of English fluency also affect degrees of transnational engagement since immigrants often seek the comfort of the home language and culture for friendships, for consumption of home country cultural products and consumer goods, for co-ethnic church membership, and for patronage of co-ethnic businesses, to name a few (Lee 2004; Park 2009; Son 2015; Yin 2015).

The proportion of Korean Americans (17.9%) speaking only English (five and older) was the second lowest after the Vietnamese (11.6%).[23] Although U.S.-raised Korean Americans were likely to be fluent in English, first-generation Koreans, on the other hand, were particularly hampered by difficulties with English. Regarding the proportion who "spoke English, but not well," Korean Americans (19.4%) again ranked the second lowest after the Vietnamese (20.3%). Because Filipinos and Asian Indians were fluent in English owing to legacies of colonial rule under the United States (the Philippines) and Britain (India), only 2.7% of Filipinos and 4.2% of Asian Indians indicated that they did not speak English well.

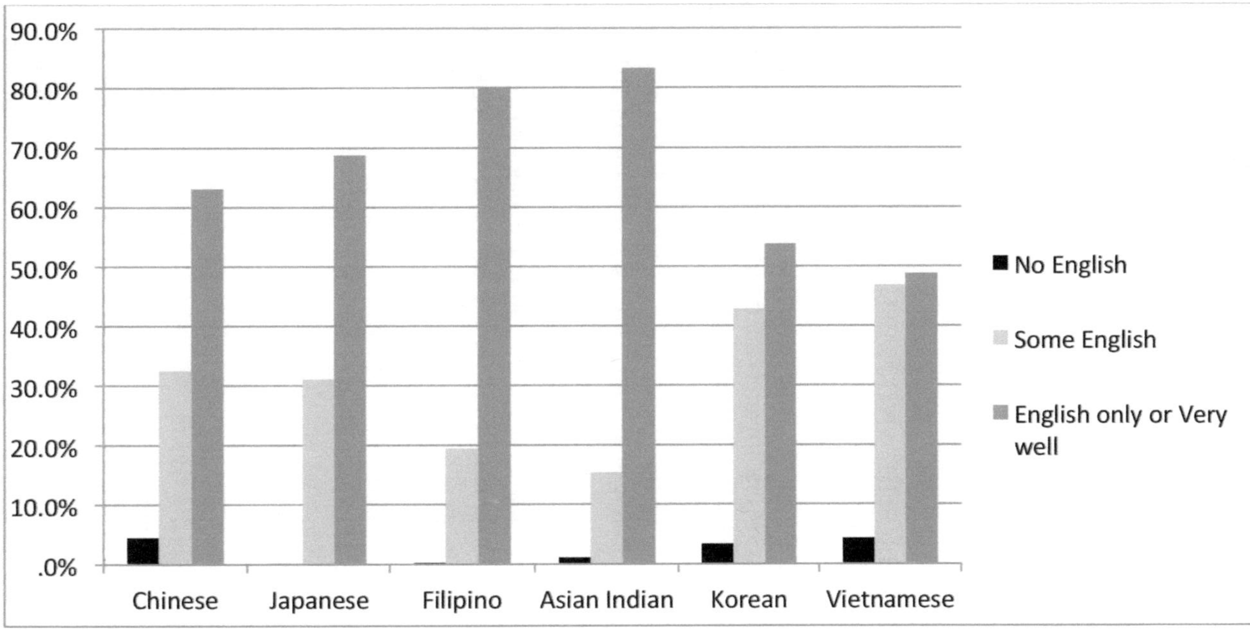

Figure 1.8 English-speaking ability by select Asian groups, five and older, ACS 2009–2011, Washington-Baltimore region. *Note*: Chinese (N=110,135); Japanese (N=14,379); Filipino (N=75,632); Asian Indian (N=144,294); Korean (N=99,783); Vietnamese (N=63,113); Total (N=507,336). Graphic courtesy of the author.

Despite lower levels of education, but similarities in the language structure between English and Spanish, only 16.0% of Latinos did not speak English well compared to 19.4% of Korean Americans and 20.3% of Vietnamese who had the most difficulty speaking English of all groups.

The 2003 D.C. Korean community survey also found that fewer than a quarter (23%) were fluent or had no major problems speaking English during conversations. Only one-sixth (14%) spoke English only at home. The variation in English proficiency across the three communities was not considerable, with a slightly higher proportion of Koreans in Los Angeles (26.3%) and New York (20.3%) unable to speak English well than Koreans in Washington, D.C. (19.4%).

CITIZENSHIP AND NATURALIZATION

The transnational literature finds contradictory tendencies on immigrant political participation. On the one hand, participation in home country politics often gives the impression that loyalties are divided, making migrants suspect for many receiving governments (Portes and Rumbaut 2014, 163). But others find that increased participation in homeland politics is precursor to greater participation in the host country since political apathy is the norm for most citizens (Foner 2005; Portes et al. 2002; Portes and Rumbaut 2014, 182). It is, thus, important to consider rates of citizenship and naturalization, as they represent the first critical steps toward participation in electoral politics.

Korean Americans in Washington, D.C. still face major challenges in participating in local and national elections as roughly three-fourths (74.5%) of first-generation Koreans were foreign-born and 60.5% were naturalized (ACS 2009–2011).[24] Compounding the high foreign-birth ratio, Korean Americans, especially the first generation, also had lower rates of naturalization compared to other Asian American groups. Korean Americans (60.5%) ranked second in naturalization after the Vietnamese (76.9%). Given that many Japanese Americans captured in the American Community Survey for this region may be managers and subsidiary workers for Japanese corporations and therefore temporary residents who may be unable to become naturalized, Korean Americans actually had the second lowest naturalization rate of all Asian Americans in the area.

Yet, the proportion naturalized among Korean and Asian Americans was still promising when compared to rates of naturalization among Latinos in the region, who, at 27.0%, had the lowest naturalization rate of all groups.[25] In fact, a whopping 73.0% of foreign-born Latinos in the Washington, D.C. region were not citizens, suggesting legalization challenges afflicting Salvadorans and Guatemalans who hold Temporary Protected Status (TPS).

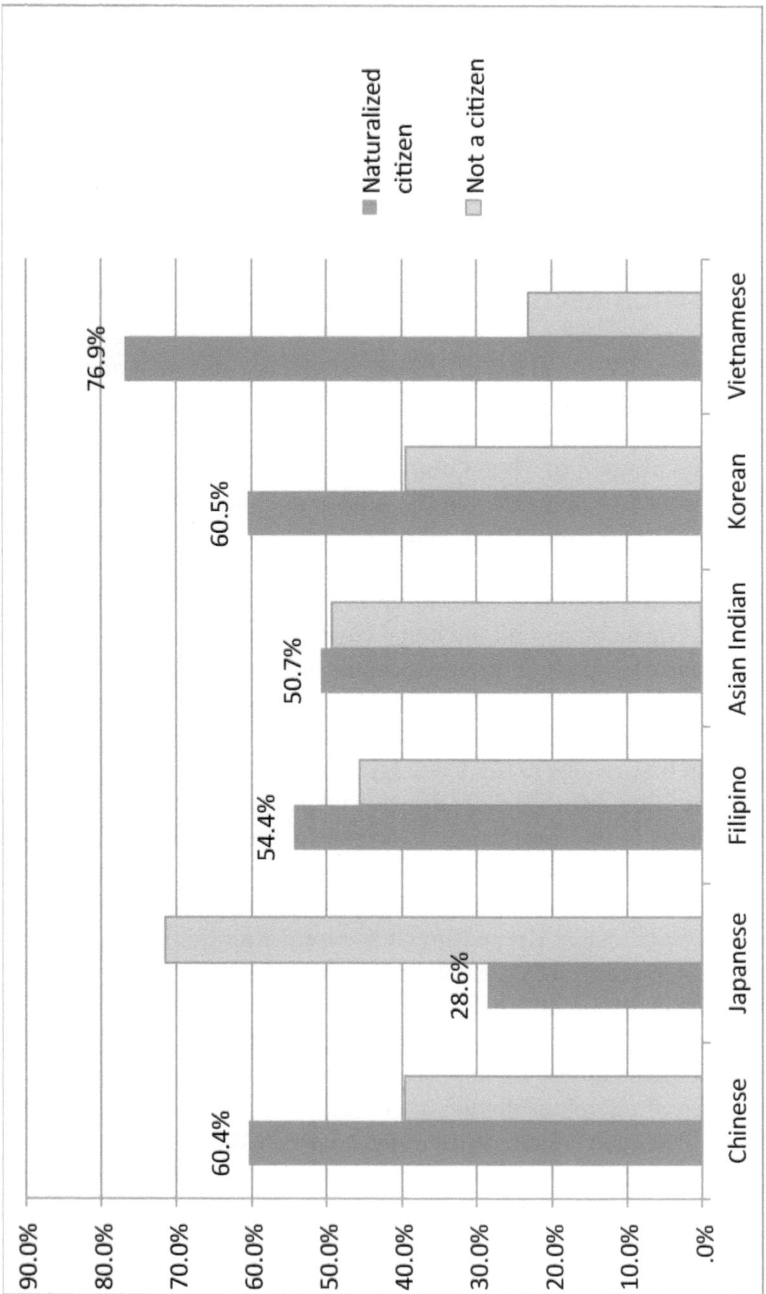

Figure 1.9 Citizenship status, select Asian groups in the Washington-Baltimore region, ACS 2009–2011. *Note*: Chinese (N=81,624); Japanese (N=9,252); Filipino (N=57,832); Asian Indian (N=111,337); Korean (N=77,795); Vietnamese (N=47,679); Total (N=385,519). Graphic courtesy of the author.

Cross-metropolitan comparisons find that the rate naturalized was on par for Koreans in all three communities. The rate of naturalization was also much higher for Korean women (59.1%) relative to men (40.9%). Interestingly, most Asian American women had higher rates of naturalization, except for Asian Indians and Vietnamese, suggesting the tendency of women to establish more permanent roots in the host country, while men seek to maintain transnational ties with the homeland (Foner 2005; Goldring 2002).

RELIGIOUS AFFILIATION AND PARTICIPATION

Portes and Rumbaut (2014, 319–320) observe that many transnational activities involving assistance to families and communities back home are either motivated by religious convictions or channeled via religious institutions. Even the "civic-cultural" or "hometown committees," which transnational organizations formed to help develop the village communities in the homeland, often had religious overtones or take on a religious character (Portes and Rumbaut 2014, 319). Hence, the scope of migrant religiosity such as religious affiliation and participation is helpful in understanding the forms and levels of transnational engagement with the home country.

Korean immigrants, just like their concentration in self-employment, are distinguished by an overrepresentation of Christians in the community. Up until recently, Christians were a smaller share of the population in Korea, yet most Korean immigrants to the United States have been overwhelmingly Christian (Kwon 2003; Min 1992, 2010).[26] A major reason for the high incidence of Christians in the community is the selective migration of Christian groups during various phases of Korean immigration to the United States, including the early Korean community in Hawaii. Second, there is substantial conversion of non-Christian Koreans to Christianity after immigrating to the United States given the church's pivotal role in the adaptation of new immigrants (Kwon 2003; Min 1992, 2010).[27]

In fact, various regional surveys corroborate the dominance of Christianity within the Korean community, as indicated by Korean immigrants' exceptional rates of church affiliation and weekly attendance. For example, in the 2003 D.C. Korean community survey, 85% of Korean Americans had a religion, out of which more than three-fourths (i.e., 78.7%) identified as Protestants, followed by 17.4% of Catholics and 3.5% of Buddhists. Among these religious practitioners, close to three-fourths (72.8%) of parents and 81.6% of the children attended church more than once a week. The vast majority of churchgoers (94.7%) also attended Korean churches, a pattern which diverged sharply from other Asian groups.[28]

Accompanying high rates of church affiliation have been the exponential growth of Korean churches over the forty-year period. For instance, the number of Korean churches nationally was 100 in 1970; by 2000, 3,402 churches were established, registering a thirtyfold growth over a thirty-year period. Korean churches in the Washington-Baltimore region recorded similar growth, starting with five churches in 1970 but growing to 187 in 2000.[29] By 2015, there were 368 Korean churches in the greater Washington, D.C. area, four more than in the previous year (Lee 2015b).[30]

Given the various social functions churches provide for the immigrant community (Min 1992), as well as critical roles they have played in the formation of the Korean community, Korean churches continue to exert a strong influence in community affairs.[31] As Okyun Kwon (2003) observes, the close relationship between the Korean church and the immigrant community continued even when many ethnic voluntary organizations were established with the growth of the Korean population. Although social service organizations serving the Korean community have appeared in recent years, the significance of the church has not declined and immigrant churches continue to play an active role in the lives of Korean Washingtonians, serving the role of both religious and community centers.[32]

Future studies need to examine more carefully the scope and intensity of religious transnational activities as immigrant churches serve as conduits for transnational engagement. For instance, many pastors travel regularly to the home country to coordinate various church and missionary activities with homeland churches and religious organizations. Sermons also routinely feature references to the home country, and pastors from Korea make frequent visits to give sermons in immigrant churches, reinforcing transnational ties. Additionally, many Korean foreign students, *jujaewons*, *girogi* families, and temporary visitors also participate regularly in church activities, leading to increased interactions and possibly the transmission of social remittances that reinforce transnational ties with Korean Americans.

CONCLUSION

This chapter examined key demographic and socioeconomic characteristics of Korean Americans in the Washington-Baltimore region and their prospects for transnationalism. The foreign-born still represent a larger share of the Korean population in the Washington-Baltimore region, but with the aging and retirement of the cohort that arrived in the 1960s and 1970s, the growth of the adult Korean population is being driven in large part by the coming of age of the 1.5 and second generation and the influx of Korean immigrants during the 1990–2010 period. This suggests that there will be a bifurcation in the transnational activities within the community, with the recent cohorts being more transnational while the 1.5- and second-generation Koreans becoming less connected with the homeland (see also chapter 6). Compared to other groups with lower rates of marriage, the higher proportion of married among Korean Americans suggest that there will be fewer reasons to engage in transnational activities since their immediate family members reside in the United States. However, among recent cohorts, given their younger age, it is likely that their parents are still alive and reside in Korea, requiring frequent transnational communication with them.

Educationally, Korean Americans in the region are well educated, suggesting they have the educational and financial stability to engage more actively in transnational activities as Portes et al. (2002) found among the well educated and financially stable. However, given that the Census does not ask questions that track immigrant transnational activities, we are not able to discern if high levels of education lead to greater transnational participation among Korean Americans. Nor do high rates of self-employment typical of Korean immigrants offer clues about their transnational activities.

With the explosion of the Korean population in the Washington-Baltimore region starting in the 1980s and 1990s, ethnic enclaves have formed in both Annandale and later in Centreville. The end result of such geographically based enclaves has been not only Korean-owned businesses catering to a co-ethnic clientele, which began to appear as quickly as co-ethnic customers created a demand for consumer and cultural products from the home country, but also growing transnational influences that have brought numerous home country food and consumer goods for sale at H-Mart, Lotte, and Home and Home (imported Korean housewares) to the globalization of Korean corporate chains, including Tous Les Jours bakery and Bonchon chicken, to storefront signs that incorporate the latest designs and slogans, to newest forms of leisure fashionable in the home country such as Korean-style saunas (Spa World).[33] To be sure, these transnational influences were beginning to form even in the early 1970s and 1980s, but the ease, speed, and volume with which these food and consumer items appear is quantitatively and qualitatively different from the past.

Although geographically based enclaves still anchor Korean immigrants' transnational practices via the consumption of homeland consumer goods, ethnic and transnational engagement today is no longer bound by geography given that ICT also enable the consumption of transnational media anywhere anytime (Yoon 2016). For instance, many popular homeland food and consumer goods can now be shipped from major websites and co-ethnic retailers, but some items can also be shipped internationally from the home country. Still, proximity does matter given the convenience factor as well as the ease with which cultural and consumer products can be acquired in the enclave, underscoring the continued significance of both business and residential enclaves on immigrant transnational participation.

Moreover, the development of ethnic enclaves into spaces of transnational consumption is leading to the formation of what Jinwon Kim (2016) calls transclaves, or "a commercialized ethnic space that exists exclusively for consumption, leisure, and entertainment; it is a space where transnational consumer culture from a sending country is embedded within a physical space in a receiving society, reflecting the landscape of the sending country's consumer culture through the physical appearance of buildings and stores, and the inclusion of franchise brands." Koreatowns in Manhattan or Centreville, thus, represent spaces where nation branding and Korean culture is promoted via the auspices of the Korean state and the globalization of Korean cultural industries, resulting in ethnic renewal and marketing of ethnicity to non-Koreans. Indeed, South Korean food and cultural industries such as bakeries (Tous Les Jours), fried chicken restaurants (Bonchon), South Korean-style spas (Spa World), and meat grilling eateries (Honey Pig) not only cater to co-ethnics but have also become increasingly popular with non-Koreans (Lee 2015a), expanding their clientele base beyond Koreans, but also creating pulls for Korean Americans whose lives, culturally and consumer-wise, are increasingly in sync with their counterparts in Korea. As Min (2012) notes, by serving as vehicles of globalization of Korean food to non-Koreans, Korean immigrants' cultural transnational ties have been strengthened. The same can also be said of South Korean franchises, whose business expansion in the United States to globalize their markets have also helped to extend Korean Americans' transnational ties (Min 2012, 69).

The implication of such transclaves for the Korean community, whether in Manhattan or in Centreville, is again the reduction of the transaction costs for engaging in transnational cultural and consumption activities, as they require little thought and effort, becoming part of what it means to be a Korean American in the age of ICTs and living lives that are in greater sync with the homeland.

NOTES

1. In California and Hawaii, Japanese Americans are predominantly U.S.-born given their long histories in those states. In other parts of the country, especially New York and Washington, D.C., they are more likely to be foreign-born since many Japanese Americans in these metropolitan areas tend to be Japanese subsidiary managers, branch workers, and students coming for work and education.

2. The large share of the foreign-born relative to the U.S.-born among Korean Americans (for that matter immigrants in general), as illustrated in the previous

section, may give an erroneous impression that most Koreans are recent immigrants with limited English fluency. Post-1960s Korean immigrants, unlike the split Asian American households of the past, have been immigrating as families, which means there are a considerable number of foreign-born Koreans who also arrive as children and are raised in the United States. This is the phenomenon that social scientists have dubbed as the "1.5 generation." Because the addition of the 1.5 generation appreciably expands the pool of those raised in the United States, it is important to consider the 1.5 generations with U.S.-born Koreans. For example, when 1.5 generation and U.S.-born Koreans are combined, the share of those raised in the United States jumps to 44% of the Korean American population. In using age of entry into the United States as a principal criterion for operationalizing generation, the proportion of either the first or 1.5 generation can expand or shrink depending on which age range is used to demarcate generation since those who arrive to the United States between the ages of thirteen and seventeen can be collapsed with the first generation, placed into a category of its own, or removed entirely from the analysis. If the 1.25 generation is dropped from the analysis, one option is to define the 1.5 generation as those who arrived at fifteen and younger, while the first generation is defined as those who arrived at age sixteen and older. In this book, I have decided to create a separate 1.25-generation category as these young adults do not quite fall in the 1.5-generation or 1.0-generation category, given that they have immigrated as teens during junior high and high school. I define the 1.25 generation as those who were born in Korea but arrived to the United States between the ages of thirteen and seventeen.

3. While Asian Americans (52.2%) had much higher proportions of the first generation compared to Latinos (38.7%), whites and blacks, as native groups, were disproportionately U.S.-born.

4. It should be pointed out that other demographic and socioeconomic characteristics of immigrants as well as levels of sending countries' economic development will also impact the scope and intensity of transnational activities practiced. For example, remittances are a big part of the foreign exchange earned by the Philippines.

5. Latinos (51.8%), on the other hand, were somewhat skewed toward men, which may reflect a tendency among Latino men to migrate for economic reasons as target earners but increasingly bring their wives and children along to reunite with them.

6. Asian Indians had the highest proportion married (71.0%).

7. Nationally, 55.2% of Koreans (Korean alone, twenty-five- to sixty-five-year-olds) held a bachelor's degree or higher compared to 33.4% of whites, 17.9% of blacks, 51.9% of Asians, 12.7% of Latinos, and 12.8% of Native Americans (ACS 2010).

8. Many women who drop out of the labor force due to childbirth usually reenter the workforce as soon as their infant children are placed in daycare. Although this may well be the course of option for Korean American women who give birth, some Korean American women, as the numbers indicate, may be opting to raise their children themselves until they enter kindergarten, delaying their entry into the labor force.

9. Operating numerous retail and wholesale ventures, Korean Americans have created well-known niches in green groceries, nail salons, dry cleaners, wig and beauty supply stores, delicatessens, variety shops, convenience stores, fish markets, and ethnic food markets. They have also diversified into clothing, jewelry, gift, stationery,

liquor, hardware, home-improvement, educational institutes, pan-Asian ethnic foods, and information and technology businesses. Furthermore, unlike the "mom and pop" retail shops of the past, Korean-owned businesses have also expanded into mid- and large-size as well as high-tech-oriented businesses (Yoon 1997). This expansion in the number and type of small businesses has also been followed by another trend, a shift away from "middleman minority" businesses serving a minority clientele to one catering to co-ethnics (ethnic enclaves) and mainstream customers. By and large, the shift from a minority to a co-ethnic and majority customer base is a natural outcome of the maturation of the community as the Korean American ethnic economy has grown to serve a larger Korean population, new niches serving a mainstream clientele have been carved out and consolidated, and new cohorts favor professional occupations and business services instead of labor-intensive, middleman minority businesses (Min 2013a).

10. Small business listings information were drawn from the KAFGW's (2009) compilation of businesses from the Giant directory, a published Korean telephone directory distributed for free each year. The years are 1985, 1994, 2004, and 2014. The compilation and analyses of business listings of the 2014 Giant business directory are my own. These business listings cater to a Korean clientele, and therefore, do not include businesses that do not market themselves in published Korean telephone directories such as dry cleaners, delis, convenience stores, and beauty supply (Lee 2014a).

11. Lee (2013a) reports that when Korean immigrants purchased their first homes in the Washington-Baltimore region in the 1970s, it was almost a community event that even made the news in Korean newspapers. The first Korean-owned real estate company to serve exclusively Korean customers in the area was Tae Kwon Lee's Dongnae Bangnae Realty, which opened in 1974 at the current location where New Star Realty, the largest Korean-owned real estate company in the region, is housed (RT 50, Fairfax). The first Korean American realtor in the region was Smith Kim who served mostly a white clientele.

12. In the latest analysis of the published telephone directory from the *Korea Times* (2015) by Lee (2014a), he found a total of 5,757 Korean-owned businesses in 2015, thirteen more than the previous year. There were 833 real estate agents, 79 mortgage brokers, 243 insurance agents, 188 lawyers, 137 accountants, 517 medical offices, 68 chiropractors, 172 dentists, 91 acupuncturists, 242 construction firms, 119 beauty/hair salons, 358 auto sales/service, 41 travel agencies, 188 hagwons or cram schools, and 368 churches/religious organizations.

13. Real estate, mortgage, and insurance companies registered continued growth, while construction, beauty/hair salons, and auto sales/service companies had their numbers fall from the previous year. Lee (2014a) also reports that siding, dry cleaning, and grocery were the most affected during the economic recession according to interviews he conducted with Korean certified public accountants. Korean restaurants also recorded growth despite competition and the economic recession. Before the slowdown in 2015, beauty/hair salons continued to grow as they were relatively easier to open and start.

14. Similar to other metropolitan regions where Koreatowns have been formed, there have been some conflicts with local residents over Korean-language signs and

criticisms involving their unwillingness to participate in local town hall meetings (KAFGW 2009, 62).

15. A small Koreatown has also appeared in Ellicott City, MD, the largest Korean CDP in the Maryland suburbs.

16. In order to cater to an increasing Korean population, many Korean-owned businesses in Annandale have either opened new branches in Centreville, or started entirely new businesses there (Lee 2014b, 2015a). Along with Korean restaurants, supermarkets, banks, and *hagwons* or after-school, private learning centers, Centreville has become home to the largest Korean church in the region, the Korean Central Presbyterian Church, which claims up to 5,000 members.

17. Centreville also has one of the lowest rates of crime and a household income that is 78% above the median state household income.

18. The same clustering of Korean businesses also formed in Centreville Crest Shopping Center, which houses not only Lotte Plaza, but also Kang Chon restaurant, Columbia College, Vitgoeul Tofu restaurant, and Shilla Bakery among others, and in Centrelee Business Park, an office/condo complex purchased and developed by Utopia Realty owner, Chul Kim, in 2001, where office and condo spaces were leased to Korean-owned insurance firms, Asian medicine, and photo studios (Lee 2014b).

19. The top ten industries where Korean Americans labored in were restaurants and other food services (8.4%), followed by hospitals (4.3%), dry cleaning and laundry services (4.0%), colleges, universities, and professional schools, including junior colleges (3.0%), grocery stores (2.7%), elementary and secondary schools (2.7%), construction (2.5%), clothing stores (2.1%), computer systems design and related services (2.0%), and religious organizations (1.7%), respectively.

20. Another way to examine the relative well-being of a group is to consider family income. According to ACS 2009–2011, there were 310,120 Korean families in the region. Median family income for Korean Americans ($79,775) was lower than that of white families ($110,000), but slightly above that of black ($70,600) and Latino ($60,000) families. Nonetheless, among Asian American families, Korean families again had the lowest median family income, far lower than that of Vietnamese families ($92,000). Asian Indian ($130,000) and Chinese ($105,140) families had the highest and second highest family incomes of all Asian American families.

21. Korean household and family incomes (18–64, NIS, working) were the lowest of all Asian groups in the Washington, D.C. region. They were lower than Vietnamese households even though the proportion of college graduates was higher for Koreans. In terms of personal income (18–64), Koreans had the second lowest income after the Vietnamese. Returns on education for Koreans were not as high despite the higher proportion of college graduates among Koreans as the Vietnamese. One possibility is that Koreans might be underreporting their income due to high self-employment rates (Min 1996), or there may be more earners among the Vietnamese than Koreans. When incomes are examined across generations, the lower labor force participation of Korean women seems to affect household and family incomes since there were fewer earners among Koreans. For instance, 49% of first-generation Korean women (eighteen to sixty-four) were not in the labor force, which was the highest of all groups. Generationally, higher proportion of 1.5 and U.S.-born Korean women, relative to

other 1.5 and U.S.-born Asian groups, were not in the labor force, although this proportion was lower than those of first-generation Korean women. 1.5 and second-generation Korean households were comparable to Vietnamese and other groups in income but it was first-generation Korean households that had the lowest household incomes, much lower than first-generation Vietnamese households. Also 1.5 and especially second-generation Vietnamese households had slightly higher household incomes than their Korean counterparts. This suggests that Korean women's lower labor force participation across generations seems to be driving the household income of Koreans, which raises questions as to why fewer Korean women were in the labor force. Another possibility is that some of them work in family businesses and are unpaid family labor. They may be working but are not being reported as such. Third, it could also be the case that many Korean families are still subscribing to middle-class ideals of the male breadwinner where wives opt out of the labor force and stay home as homemakers, although this ideal has been undergoing significant changes in Korea.

22. After implementing the Affordable Care Act in 2010, the proportion of those uninsured among Korean American went down considerably from a high of 27.1% in 2009–2011(ACS) to 22.4% in 2013, 17.2% in 2014, and 12.2% in 2015. With the election of Donald Trump and his campaign promise to remake "Obama Care," it remains to be seen how Korean immigrants' health coverage will be affected in years to come.

23. The 2012 Pew Research Center's Asian American survey (94) also found that after the Vietnamese (21%), only less than a third (30%) of Koreans indicated they could carry on a conversation in English "very well," the second lowest of all Asian groups. Korean Americans, among the six select Asian groups in the survey, also attached the most significance to speaking the Korean language for future generations. For example, 62% of Korean Americans saw it important to maintain the native language compared to 52% of Chinese, 29% of Asian Indians, and 25% of Japanese Americans (The 2012 Pew Research Center, 92).

24. Several recent surveys of the Korean community (published as reports), in particular the 2003 D.C. Korean community survey (N=303) and the 2006 Southern California survey (N=1,047), provide some information about the proportion of citizens among Korean Americans. In the 2003 D.C. Korean community survey, 58.1% of respondents reported being citizens while 29% were permanent residents and 10.2% were non-immigrants. In the 2006 southern California survey, the proportion of citizens was 39% while 33% were permanent residents, and 27% belonged to the other category (not specified).

25. With their concentration in important inner suburbs, Korean Americans are certainly becoming more visible and beginning to flex their economic and political clout in the region. In recent years, Korean Americans' ability to wield political influence has grown as the number of Koreans in the area has swelled, creating areas of significant concentration that compel elected officials from those districts to pay close attention to potential voters. In Northern Virginia suburbs such as Fairfax County where many Koreans reside, the community has been able to draw the attention of and recognition from politicians, electing as a result, the first Korean American, Mark Keam, to the Virginia House of Delegates (35th District). There are other notable

political figures such as Ilryong Moon, who is currently serving as chairman and member at large of the Fairfax County School Board (Gjelten 2016, 190). Recently, despite intense lobbying from the Japanese government, the Virginia House of Delegates and Senate passed a joint resolution to rename the Sea of Japan as Sea of Japan/East Sea in school textbooks, which was signed by Virginia governor Terry McAuliffe on April 2014. Electoral district leaders within Fairfax County have also started to pay greater attention to Koreans, given their size in the county, especially in places like Centreville. Lee (2015a) reports that many politicians such as Bob McDonnell and Terry McAuliffe, past and current governors of Virginia, have campaigned in Centreville during local and national elections, meeting with Korean business owners there. During the national Congressional and Senate elections, Mark Warner (current senator representing Virginia) and Gerry Connolly (Congressman representing Virginia) have also visited and spoken at the Korean Central Presbyterian church to garner Korean American votes.

26. A previously conducted nationwide survey of the adult population (ages eighteen to sixty-eight) in Korea found that the Christian population (21.1% including 4.9% of Catholics) was actually smaller than the Buddhist population (24.4%). But in recent years, among the religiously active population (51%) in Korea, Christians (51.8%) have begun to overtake Buddhists (45.6%), who, at less than 5%, constitute a smaller portion of the Korean population in the United States (Hurh and Kim 1990; Kwon 2003). With the rapid swelling of the Christian population in South Korea to roughly one-half of the Korean population, Korean immigrants are no longer emigrating from a non-Christian country.

27. There are three major reasons why church building has been at the centerpiece of community formation. First, there is a vacuum in community-based service organizations within the Korean community. Second, Korean immigrants often lack familiarity with local, state, and federal political and service organizations. Third, there is ample supply of Protestant leaders seeking to assume positions in the ethnic church. For instance, one striking feature of top occupations among first-generation Koreans was religious organizations, which goes to explain the proliferation of Korean churches in many metropolitan areas as there is an abundant supply of ministers seeking to serve established churches or start their own congregations.

28. For example, approximately 17% of first-generation Filipinos in the United States attended co-ethnic churches or temples, while 32% of Chinese in Chicago, 37% of Japanese in Chicago, and 65% of Asian Indians and Pakistanis in Canada did the same (Hurh and Kim 1990).

29. The first Korean church in the area was established on October 14, 1951 by Reverend Tae Mook Kim whose worship service with thirty-two Koreans marked the beginning of the Washington Korean Methodist Church (KAFGW 2009, 32, 66). Soon after, a second Korean church, a Korean Baptist church, was launched in 1955 by Reverend Chang Soon Kim who received support from the Baptist Church Promotion Headquarters in Korea (KAFGW 2009, 32). In 1965, Elder Kyung Ok Kang and Reverend Won Bong Park started a third Korean church, a Presbyterian church, in the metropolitan Washington-Baltimore region (KAFGW 2009, 32).

30. My analysis of the 2014 Giant business directory also found that there were 337 churches in the area, a slightly lower figure than the 368 reported by Lee (2015b) in his analysis of the *Korea Times* telephone directory, but high nonetheless.

31. Given their large numbers and visible role in the community, I examined the total annual budget and membership for select Korean churches in the Washington-Baltimore region. Based on information collected by the KAFGW (2009) on the most prominent churches in the area, I calculated the total annual budget and membership. Among the fourteen most prominent churches in the area, the total annual budget topped $26 million with a membership of 17,000. Assuming an annual budget of $100,000 (low end) to $200,000 (high end) per church, and a total of 300 churches in the area, the combined annual budget of these churches reached approximately $56–$86 million. While these figures are ballpark estimates, they still provide us with the membership size and financial scope of Korean churches, which are substantial. The church that I currently attend, Open Door Presbyterian Church in Herndon, which has more than 3,000 members in Virginia, is the second largest church in the region. Along with the senior pastor, there were ten other pastors in ODPC in 2016. The church houses both Korean-language and English-language congregations, holding separate services during the busy Sunday mornings.

32. The church has also played an integral role in preserving the ethnic culture, language, and identity for Korean Americans (Park 2009, 83). According to Park (2009, 102), given Korean immigrant women's newly found religious identity through the ethnic church, church communities can also be described as ethnic communities. In fact, much of the sense of belonging to the community takes place through the co-ethnic church (Park 2009, 103).

33. Korean-owned grocery stores first appeared in the Washington-Baltimore area in 1975. By 1980, there were thirteen grocery stores in Northern Virginia (KAFGW 2009, 44). Initially, most of the merchandise was obtained from wholesalers in New York and JFC, a Japanese wholesaler in Virginia. Since the opening of Rhee Brothers in Baltimore, however, nearly 70% of the groceries were sourced from local wholesalers and grocery importers (KAFGW 2009, 44). In the 1980s there were only twenty wholesalers in the area, but their numbers have since risen to forty. Florida Market (Capitol City Market now), which had been dominated by Jews, Italians, and Greeks in the past, has become home to close to fifty Korean-owned businesses in the 1980s (KAFGW 2009, 46). Located on New York Avenue and Florida Avenue in Washington, D.C., the wholesalers supplied groceries, liquor, vegetables, and other tourism-related products (KAFGW 2009, 45). A new development since 2002 in the grocery business has been the proliferation of large Korean/Asian/International grocery stores or mega supermarkets (KAFGW 2009, 49). Among them, Global Food, LLC., in Manassas, Virginia, and Woodbridge, Virginia, started by Jong Il Kim who had run a window manufacturing business (Home Kim Group) before venturing into the grocery business, catered primarily to Hispanics and Koreans in Prince William County. Another successful entrepreneur who began to open a series of Grand Mart stores in Centreville, Germantown, Gaithersburg, Annandale, and Baltimore was Min Sik Kang of Kang Foods (from Florida Market). But the two biggest supermarket retailers were H-Mart and Rhee Brothers operating under the Lotte and Assi Brands.

Rhee Brothers, headquartered in Hanover, MD, was founded by Seung Man Rhee, who began his grocery business in 1976 (KAFGW 2009, 49). A major importer and distributor of international groceries and food products, Lotte and Assi supermarkets have spread throughout the area, running ten supermarkets in the Washington-Baltimore region (see Lotteplaza.com). All in all, Rhee Brothers ran a hugely successful import and distribution business, along with mega supermarkets in California, New York, New Jersey, Philadelphia, Washington, D.C., Atlanta, and Chicago, recording annual sales of $500 million in 2006 (Mui 2006). The other major player competing against Lotte and Assi Plaza, both regionally and nationally, is H-Mart. Han Ah Reum first began in Queens, New York in 1982 and has been opening numerous Super-H and H-Mart supermarkets in Fairfax, Centreville, Burke, Wheaton, Catonsville, to name a few, as well as expanding into other major metropolitan areas of Korean settlement (McCart 2009). To date, there are ten H-Mart supermarkets in the Washington, D.C. area (hmart.com), matching Lotte's stores regionally but surpassing them nationally with over forty supermarkets. According to the National Retail Federation's "Hot 100 Chart 2014," H-Mart's annual sales topped $1 billion in 2014.

Chapter 2

Connecting with the Home Country

Information and Communication Technologies (ICT) and Transnational Media/Television

The world we live in today, especially following the vast advances that enable connecting and communicating instantaneously with others in far-flung places, is beyond recognition from earlier periods of human communication and interaction. With each innovation, information and communication technologies (hereafter ICT) have been continuously revolutionizing and remaking the way we communicate with others, bringing profound changes to our lives, including the lives of migrants and their families. From past ICT of choice such as letters, cassette and video tapes, landline telephone calls, and calling cards to the newest ICT, including email, VOIP voice over Internet protocol, mobile phones, Short Message System (SMS) and mobile instant messaging (MIM) text messaging, smartphones, and social network services (SNS), migrants and transnational families, given their separation from family and friends and desires to maintain cultural traditions abroad, have been at the forefront of ICT adoption and usage, both old and new (Bacigalupe and Lambe 2011, 14; Karim 2003; Madianou and Miller 2012; Parrenas 2005; Wilding 2006, 130).

An important question arising with extensive use of ICT and new social media is their impact on human behavior and the larger society as they get widely adopted and integrated into daily life. Do new ICT transform the way people communicate with each other, or are there continuities in the purpose of and experience with them? Debating whether transformative technologies have utopian or dystopian implications, some regard ICT as emancipatory spaces, while others see them as superficial and depthless when compared to face-to-face interactions (Miller and Slater 2000, 4; Wilding 2006, 126). Some researchers, taking a technology-oriented view of ICT, regard features inherent in these technologies as shaping the use and scope of ICT (check Yoon 2015, 4), while for others, it is not the technical or technological dimensions, but the social and moral, that decide their use, along with its affordability and users' digital literacy (Madianou and Miller 2012, 3).

Though ICT enable more and more people to overcome information and networking constraints, scholars also observe growing digital divide along age, social class, occupation, and nation, not only continuing and exacerbating old inequalities but also creating new ones (Benitez 2006, 187; Wilding 2006, 127). Among them, age divide in the use of ICT is arguably one of the more apparent disparities in transnational communication. For instance, Wilding (2006, 135) found that some older parents in her study opted to not purchase computers and participate in transnational communication with their children because of their difficulties in learning to use them. Denison and Johanson (2012, 237) found that younger Chinese tended to adopt the newest ICT, including mobile phone apps such as QQ (Chinese MIM text messaging app) and MSN messenger, while older Chinese relied on old-fashioned and less demanding ICT such as television, radio, newspapers, and fax. The same was true among young EU migrants who were using computers to watch DVDs and television, to listen to radio and music, and to read the news, while older adults obtained their entertainment and news from satellite television (Metykova 2010). In fact, computers and mobile phones, rather than landline telephones and traditional television and radio sets, were the ICT of choice among young EU migrants (twenty- to twenty-three-year-olds) since, like others in that age group, they were computer savvy and educated (Metykova 2010). In addition, as ICT use spreads globally, there is also a North-South divide in access to and use of the Internet and mobile phones (Hamel 2009, 4), with young urban adults in high-income countries having more extensive knowledge of and skills in ICT use than their counterparts in low-income nations.

ICT AND CONNECTED MIGRANTS

One of the distinguishing features of migrants in the digital age is their mobility and connectivity. According to Diminescu (2008, 568), the goals of today's migrants may not be assimilation but to "circulate and keep in touch," producing the "age of the connected migrant," the "interconnected immigrant" (Ros 2008), or the "connected transnational family" (Madianou 2014, 673; Madianou and Miller 2012, 1). For these migrants, the Internet, mobile telephones, and text and instant messaging are no longer simply items of occasional use, but integral to their lives, serving as essential components of daily life. Consequently, the transformations brought by ICT enable a new "transnational habitus" for migrants, or new networked lifestyles that enable multiple belongings, deterritorialized identities, and cosmopolitan values (Nedelcu 2012, 2).

ICT can be classified on the basis of "big" mass media or transnational media, "small" media such as telephones, letters, and family videos (Hepp et al. 2012, 173), and digital media such as the Internet and mobile phones and smartphones. In the age of the connected migrant (Diminescu 2008, 568), migrants do not rely exclusively on a single media but integrate various media within their lives to stay connected, using both mass media and the media of personal communication (Madianou and Miller 2012, 3). In their use of ICT, origin-oriented migrants, because of their orientation toward the home country, tend to be more reliant upon home country media (satellite television, radio, newspapers) (Hepp et al. 2012, 179) than ethno-oriented migrants, or those with dual identities with the host and home countries, and world-oriented migrants, whose focus is more European and global and hold cosmopolitan identities (Hepp et al. 2012, 180).

SCOPE AND FORMS OF ICT USED

The literature on ICT adoption and use vary notably by social class and ethnicity. For instance, middle-class immigrants such as Asian Indians and Filipinos had higher rates of Internet use than the native born, while Mexican Americans, in part due to family income and education, had one of the lowest rates of Internet use (35%) (Hamel (2009, 8). In Australia and Canada, where selective immigration policies brought well-educated immigrants, the native born trailed slightly behind immigrants in their use of ICT (Hamel 2009, 8–9). For example, while three-fourths (75%) of native-born Canadians used the Internet, 78% of immigrants were using it (Hamel 2009, 8–9). The same patterns also held true among migrants in Germany according to a 2006 survey, with migrants exhibiting higher rates of ownership of cell phones and desktop and laptop computers than the native German population, but lower use of the Internet (Kluzer and Codagnone 2012, 192). By contrast, in a 2008 survey in Spain, Internet use was higher among foreigners than among Spaniards (Kluzer and Codagnone 2012, 194).

Among the most important reasons for engaging in frequent communication with family and friends through ICT is, without doubt, to sustain intimacy from afar. For instance, Nedelcu (2012) found that Skyping once a week with family members helped migrants to establish a sense of intimacy despite the physical distance. Emails also enabled migrants to maintain intimacy by sharing everyday life experiences. For others such as EU nationals, photos, films, music, news stories, and web links shared with family and friends via ICT helped to create what researchers call the exchange of everyday stuff or the mundane, resulting in routinized communication across national borders (Metykova 2010). By the same token, while most of these

ICT-mediated conversations centered on the mundane stuff regarding daily life, as Wilding (2006, 132) observes, what was central was not the actual content but the exchange, which was what reinforced and helped to sustain intimacy with family members, blurring the distinctions between absence and presence (Hamel 2009, 28).

While the need to maintain intimacy with family members is a major driver of ICT usage among migrants, other factors, including cost, entertainment and news (information), and familiarity and continuity, among others, are also behind the wide adoption and use of ICT. For instance, cost was a major factor in the type and scope of ICT used for engaging in transnational communication. According to Metykova (2010), EU nationals in her study favored the Internet, especially Skype, email, and Messenger because of their affordability and accessibility. Skype was particularly preferred because it was free, allowed making cheap telephone calls to both cellular phones and landlines and did not require a computer to use it. Cost was also an important consideration in mobile phone use among these young adults, who, seeking to reduce international calling fees as soon as they settled in the United Kingdom, obtained two telephone numbers or two subscriber identity module (SIM) cards, one with a UK number to make calls within the United Kingdom and the other (home country number) to make "local" calls to the home country (Metykova 2010).

In addition to cost, communication with family and friends, unsurprisingly, represents one of the key uses of ICT. According to a Pew survey, one of the primary reasons for using social networking service/site (SNS or social media) was to stay in touch with current friends (67%) and family members (64%). This was also the case among EU nationals in Metykova's (2010) study who used ICT for interpersonal communication and for entertainment and news. More than three-fourths (77%) of Chinese migrants in Italy also used the Internet, which was accessed from Internet cafes, for chatting and relaxation, while one-half (49%) used it to play online games (Denison and Johanson 2012, 233–234). Greeks in Canada also utilized ICT, including computers and transnational media (television), to connect and interact with other Greeks around the world (Panagakos 2003, 201). Second-generation Greeks turned to Napster, especially its chat feature, to not only listen to Greek music, but also to connect with other Greeks (Panagakos 2003, 208).[1] Internet games, especially Greek online games, brought and connected Greeks together from all over the world (Panagakos 2003, 209).[2] Taken together, through the Internet, emails, and satellite television, along with the local Greek Orthodox Church and community centers and Greek cultural festivals, ICT helped second-generation Greeks to connect with and express their ethnicity (Panagakos 2003, 202).

Furthermore, as ICT, especially smartphones, become increasingly integrated into the daily lives of transnational families, they enable immigrants to achieve simultaneity and continuity. For example, among Korean transnational families, smartphones offered a "sense of continuity, consistency, and coherence" as they were always online (Yoon 2015, 6–7). Mobile communication, at least for some Korean transnational families, also had the unintended effect of expanding communication between parents and children, increasing the frequency and amount of conversations parents had with children compared to past face-to-face interactions. According to Yoon (2015, 6), Korean fathers were talking more frequently over the phone than they did in person because some of them felt more comfortable with mediated communication when talking to their daughters. Yet, as Metykova (2010) argues, many of the daily activities migrants engaged in via ICT were not new behaviors that emerged with migration, but were carryovers from the home country, suggesting that ICT provided continuity to migrant lives in the host society.

Another major use of ICT is to obtain news and information from the home country, which again assists immigrants to stay connected with the homeland. Among immigrants in Canada, ICT were primarily used to obtain the news (75%) and to make telephone calls (26.8%) (Hamel 2009, 9). Migrants in Europe were also using ICT to communicate with family and to access the news and other cultural content (Hamel 2009, 9). Wilding (2006, 132) observes that websites were primarily used for reading the news, for viewing photos, and for participating in chat room discussions. Salvadorans, according to Benitez (2006), were using the Internet to read home country newspapers, to listen to radio stations, and to communicate with family and friends. One of the websites, Intipuca city site, was used not only for personal but also collective purposes such as local development projects, political practices, and cultural expressions (Benitez 2006, 189). Centro Deportivo, a website where soccer was the main attraction, also drew many Salvadoran immigrants to share and view photos together. In sum, by accessing home country news and obtaining up-to-date information on sports, politics, social life, and culture, migrants were able to develop a sense of connection and involvement with homeland events (Benitez 2006; Bernal 2006).

ICT also facilitate the gathering of critical information and building of social networks among migrants, helping to develop social capital. For instance, popular Korean immigrant websites like MissyUSA.com not only provided useful information to Korean immigrants, easing their adjustment to the host society (See Lee and Katz 2015; Oh 2016), but also mobile communication (Kakao Talk[3] and Line apps) and online communities such as Missy USA.com, HeyKorean.com enabled Korean immigrants to maintain close social networks with fellow Koreans, becoming important sources of social capital (Lee and Katz 2015, 615–616; Oh 2016, 2016b). Interestingly, the scope and intensity of the applications used, whether on mobile phones or personal computers (PC), had an effect on the density of social ties. For example, voice calling and MIM apps for text messaging (Kakao Talk) tended to create strong ties but narrow social networks, while PC emails and SNS apps (Facebook) produced weak ties but diverse social networks among Korean immigrants (Lee and Katz 2015, 619). Relatedly, Ghanaians in Britain also drew upon ICT to not only communicate with co-nationals and connect with the homeland, but also to break from the insular ethnic community, helping to diversify social networks beyond co-nationals and the homeland (Burrell and Anderson 2008, 204).

Another important function of ICT, through the interactions users have on websites and in online chat rooms, is creating a sense of community. For example, Greschke's (2012, 127) study of Cibervalle, although not based on kinship or personal relations, showed that the website, over time, helped to establish a close-knit community among Paraguayans. Cibervalle initially began as a forum to invite friends among Paraguayans interested in accessing it from abroad as well as from Paraguay. For those in Paraguay, the site appealed to them because it made virtual travel abroad possible, while for Paraguayan expats, the site became a regular, intimate place for things Paraguayan. Through routine postings of pictures, jokes, and comments, which became part of users' daily activities, the website became both a "site of belonging to Paraguay and site of being with Paraguayans at a distance" (Greschke 2012, 128).

In addition to the various uses mentioned above, there are a few other unique uses of ICT, including using computers and the Internet to enhance migrant children's education (Kluzer and Codagnone 2012, 196). Another was the role ICT plays in facilitating and promoting further migration, both legal and undocumented, as they offer would-be migrants detailed information about migration, assisting them not only with the migration process but also helping them to develop more realistic expectations of the host society (Hamel 2009, 1). For example, through websites dedicated to providing specific details about migrating clandestinely across national borders, ICT helped to promote irregular and undocumented migration (Hamel 2009, 17). Along these lines, the newest ICT such as mobile phones (and now smartphones) were proving to be critical for coyotes or smugglers coordinating desert crossings through the U.S.-Mexican border (Hamel 2009, 18). Furthermore, by serving as tools of socialization for future migrants, Nedelcu (2012,10) found that websites as well as email and discussion forums dedicated to guiding newcomers to Canada not only eased their adjustment to the host society but also encouraged more migration.

Lastly, ICT enable the circulation of social norms and values, namely social remittances, between migrants and nonmigrants. According to Levitt

(1998, 926), migrants not only sent money home, but also sent social remittances, namely values and ideas to family and friends in the home country. Given that the lives of nonmigrants were being touched by migration and transnational ties, regular contact between migrants and nonmigrants intensified transnational social networks, creating and leading to the institutionalization of social fields (Levitt 2001b, 8). For example, through regular conversations one of the fathers in Romania had with his son in Canada via ICT, the father learned to better appreciate and understand cross-national cultural differences, especially the ethnic and racial diversity of Canada which differed sharply from Romanian ethnic relations, which were relatively homogenous (Nedelcu 2012, 12). The circulation of social norms and values was also visible in the interactions between a grandmother in Romania teaching her granddaughter in Canada Romanian language and cultural traditions and her granddaughter teaching her Canadian multiculturalism, illustrating the two-way street of transnational communication and interaction (Nedelcu 2012, 14).

LIMITATIONS OF ICT

Although innovations in ICT have certainly facilitated and increased the quantity and quality of transnational communication, helping to recapture old ties as well as create new ones and giving migrants a sense of proximity or semblance of co-presence, despite geographic distance (Benitez 2012, 1446; Wilding 2006), Wilding (2006, 134) finds that these do not fundamentally alter past social networks and relations. Instead, relations prior to ICT remain the same with use of ICT and the effects of distance are not fully eliminated with their usage, pointing to the constraints of physical separation and distance (Waldinger 2015).

Moreover, while ICT assist in immigrant integration, there are also downsides to dense social networks via ICT: insularity and delayed acculturation. For instance, in answering the question of whether ICT enable Korean immigrants to establish new social ties beyond their preestablished social networks, Lee and Katz (2015, 617) found that ICT alone could not create new social networks. Instead, they helped to simply maintain and reinforce existing social ties. Similarly, among Korean foreign students in New Zealand, Cyworld *homepys* (modified form of blog) were unable to help the students develop new social ties; instead, social ties begun offline were simply extended through online communication (Collins 2009, 854). Hence, ICT were seen as delaying their acculturation precisely because mobile communication intensified existing social ties with family and friends, but did not help to produce new social ties with non-Koreans. Moreover, the use of these *homepy's*, while soothing feelings of homesickness, prevented Korean students from learning English and establishing new relations outside of their preestablished networks (Collins 2009, 855). Still, the longer students spent living and studying in New Zealand, local networks did expand over time and their use of Cyworld mirrored that expansion (Collins 2009, 856).

Although migrants can establish a semblance of co-presence with families despite separation, transnational communication via mobile or cell phones does not displace and replace face-to-face interactions (Benitez 2012, 1443; Hiller and Tara 2004; Horst and Miller 2006; Panagakos and Horst 2006). For example, while ICT certainly enabled Korean transnational families to communicate more frequently and abundantly, mediated communication did not and could not make up for face-to-face interactions. In fact, many Korean children described feelings of emotional distance from parents due to the separation they experienced during adolescence, noting that mediated communication was unable to make up for close physical proximity and face-to-face interactions (Yoon 2015, 9). What children wanted instead was face-to-face communication because of the inherent limitations of mediated communication such as miscommunication and the inability to fully express themselves. Though frequent mediated communication was still far better than none, children did not find them to be as meaningful as face-to-face interactions.

ICT can also create burdens for migrants who, with increased communication with family and kin, were being asked by kin to send remittances more frequently than before (Wilding 2006, 135). Moreover, while resolving some hurdles of distance, ICT were unable to resolve the day-to-day needs of caring for aging parents from abroad, which could not be handled from far away since these required physical co-presence (Wilding 2006, 134). In sum, while ICT and mediated communication offer virtual togetherness, they certainly are unable to replace physical togetherness, attesting to the significance of distance despite revolutionary ICT that shrink the constraints of time and space. To be sure, by offering an appearance of co-presence, ICT do reduce transnational families' separation and anxiety, and as a result, enable and promote migration, including transnational parenting from afar.

EVOLUTION OF ICT: FROM LETTERS TO TELEPHONES TO MOBILE/SMART PHONES

In the past, the preferred method of transnational communication among migrants was, without doubt, letter writing due to its ease, dependability, and cost (Wilding 2006, 15). In fact, even until the mid-1990s letters were still preferred among some migrants since it was more expensive to call and telephones were also unreliable (Wilding 2006, 130). Starting in the late 1990s, however, as cheap international calling cards came on stage, significantly reducing the cost of international telephone calls (Vertovec 2004; Wilding 2006), not only has contacting family and friends become much easier and more regular but also weekly phone calls of thirty minutes or more have become the norm, making, among other things, transnational mothering and split households a lot more possible than before (Hamel 2009, 26–27; Madianou and Miller 2012, 7; Vertovec 2004; Wilding 2006, 130).

In addition to international telephone calls, video tapes were also used to communicate with family members. For instance, among Salvadoran immigrants, video tapes capturing family events, soccer games, patron saint and other cultural celebrations were routinely sent back and forth between El Salvador and the United States (Benitez 2006, 192) (See also Adler's (2004) study of Yucatecans' use of video tapes). According to Benitez (2006, 192), "these images encompass narratives, stories and symbols that travel through the transnational communicative circuit and create new transnational spaces of experience." What should be noted about the use of ICT among Salvadoran immigrants, however, is that many of them had no choice but to rely upon mediated forms of transnational communication such as telephone calls, video teleconferencing, letters, photos, and video tapes, since they were unable to travel back regularly due to the civil war and their Temporary Protected Status (TPS) (Benitez 2006, 195).

Beginning in 2000s, more than any other medium, the advent of the Internet ushered in a watershed moment in ICT development, dramatically altering the scope and intensity of transnational communication and interaction. Initially in the early stages of the Internet, transnational communication was constrained by technological limitations of the new technology. Still, the impact of these innovations was undeniable (Greschke 2012, 129). For instance, when the Cibervalle website was first introduced, a time when there were no broadband connections to speak of and dial-up modems were excruciatingly slow, technological limitations made postings of photos or member profiles almost impossible. Moreover, unlike today there were no communication tools that could start personal relationships such as instant chat, messenger, and voice or video chats. As Greschke (2012, 129) observes, in this early and rudimentary stage of the Internet, the exchange was of "unformatted text," and the most users could do to "enrich their communication" was to rely on different fonts or colors to express emotions.

But with technological improvements, photos and member profiles were soon added, helping to overcome user anonymity (Greschke 2012, 129).[4] More importantly though, the rudimentary online interactions often crossed over into face-to-face interactions when users took initiatives to create "encuentros," or meetings, among Paraguayans living in Argentina or among users in Paraguay. Immediately after these meetings, pictures and comments of the event were posted on the website, drawing those abroad to take virtual "daily trips to Paraguay" (Greschke 2012, 135), helping to soothe, what Urry (2002) observes, expats' nostalgia for the homeland. All in all, what these activities on the Internet, particularly on Cibervalle website, created was a sense of being together despite the geographic separation (Greschke 2012, 133).

What this brief overview of the evolution of ICT reminds us is that new ICT continuously appear, with some older ICT giving way to new ones, while others continue to find novel ways to adapt alongside them (Madianou and Miller 2012, 7). For instance, although Horst's (2006, 143) study of mobile phone usage among Jamaican transnational migrants found that mobile phones were indeed displacing older ICT, Wilding (2006, 131) found that newer ICT were not necessarily displacing and replacing older communication mediums, but were being added on to older ones. Similarly, although letters were no longer being sent as often with extensive use of telephone calls, transnational migrants were still using email and SMS text messaging to signal telephone conversations (Wilding 2006, 131). Moreover, although many ICT lose their utility when the most up-to-date ICT appears, some ICT such as email have actually found a way to stay relevant with the arrival of the newest ICT. In fact, email still remains hugely popular and has successfully crossed over onto the smartphone platform, serving as a useful medium of transnational communication for migrants and their families. Equally, even with the advent of smartphones and expansive use of Kakao Talk app, Yoon (2015, 8) found that MIM text messaging was not replacing voice calls. Instead, they were being used to signal to family members that they were ready for voice or video calls similar to Filipino families' use of email or SMS text messaging to check if family members were around for telephone calls. This means that any discussion of ICT is like a moving target that by the time researchers study and discuss them, there will be newer ICT that may or may not overtake previously popular ICT. As a result, by the time studies on ICT use by migrants and transnational families are published, the ICT discussed in these studies become dated as the newest ICT are adopted and integrated into migrants' daily life.

MOBILE PHONES

As discussed earlier, innovations in telephone technology, especially cost reductions in international telephone calls using calling cards, were undoubtedly at the forefront of transnational communication (Vertevoc 2004). Still, telephones were expensive and inconvenient to use in many places before

1995 (Horst 2006, 145). For example, not only did families in rural Jamaica have to wait from thirty minutes up to three hours for a five-minute international telephone call to use the local phone box, but also there was very little privacy. Even when landlines were introduced in rural Jamaica in the late 1990s, ushering in the era of home telephones, many migrants and their families still wrote letters and called sporadically during the year, relying more heavily on collect calls until 2001 despite having purchased calling cards (Horst 2006, 146).

But starting in the millennium, the combination of continuing declines in the cost of international calls, along with the mainstreaming and penetration of basic mobile phones, led to a turning point in transnational communication, ushering in the era of mobile phones, and soon afterward, smartphones (Bacigalupe and Lambe 2011, 13; Cabanes and Acedera 2012, 918; Horst 2006, 147). For instance, with an 80% penetration rate in the Philippines, mobile phones were the primary means of communication among Filipino transnational families (Cabanes and Acedera 2012, 917). In El Salvador, Benitez (2012, 1445) also found that 78.4% of Salvadoran households owned mobile phones, with 70% of them using it to converse about everyday life.

Among the various uses of mobile phones, one of the more common one is, not surprisingly, making international telephone calls, whether through calling cards or collect calls. But SMS, namely mobile phone text messaging via telcos (telecommunication operators), are also one of the most significant uses of mobile phones among migrants, especially Filipina migrant workers who were using it to communicate with children and spouses. For example, Chib et al. (2014, 78) found that Filipina and Indonesian domestic workers in Singapore used mobile phones to send SMS text messages, to make telephone calls, and to access new social media such as Facebook. In fact, many of these women were text messaging their children regularly throughout the day. Another interesting finding from Chib et al.'s (2013) study was that, reflecting the time of their research, mobile phones were beginning to overtake computers as the communication device of choice, underscoring their portability and increasing computing power (Chib et al. 2013, 26).

Similar to migrants' typical reasons for ICT adoption and usage discussed earlier in the chapter, mobile phone-based communication helped to ease the separation between mothers away and their children (Cabanes and Acedera 2012, 917; Madianou and Miller 2011; Paragas 2009; Parrenas 2005; Uy-Tioco 2007). For instance, Filipina mothers away have been able to maintain intimacy with family members through letters and especially telephone calls and SMS text messages (Parrenas 2001, 374).[5] Through regular calls every Sunday afternoons (Parrenas 2005, 326) and frequent SMS text messages to the children (Parrenas 2005, 328), transnational families were able to achieve stability and continuity.[6] Yet, while mobile phones helped to make up for the separation, it also led to increased surveillance of the children from far away, often monitoring children's activities by following their Facebook messages (Chib et al. 2014, 81; Parrenas 2005, 76). All in all, through letters, telephone calls, and SMS text messaging, transnational communication enabled Filipino transnational families to not only maintain family intimacy (Parrenas 2005, 328), but also gave mothers away a say in how the house was to be run and children to be disciplined (Madianou and Miller 2012, 2).[7] Among Jamaican migrants and their spouses, mobile phones also made separation less taxing, easing wives' worries of husbands' health and their whereabouts (Horst 2006, 149).

Mobile phone-based transnational communication also alleviates parents' decisions to leave children in the care of relatives and migrate abroad as they are able to participate in transnational parenting using mobile phones (Horst 2006, 149). Frequent transnational communication via mobile phones helps would-be migrants to develop more realistic expectations of migration in the receiving country (Horst 2006, 155). Another function of mobile phones and transnational communication for Indonesian women migrants in Singapore has been the reduction of stress and provision of social support (Chib et al. 2013, 27).

Lastly, ICT, especially mobile phones, helped to sustain economic transnationalism by creating efficiencies in sending remittances to the home country. Compared to the past when couriers were used for sending remittances, which carried steep fees, it is now much cheaper, easier, and faster to send remittances via Western Union and Money Gram as mobile phones greatly improve the sending and receiving of remittances (Foner 2005; Hamel 2009, 20; Horst 2006, 153).

Limitations of Mobile Phones

Though mobile phones, through regular transnational communication, certainly bolster family relations and give the impression of co-presence with children and spouse, they do not necessarily deepen family bonds with repeated use (Cabanes and Acedera 2012, 920; Madianou and Miller 2011). In fact, scholarly studies find that children often feel estranged from their mothers with prolonged separation and absence (Cabanes and Acedera 2012, 926; Parrenas 2005).[8] For instance, a number of children explained that they were unable to fully express their feelings to their mothers away through text messages. In other situations, the constant text messaging between migrant mothers and children made the fathers feel excluded in their relations with children (Cabanes and Acedera 2012, 926). Thus, despite their rapid adoption and integration into migrants' lives, mobile phones were unable to fully surmount the constraints of physical separation and geographic distance

(Wilding 2006, 76). Furthermore, frequent, real-time transnational communication using text messages had the effect of burdening migrants, as Filipina mothers away were seen as "walking ATMs" by family members, prompting them to use email instead of text messaging to delay their response time to monetary requests (Madianou 2014, 676). Extensive use of mobile phones also increased the surveillance of partners in the home country from migrants residing abroad (Horst 2006, 155). Finally, despite efforts at intensive mothering, ICT and transnational communication failed to alter traditional gender norms as left-behind fathers continued to disengage from housework and childcare, forcing migrant mothers to play not only the breadwinner but also nurturer roles from abroad (Parrenas 2005, 333).[9]

SMARTPHONES

It can probably be argued that the evolution of and morphing from mobile phones into smartphones, featuring portability, network connectivity, and computing power, represents, undeniably, to date the most sweeping innovation in ICT, revolutionizing communication for millions of people, including migrants and their families (Madianou 2014, 667). For instance, the 2012 World Bank study estimates that there were approximately six billion mobile subscriptions worldwide (Madianou 2014, 669). According to a Pew survey, close to half (45%) of the adults in the United States owned smartphones in 2012. Statistica Digital Market Outlook (DMO) (statistica.com) estimates that 64.1% of the U.S. population used a smartphone in 2016, and among U.S. mobile subscribers (13 and older) in 2015, 79.3% owned smartphones (comScore.com). Additionally, Statistica DMO (statistica.com) estimates that 1.42 billion smartphones were sold throughout the world in 2015.

The main catalyst behind the mass penetration of smartphones among consumers has been indisputably the introduction of the iPhone in 2007 (Chen 2011; Goggin 2009), immediately followed by Android-based smartphones (Goggin 2012). With widespread penetration and use of smartphones today, we certainly take being online for granted (Madianou 2014, 674). As Madianou (2014, 669) observes, smartphones represent the convergence of mobile technology with personal computing and network connectivity. Not only is it easier to carry smartphones around anytime anywhere, and apps such as Facebook are open most of the time (Madianou 2014, 674), but also users can now deploy a single device to complete multiple tasks. For example, smartphones are no longer about making and receiving telephone calls, but also serve as MP3 or MP4 players, radio, television, digital cameras and video recorders, and Internet browsers, along with checking MIM text messages and email, and getting on Facebook, to name a few (Chen 2011; Law

2012, 209; Yoon 2015, 7). Hence, the ubiquity of mobile phones/smartphones is clearly discernible in the increasing number of families today relying on cellular lines as their main telephone in their homes compared to couple of years ago when mobile phones were a lot more expensive to use than land lines (Law 2012, 209).

Forms and Use of Smartphones

Research on mobile phones/smartphones finds multiple uses for these devices, including calling family and friends, sharing photos and music, looking for jobs, to name a few. For example, before widespread diffusion and use of smartphones in China, Law (2012, 210) found that many rural Chinese workers migrating to large Chinese cities in the 1990s relied upon weekly letters to keep in touch with family when landlines were not available. With extensive penetration and integration of mobile phones, however, Law (2012, 210) found that many workers were no longer calling as often, in fact, calling much less than when they had sent letters to family members. Instead, mobile phones were being used for calling and talking to friends (Law 2012, 210). Cheng's (2012, 218) study of Chinese factory workers found that workers were using Mobile QQ, that is, Chinese Instant text messaging app on smartphones (similar to Kakao Talk), to connect with other workers. Many of them were also using mobile phones to download the latest music recommended by Baidu, a popular Chinese website (Law 2012, 211). Because Mobile QQ was cheaper to use than SNS packages, workers used them to share photos and songs, enhancing face-to-face, in-person interactions with friends and coworkers (Cheng 2012, 218). Some rural Chinese workers also used mobile phones to access job vacancy information, serving as mediums for job search and mobility (Law 2012, 212).

MOBILE INSTANT MESSAGING APPS VERSUS SHORT MESSAGE SERVICE TEXT MESSAGING

While smartphones today far outpace early mobile phones in many key features, one key innovation that needs fuller discussion to better understand the appeal of Kakao Talk and other MIM apps such as WhatsApp and Line is the text messaging feature. In fact, MIM apps are far more popular than SMS and multimedia messaging service (MMS) because of their cost and speed. For instance, SMS, provided by telecommunication operators (telcos), relies on users' telephone numbers to send text messages (Oghuma et al. 2015, 659). Although text messaging these days is a regular feature of most monthly plans in cellular telephone plans with unlimited calling and text messaging from carriers like AT&T, T-Mobile, Verizon, and Sprint, when smartphones were first introduced, text messaging incurred a nominal cost on mobile phones, while MIM apps such as Kakao Talk had no user fees, ran on multiple platforms (iOS and Android), had group chat functions, and unlike SMS, were not tied to particular telcos (Oghuma et al. 2015).

Especially for migrants and transnational families, the cost of sending text messages internationally through SMS, along with international telephone calls, took a toll on their monthly budgets, while MIM apps such as Kakao Talk helped to significantly reduce the cost of transnational communication. As mobile phones evolved into smartphones and new features began to coalesce around them, MIM text messaging soon overtook mobile phone-based SMS text messaging. Furthermore, as smartphones and monthly data plans rapidly came down in price, were widely adopted, and MIM apps began to incorporate additional features such as voice and video call functions, they soon outcompeted SMS text messaging, resulting in huge losses in revenue for telcos.

FROM PC-BASED CYWORLD TO SMARTPHONE-BASED KAKAO TALK

South Korea boasts one of the highest mobile phone, smartphone, and Internet penetration rates in the world (Yoon 2015, 2). For example, mobile phone penetration was at 110% in Korea in 2013, out of which 78.5%–80% were smartphone users (Oghuma et al. 2015, 660; Son 2013, 381). According to estimates by Statistica DMO (statistica.com), the share of South Koreans using a smartphone in 2015 was 76.4%, while Korea's Internet penetration rate in 2013 was a whopping 82.7% (Son 2015, 381).

Among the first social networking sites to become hugely popular and widespread in South Korea was Cyworld. Started in 1999, it claimed a user rate of 90% of all Koreans aged between twenty and twenty-nine in 2006. Accessed via the PC, many used Cyworld to connect with friends in the homeland (S. Kim 2011, 94). In one of the few studies on Cyworld, Collins (2009) examined the use of Cyworld among Korean foreign students studying in New Zealand. He found that Cyworld's *Mini hompy* and New Zealand story (*Iyagi*) were the two most popular websites used by Korean students. The former was, until the advent of Facebook and Kakao Talk, the most popular SNS site, similar to Myspace and Facebook, used for communicating with friends and family in the home country, while the latter (*Iyagi*) was an information-sharing site for adjusting to New Zealand (Collins 2009, 846). *Homepys* were mainly used to keep a record and diary of Korean students' everyday experiences in Auckland, namely an online transnational diary

(Collins 2009, 849). What is interesting about the social ties these homepys maintained through the *Ilchon's* or friends was that they mostly involved other international students in New Zealand or homeland friends but few local Korean New Zealanders (Collins 2009, 852).

With the explosion of Facebook in Asia in 2011, Korean users, known for adopting the latest technology, began to rapidly migrate out of Cyworld to Facebook (Shim et al. 2013) as PCs, which was how Cyworld was accessed, gave way to smartphones. Not only were they convenient to carry around but also smartphones began to match the computing power of PCs, enabling smartphone users, for example, to open Facebook via its dedicated app. In fact, as Shim et al. (2013) found, among the 100 college students they surveyed, most preferred to use SNS via smartphones rather than via personal computers. In another study, one-half (50%) of Facebook users relied on smartphones to access the application (Mansumitrchai et al. 2012, 142).

While new social media apps such as Facebook, Twitter, and others continue to be very popular in Korea, the application most used on smartphones today is no other than Kakao Talk, the number one app in SNS, with 79.9% using it (Mansumitrchai et al. 2012, 142; Shim et al. 2013, 488). Released in March 2010, Kakao Talk was the first and free MIM app on smartphones (Choi 2013; Yoon 2016, 7), achieving a massive penetration rate of 93.5% (Koreanclick 2011). In another study, Oghuma et al. (2015) found that 90% of smartphone users had Kakao Talk app installed on their phones. In December 2012, there were seventy million users of Kakao Talk worldwide. When other MIM apps such as Kakao Talk, WhatsApp, and Line are combined, the number of MIM users jump from 120 million in 2008 to 310 million in 2010; it is projected that by 2015, there will be 1.6 billion MIM users (Choi 2013, 64). In 2011, users spent an average of eighteen minutes per day on Kakao Talk (Choi 2013; Koreanclick 2011). By November 2012, an average of fifty-three minutes were being spent on Kakao Talk compared to seven minutes for WhatsApp. Furthermore, 4.2 billion messages were being sent per day using Kakao Talk, which amounted to 156 messages per person per day (Choi 2013, 63). Most used MIM apps for communication, with 88.2% using it to communicate with family and friends (Oghuma et al. 2015, 666).

Several reasons explain the rapid adoption and integration of Kakao Talk among users. First, Kakao Talk automatically found and entered the contact information stored on users' mobile phones, a feature common now in other MIM apps such as Line and WhatsApp but quite innovative when first introduced (Choi 2013, 65). Second, Kakao Talk was a free download on iOS and Android platforms, while WhatsApp charged a nominal fee to download it.[10] Finally, the app was also the first to enable group conversations (Choi 2013, 67), a feature used by many to set up meetings, to engage in bible study fellowships, to participate in group conversations among friends, among others.

These multiple uses of Kakao Talk have led to Kakao Talk becoming a verb like *google*, that is, *Katalk*, underscoring the app's ubiquity and huge popularity with Korean and Korean American users (Choi 2013).

In order to remain competitive against the onslaught of Facebook, Kakao Talk recently introduced Kakao Story, which has since become the number one SNS application in Korea (July 2012). While Kakao Talk features text messages and voice or video calls, Kakao Story allows users to post pictures and status messages so that they can be viewed by others who are part of the user's network. Selfies and emoticons (feelings) were also uploaded to Kakao Story, which was an add-on for Kakao Talk users (Yoon 2015, 7). Currently, Kakao Story has thirty million users (Choi 2013, 67).

In sum, this overview of the evolution of ICT from letters and international calling cards to mobile phones/smartphones and Kakao Talk illustrates migrants' rapid adoption of and adaptation to the newest ICT, helping to sustain intimacy and easing separation across national boundaries.

TRANSNATIONAL MEDIA/TELEVISION

The previous section focused on ICT, especially the evolution of older ICT into the hottest innovation, and their use and impact on transnational communication. In this section, I examine the scope and intensity of transnational media/television consumption by migrants and their impact on their adaptation and integration.

Transnational or ethnic media can be broadly defined as "media produced for a particular ethnic community" (Matsaganis et al. 2011, 5). Sometimes they can be produced by the ethnic or immigrant community, but big media organizations from the home country also produce them for consumption in emigrant communities abroad.[11] The proliferation of transnational or ethnic media providing news, entertainment, and important cultural information to immigrants via ethnically targeted television, radio, newspapers, and websites is a natural outcome of the rapid increase of immigrant populations in the United States since the 1960s and 1970s (Matsaganis et al. 2011, 3). Growing by leaps and bounds, they have become prominent and permanent fixtures in the lives of immigrants, resulting in what Itzigsohn et al. (1999, 333) delineate as regular forms of cultural transnational engagement.

Yet, their visibility and widespread use of transnational media raise important questions regarding their impact on the adaptation and integration of immigrants in their places of settlement. On the one hand, transnational media appeals to immigrants because they help immigrants stay connected and informed about current events in the home country (Elias 2008). For instance, among Hmong immigrants in the United States, homeland television shows were instrumental in renewing transnational ties with the Miao in China as these programs helped the Hmong rediscover their roots and identity (Faist 2000, 212). On the other hand, in its effort to stay relevant to immigrants, transnational media also engages in localization by providing valuable community information, which support immigrant adaptation into the host country (Matsaganis et al. 2011; Zhou and Cai 2002). For example, ethnic television and radio stations carry a broad range of programs useful to the immigrant community, including local and national news as well as information vital for adaptation in the new place of residence. Transnational media also serves to moderate the isolation immigrants face by easing their transition into the mainstream of American society (Y. Kim 2011; Son 2015; Zhou and Cai 2002). In short, through its coverage of home ownership, entrepreneurship, and educational achievement, Chinese transnational media emerged as a key social institution in the immigrant community, which provided indispensable information and promoted upward mobility to Chinese Americans (Zhou and Cai 2002).

Still, despite the many benefits for migrants, in public discussions of migrant consumption of transnational media, there is often an outcry against them because of fears of immigrant dissimilation and disloyalty. For instance, one of the many objections against ethnic or transnational media is the fear that immigrants, by connecting to homeland media, are voluntarily choosing to disengage from the host society (Aksoy and Robins 2000, 344). However, as Y. Kim (2011) observes, consumption of ethnic or transnational media, while they do affect immigrant attachment and identification with the host country, is not simply a matter of turning inward and rejecting assimilation. Instead, as Aksoy and Robins (2000, 344) note, the anti-immigrant discourse in Germany against Turkish Germans, which associated the consumption of transnational Turkish media with rejection of assimilation, was based on monolithic views of Turkish media duping the Turkish community. What such view failed to consider was that today's Turkish media was actually comprised of many commercial Turkish private channels competing for Turkish audiences abroad. Such nuanced understanding of Turkish media dispels homogenized views of Turkish media held by German commentators since in practice, many programs were far more open and diverse and were actually catering to the tastes of Turkish viewers to appeal to them (Aksoy and Robins 2000, 353). This meant that many of the shows actually tended to focus on the mundane, namely the daily lives and culture of Turks. Thus, despite public fears and concerns that transnational media may discourage and delay the assimilation of immigrants, the growing empirical literature suggests that it may actually serve a dual function of assisting immigrant adaptation and integration, while helping to stay connected to and to keep abreast of home country life.

Forms and Use of Transnational Media/Television

The literature on transnational media/television consumption finds that most immigrants, especially the first generation, prefer homeland, over host country, media. For instance, in her study of Greek immigrants in Canada, Panagakos (2003, 210–211) found that more than one-half (54%) of first-generation Greeks, especially first-generation women who were not well integrated into Canadian society, preferred to watch Greek satellite television, while only 15% of the second generation did so (Panagakos 2003,). Elias and Lemish (2008, 24) also found that close to 80% of adult immigrants in Israel regularly watched Russian-language channels, while only a quarter watched Hebrew-language ones. Indeed, the medium consumed most across age, class, ethnicity, and location among Arab speakers was transnational television (Georgiou 2012a, 6; 2012b). Katz (2010, 304) found that among Latinos, the television programming most tuned in to was *telenovelas*, becoming a taken-for-granted and routine activity for many families (Barrera and Bielby 2001, 1). Moreover, the fact that many of these low-income families prioritized cable subscriptions over Internet access suggested that more weight was being placed on entertainment than on children's education, underscoring transnational television's ubiquity and appeal (Katz 2010, 305).

Just like the age and class divide in ICT use, there is also an age and generational divide in the consumption between ethnic/transnational media and host media, with older and less acculturated immigrants favoring transnational television compared to younger and more acculturated counterparts. For example, it was the older, more recently arrived and less fluent in English who tended to watch Chinese television, while middle-class and more English-proficient Chinese accessed more mainstream websites (Zhou and Cai 2002). Younger and better educated Arab women also tended to most critically engage with soap operas, especially over gender representations, compared to their older and less educated counterparts (Georgiou 2012b, 10). In some cases though, immigrant parents preferred ethnic media for their children because they were less explicit on sexual matters than French television. Yet, parents and children generally lived in different media worlds, with parents usually watching Russian programming, while children were browsing the Internet (and emails and blogs) in Hebrew because they were looking to integrate into the local youth culture in Israel (Elias and Lemish 2008, 30). Ironically, given parent-children differences in media preferences, what served as a compromise between them was global media: Hollywood films, concerts, and international sporting events (Elias and Lemish 2008, 37).

In discussions of migrant media consumption, migrants have a choice of consuming between the host and transnational media. Elias and Lemish (2008, 22) observe that consumption of host media makes sense for migrants seeking to adapt to the host society as these provide information and serve as tools of socialization into the receiving society (Johnson 1996; Lee and Tse 1994). Certainly, some immigrants who seek to adapt quickly to the new country will pursue content related to the host society, but it is also the case that immigrants who differ culturally from the host society prefer media in the mother tongue (Elias 2008). Thus, despite the benefits of host media for information, acculturation, and integration into the host society, most research finds that migrants tend to favor transnational media/television.

Among the various reasons for consuming transnational media, a key reason why transnational television is sought in the first place by migrants is because the host media tends to misrepresent, underrepresent, or not represent racial and immigrant minorities at all (Y. Kim 2011, 553; Ojo 2006, 351). For instance, Metykova (2010) found that EU migrants in her study pursued transnational media precisely because many UK channels hardly covered foreign news or gave satisfactory coverage of ethnic news that were relevant to them. Because American media/television also offered little ethnic and world coverage, most Chinese preferred Chinese media for news, which gave continuity to and appreciation for cultural nuances (Shi 2005, 65). Y. Kim (2011) makes similar observations among Korean, Chinese, and Japanese women foreign students studying in Britain whose media needs—familiarity, content, and diversity—were not met by British media, prompting them to turn to transnational media for information, entertainment, and identity. This was also the case among Latino families who favored soap operas or *telenovelas* because of the neglect and lack of ethnic content on American media (Barrera and Beilby 2001, 1). Clearly, in the face of cultural marginalization, telenovelas, by featuring positive portrayals of Latino life, including the extended family, helped to reinforce cultural connections and ethnic identification among Latinos (Barrera and Beilby 2001, 13; Bielby 2001; Mayer 2003).

Another important reason for turning to transnational television is entertainment and relaxation. For example, Chinese Americans preferred to watch Chinese sitcoms and movies on Chinese television because they found transnational and ethnic media/television to be more relaxing and entertaining than U.S. media (Shi 2005; Zhou and Cai 2002). By contrast, Japanese women students in Britain found that British media took work and effort rather than entertainment and relaxation to enjoy it, pushing them to seek their own ethnic media spaces. This desire for entertainment and familiar content without the encumbrances of language and culture was further compounded by their difficulties in understanding British jokes, which is why Chinese women students stopped watching UK television due to lack of cultural competence (Y. Kim 2011, 103). Instead, many of them sought the comfort of home by watching Chinese dramas and eating Chinese food.

Immigrant nostalgia for the homeland, namely memories of childhood and upbringing, is surely an enduring sentiment migrants continue to hold on to, which transnational television, through its coverage of familiar places, faces, and sounds, is effectively able to meet. For example, Aksoy and Robins (2000, 359) found that Turkish television enabled Turkish Germans to reminisce about their childhood, not only fulfilling their need for nostalgia, but also helping to synchronize with Turkish events as if these immigrants were there even though they did not live in Turkey on a daily basis (Aksoy and Robins 2000, 362). Similarly, soap operas helped older women immigrants to reminisce about their childhood and memories of the home country, fulfilling their nostalgia for the homeland (Georgiou 2012b, 15). By presenting common religious and cultural themes and practices, along with familiar places (scenery of the locations) which were easily recognizable and identifiable among Latino viewers (Barrera and Beilby 2001, 8–9), *telenovelas* also helped to recreate Latino culture, serving to mitigate feelings of homesickness for migrants.

Transnational media/television also provides a sense of normalcy or ontological security for migrants. According to Metykova (2010), transnational media helped EU migrants to overcome the disruptions they encountered with migration in their quest for a sense of normalcy in the host society. For instance, a main reason why Arab respondents consumed transnational television, which covered the familiar and was predictable, was because it offered ontological security, which offered reassurance and sense of comfort for Arab viewers (Georgiou 2012a, 4). This was also the case among Korean, Chinese, and Japanese women foreign students for whom, according to Y. Kim (2011, 94), transnational media helped to establish "social ontological security in their own communication channels." Ultimately, transnational media fulfilled "a self-determined need to seek symbolic inclusion, a desire to connect with significant others back home, and a pleasure to expand the space for self-expression, understanding, and articulation in the language of home" (Y. Kim 2011, 94).

Relatedly, the estrangement and dislocation that migrants (and also foreign students) experience in new places is another reason for consuming transnational media/television. For example, Y. Kim (2011, 100) found that transnational media helped Korean, Chinese, and Japanese women students studying in Britain to deal with their isolation and disruption during their adjustment in Britain (and also elsewhere). Ethnic or transnational media space, Kim argues, should, thus, be seen as defensive mechanisms against racial and cultural marginalization in everyday life (Y. Kim 2011, 96), that is, coping mechanisms against loneliness and exclusion (Y. Kim 2011, 97). They are also efforts to create self-respect against racial and cultural denigration in Britain as foreign minorities, giving rise to diasporic nationalism

(Y. Kim 2011, 95). Ironically, rather than making them more globalized and cosmopolitan, their globalization through study abroad had the opposite effect of making them re-nationalized and re-essentialized in transnational social fields, prompting them to retreat to the ethnic enclave physically, psychologically, and symbolically (Y. Kim 2011, 95–96).

Transnational media/television also helps migrants and diasporic groups to take part in a collective transnational culture and identity. In a study of transnational media consumption among Chinese Malaysians, Carstens (2003) found that consumption of Chinese popular culture enabled Chinese everywhere to participate in a common transnational Chinese culture, helping to maintain transnational ties and identities. Ethnic media also provided Chinese students studying in the United States with common reference points, such as the news and other events, which they could share and discuss with family members in the home country (Shi 2005, 66). For these students, keeping up with trends and events in the homeland was actually in their own self-interest since many of them were planning to return back after completing their studies (Shi 2005, 76). The same was true among Mexican immigrants, who, by consuming Mexican media and *telenovelas* and engaging in telephone conversations with family and relatives in Mexico about the latest Mexican television and music, were able to participate in the sharing of a common culture (Mayer 2003, 485).

Social closure within the immigrant group is another significant reason for keeping up with transnational media/television. According to Panagakos (2003), by watching Greek satellite television and keeping abreast of popular television shows, Greek actors, and news, Greek immigrant women were not only able to build friendships and bonds with co-ethnics, but also such knowledge created social closure between those who were regular viewers and those who did not watch Greek television (Panagakos 2003, 214–215). This was also the case among second-generation Koreans, where knowledge of Korean popular culture, namely Korean dramas, served as means of defining ethnic authenticity among second-generation Koreans, establishing social closure between the more ethnically oriented second generation and the more assimilated Korean "twinkies" (Oh 2012, 2015).

Another important function of transnational media for migrants is its role as outlets for expressing ethnicity, commonality, and belonging (Panagakos 2003, 216). According to Aksoy and Robins (2000), transnational television helped Turkish Germans to express multiple ways of being Turkish. Georgiou (2012b, 3–4) also found that by consuming the same transnational media such as soap operas, a sense of belonging and commonality was engendered and reinforced among Arab women.

Transnational media/television is also often favored by some ethnic groups because of the low quality of host media/television programs. For example, even before Hong Kong and Chinese serials began to be routinely featured during prime time hours on Malaysian channels, becoming the most watched program among Chinese and non-Chinese Malaysians (Carstens 2003), many ethnic Chinese in Malaysia were renting transnational Chinese videos despite the fact that many of them did not speak and understand Cantonese. One reason had to do with the fact that there was limited programming in Malaysian television, but it was also because many Malay programs, even with state support, failed to attract Malaysian Chinese due to their low quality.[12]

Finally, soap operas are popular with immigrants due to their role in maintaining fluency in the mother tongue. For example, Barrera and Beilby (2001, 10) found that *telenovelas* helped Latinos, even among those who were proficient in English, to maintain their fluency in Spanish. Furthermore, the time when telenovelas were viewed were considered treasured private spaces for Latina women, who, in the companion of other women, sought to resist male authority (Mayer 2003, 486).[13] But similar to the role of television in general, soap operas, were also a source of escapism from daily life for migrants (Georgiou 2012b, 15).

CONCLUSION

Transnational communication via ICT and transnational media/television fulfill important needs for migrants, including easing separation with family members and providing entertainment and information. The main reason why migrants and transnational families deploy ICT is invariably their need to sustain family intimacy from afar, usually by engaging in the exchange of everyday stuff, that is, the mundane, which helps to blur absence and presence. Other reasons for transnational media consumption include the need for entertainment and news, which help migrants stay connected with the homeland, giving them a sense of familiarity and continuity. In fact, as several research studies find, these were not new behaviors which appeared as a result of migration, but were carryovers from the home country. Still, while ICT provide a sense of proximity or semblance of co-presence, ultimately these were unable to overcome the constraints of distance and replace face-to-face interactions. ICT use also led to the reproduction of dense social networks, which had the effect of increasing insularity and delaying acculturation.

Equally, transnational media/television was also consumed to fulfill migrants' need for entertainment and relaxation, to stay connected and informed of homeland events, and to preserve the ethnic language and to participate in a common culture. But the reasons for turning to transnational media were also due to the fact that the host media offered little to no ethnic programming relevant to immigrants, refuting host society's fears of dissimilation with transnational media consumption. Yet, given immigrants' preference for transnational media due to language barriers and cultural unfamiliarity, the consumption of transnational media/television did lead to some insularity and delayed acculturation. For example, although Korean immigrants' use of homeland media did not differ much from other immigrant groups (Kama and Malka 2013; Son 2015; Yin 2015), their expanded and extended use did lead to separation from the host society, exposing them far more to Korean than host language and culture, creating what Yoon (2016, 13) calls an "ethnic island." However, delayed acculturation among Korean migrants was not simply a question of their failure to assimilate but also an option they could exercise under the constraints they faced in the host society (Son 2015). As other studies have found, in their effort to carve out their own spaces of control through own communication channels and mediated networks, the end result was also limited social interactions with dominant groups (Y. Kim 2011, 96).

NOTES

1. Greek music was also downloaded, burned onto a CD, and then played among their second-generation Greek friends (Panagakos (2003, 210).

2. Panagakos (2003) notes that with socioeconomic assimilation, there was a loss of the mother tongue among second-generation Greek Canadians, with few being able to speak the Greek language at home. One of the ways by which second-generation Greeks preserved transnational ties, in addition to ICT use, was by participating in Greek community activities, especially Greek cultural and food festivals, as well as spending summer vacations in Greece (Panagakos 2003, 206).

3. Kakao Talk is a free MIM text messaging app offered by a new Korean startup company (now owned by Daum portal site) that has basically replaced traditional mobile telephone SMS text messaging service. It has more than 190 million users, and smartphone and tablet users can download the app in both android and iOS (Apple) formats. The advantage of Kakao Talk and other MIM apps like WhatsApp and Line (another popular MIM app in Korea) is that the app will automatically find and add the contact information from users' phone book on their smartphones/tablets. Moreover, users can also make free domestic and international voice and video calls using Kakao Talk, in addition to free text messaging, making the app extremely popular. I can also attest to the ubiquity of this app as I use it to communicate with most of my friends and also my own family members.

4. Another was the expansion of topics in the forums, adding mundane topics such as films, food, jokes, teasing, quarrels, and debates. Discussion threads also enabled both frequent users, those who were online frequently to communicate in real time, and irregular users, those who were online intermittently, to follow the threads that had been posted earlier and post their comments afterward (Greschke 2012, 130). Given that users can be in different time zones, the "condition of asynchronicity" also enabled communication across different time zones (Greschke 2012, 130).

5. But how often and for what purposes mobile phones get used, including their regularity, are also affected by migrant women's occupations abroad, the country of destination, and migrants' place of origin. For example, mothers away who were nurses were able to call and text message their children much more frequently than domestic workers, while migrant mothers working in rich countries were able to earn more and have more time to call than women migrants in poorer ones (Parrenas 2005, 329). The rural-urban divide also affected transnational communication since in remote rural areas where some of these women came from, there was little to no cellular phone coverage (Parrenas 2005, 330). Age of the child during parents' migration, the quality of preexisting relationships, and type of media available during the period of separation also affected the quantity and quality of transnational communication (Madianou 2014, 677).

6. Filipina mothers also participated in daily minutiae with family members via text messages sent by both the fathers and children, the former informing mothers who are away of children's transgressions, while the latter alerting migrant mothers regarding unfair punishment from Filipino fathers (Cabanes and Acedera 2012, 925). Various household tasks were assigned to children via text messaging as many Filipina fathers were still reluctant to complete household chores seen as "women's work" (Cabanes and Acedera 2012, 924). Filipina and Indonesian migrant mothers also participated actively in their children's academic and emotional life by helping them with homework during online chats (Chib et al. 2014, 79).

7. In order to resist deviant narratives of transnational mothering (Chib et al. 2014, 78), mothers who were away actively used ICT to engage in intensive mothering such as micromanaging the family budget and daily family activities (Parrenas 2005, 323). For example, in order to safeguard against the mishandling of remittances, mothers often resorted to managing the family bank accounts with oldest daughters rather than their husbands, sons, or kin (Parrenas 2005, 324). Mothers who were away also sent only specified sums of money each month to control the family monthly budget (Parrenas 2005, 326), similar to Jamaican migrant families using telephone cards to control use of telephone calls (Wilding 2006, 137). Another was Filipina mothers' attempts to monitor the family spending by calling at the end of each month to get an inventory of all the spending made by the fathers (Cabanes and Acedera 2012, 923).

8. Despite intensive mothering from afar via ICT (mobile phones), many children still placed most of the blame for this separation on the mothers but less on the fathers because of the ideology of mothers as nurturers and fathers as breadwinners in the Philippines (Parrenas 2001, 375). Subscribing to traditional ideologies of mothers as nurturers, children held the mothers responsible for their absence during critical periods of childhood, a double standard they failed to notice or acknowledge, deeming fathers' absences less detrimental than those of mothers in children's upbringing (Parrenas 2001, 385; Parrenas 2005, 333). Although many Filipino children agreed with their mothers' migration abroad for work, they still questioned the value of their separation, which the young adults considered to be less worthwhile despite the education and material benefits that came with their mothers' sacrifice. As Parrenas (2001) observes, what many middle-class children failed to realize, despite their claims that what they wanted and needed was more intimacy with mothers during childhood than all the care packages and material comfort, was that they were taking

their own mothers' ability to migrate abroad and support them materially for granted, overlooking many working-class Filipino families' challenges in migrating with comparable ease (Parrenas 2001, 385). Furthermore, without the sacrifice of migrant mothers and her remittances, the children's education and their middle-class lifestyles were sure to suffer, forestalling their upward mobility (Parrenas 2001, 385).

9. Parrenas (2008, 1058) notes that transnational fathering was no different from conventional fathering since many fathers still kept their authority and followed traditional scripts of fathering. For example, asserting their presence transnationally through the remittances they sent home, especially the houses their earnings helped to build, fathers were able to reinforce their breadwinner role (Parrenas 2008, 1063). Interestingly, Parrenas (2008, 1064) found that compared to fathers in families where the mother is away, migrant fathers, having fulfilled their breadwinner role, were less afraid to do housework when they were home as their masculinity was not threatened by "women's" work. However, many children reported emotional distance and discomfort when interacting with their fathers after long periods of absence and separation (Parrenas 2008, 1065). More importantly though, migrant fathers were still hardly involved in nurturing their children, communicating sporadically for disciplining purposes, but leaving the bulk of emotional and nurturing work to mothers. Not surprisingly, what the children wanted from their migrant fathers was precisely the opposite: to play a more nurturing, rather than a disciplinarian, role (Parrenas 2008, 1069).

10. WhatsApp is now a free download, but given the rapid adoption of Kakao Talk by Korean and Korean American users, and because WhatsApp has no particular advantage over Kakao Talk on features, Kakao Talk has become the MIM app of choice for Korean users.

11. While there are slight differences between the terms ethnic, immigrant, diasporic, and transnational media (Matsaganis et al. 2011), the term transnational media, rather than immigrant or ethnic media, is used because the focus is on media produced in the home country (especially television) for consumption in the immigrant community.

12. In Ipoh city where two-thirds of the population was Chinese, adult women there tended to watch more Chinese serials than men. Also among the videos that were rented, Western films tended to be more popular than Chinese films because of their technical superiority and variety (Carstens 2003).

13. Mayer (2003, 486) also found that the men and the boys, who regarded telenovelas as low class and feminine, tended to not admit that they also watched telenovelas, or were likely to say that they watched them because they had been forced to by their mothers.

Chapter 3

Transnational Activities of Korean Immigrants

Korean immigrants today, unlike past cohorts who came with little information and with the goals of settling down permanently in the United States, know far more about the country to which they migrate. More importantly, they are ostensibly more oriented to the home country since they no longer see migration as irreversible (Park 2009). For these new immigrants, the pursuit of instrumental citizenship is not only normative, but also integral to their goals of maximizing opportunities and reducing uncertainties in a fast-changing world. As a result, immigrants no longer have to settle between assimilation and transnationalism, but instead can pursue both, fulfilling their pursuit of instrumental citizenship (Faist 2000; Foner 2005; Levitt 2001b; Levitt and Schiller 2004; Ong 1999; Portes et al. 1999; Vertovec 2007).

Yet, while transnational ties promise to become salient and routine features of and goals for recent cohorts, questions remain as to how extensively long-time Koreans are actually engaging in transnational activities and ties with the home country. For these residents, is regular transnationalism the exception rather than the rule as Waldinger (2007) argues? Or, as Itzigsohn et al. (1999) note, is the total sum of occasional transnational participation with the homeland greater than the individual parts?

Research on immigrant transnational activities, as described earlier, suggests that most immigrants engage in some aspects of transnationalism, including contacting family and friends, visiting the home country, sending remittances, and participating in homeland politics (Foner 2005; Itzigsohn et al. 1999; Portes et al. 2002; Portes and Rumbaut 2014; Vertovec 2007; Wilding 2006). Clearly, broad or occasional transnationalism is the rule and only a minority constitutes transmigrants, namely those who engage in regular or narrow transnationalism. In this chapter, I draw upon the sparse data on Korean immigrant transnationalism to assess what appears to be an ever-increasing trend among Korean Americans and other immigrants. I rely upon Noh et al.'s (2013) research, one of the first surveys on Korean American transnationalism (Korean immigrants in Toronto, Canada, N=274; twenty- to seventy-two-year-olds), to explore the nature and scope of transnational engagement among Korean immigrants.[1] I also examine the 2003 D.C. Korean community survey and interviews conducted with Korean community leaders and long-time residents to ascertain whether transnationalism is indeed turning out to be a significant component of Korean American life.

In order to address the scope and intensity of transnational engagement (regular vs. occasional), I begin with an examination of several standard measures of migrant transnationalism such as contacts with family members and friends in the home country, homeland visits, remittances, and political engagement with home country politics. This will help us gauge whether information and communication technologies (ICT) and growing transnational connections are indeed having the effects that we assume are taking place in a shrinking world as immigrants seek to maintain long-lasting ties with home countries.

EVOLUTION OF ICT USE AMONG KOREAN MIGRANTS

In the discussion on the history of ICT in chapter 2, I noted that ICT were like moving targets since with each innovation, many of them were often displaced and replaced by the latest ICT, although some were able to adapt to changing technology.

During the 1970s and 1980s, the ICT of choice among Korean immigrants was, reflecting the period, letters—given the prohibitive cost of international telephone calls. Even in 2000s, few Korean immigrant women were actually making telephone calls because it was still expensive to call internationally, relying mostly, instead, on letters to keep in touch with friends (Park 2009, 84). But as email became widely available, more of them began to use this new ICT to engage in transnational communication (Park 2009, 85).

With the advent of the Internet in 2000s, Korean migrants and their families turned to the newest ICT of the times: VoIP calling via home computers or Internet-customized telephone handsets (Yoon 2016a, 6). Many of them were also using international telephone cards to make phone calls given their lower cost, but telephone expenses were still a major burden on those transnational families since even a ten-hour card ran out quickly and additional telephone cards had to be purchased (Yoon 2016a, 7). Email was also used for transnational communication, but due to time differences, it was not as effective since there were delays in responses with email.

When Facebook, Daum, and Naver came on stage, Korean migrants, like other migrants, began to adopt them for communication and information searching (Yoon 2016b). According to Yoon (2016b, 9), while Facebook was generally reserved for social events in the host society, Daum and Naver, the most popular portal sites for Koreans, were used for connecting with other Korean immigrants in the area. Interestingly, like other studies showing the increasing trend of using smartphones instead of computers to go online, Korean transnational families were accessing the Internet via their smartphones (Yoon 2016a, 7).

Hence, this brief overview of ICT adoption and use by Korean transnational families shows a pattern of not only adopting the latest ICT, but also deploying multiple ICT to communicate with family and friends (Yoon 2016b). In fact, Yoon (2016b) found that fathers in Korea were using multiple devices, including laptops, smartphones, and office computers, as well as an array of apps such as Kakao Talk, Facebook, and Skype to communicate with the daughters in the United States.

INTERNATIONAL TELEPHONE CALLS AND TRANSNATIONAL COMMUNICATION

International telephone calls, more than any other medium, have arguably been at the forefront behind maintaining transnational ties with the home country (Vertovec 2007; Wilding 2006, 130). As Held et al. (1999, 344) observe, the volume of international telephone calls, measured in call minutes, jumped more than twelve times from 1982 to 2001. In 1982, there were 12.7 billion call minutes; by 1992, it soared to 42.7 billion call minutes and to 154 billion in 2001. Also calls made from the United States to other countries, according to the 2002 Federal Communications Commission report, rose from 200 million in 1980 to 6.6 billion in a span of two decades. Clearly, the sharp drop in the cost of international calls, made possible in large part by the emergence of Internet-based, VoIP telephone calls, has not only made it easier and cheaper to call abroad, fueling the volume of international calls, but also has extended the length of telephone conversations with family members and friends. Perhaps it is this type of transnational engagement via the telephone and the newest ICT that most enables migrants to sustain connections with the home country given their ease and speed. In this section, I examine the various ICT used for communicating with family and friends in the home country as well as the reasons behind them to assess whether the ubiquity of inexpensive international telephone calls and ICT is strengthening social ties across national borders.

In his analysis of the 2006 National Survey of Latinos, Waldinger (2007, ii) found that 41% of Latinos talked at least once a week on the telephone with family members in the home country. The frequency of calling and talking with family and relatives in the home country, however, varied with immigrants' residence in the United States. Latino immigrants who were new to the country called the home country more regularly than those who had been in the United States for a long time. For instance, two-thirds of recent arrivals called the home country at least once a week, while those who had lived in the United States for some time called less often (Waldinger 2007, 3).

Among Korean immigrants in Toronto, Noh et al. (2013, 127–128) found that 20% to 50% of Korean immigrants talked on the telephone or made online contacts regularly (at least once a week) with family and friends.[2] But the incidence of telephone calls rose most significantly if a parent still resided in Korea. In their survey, more than one half (54.6%) of respondents had a parent residing in Korea, while two-thirds (66.7%) had a sibling and 85% had extended family members there.[3] Among respondents with parents in Korea, close to one half (45%) talked regularly with parents on the telephone, while nearly 80% spoke with parents on the telephone at least once a month. Telephone calls, in short, were the preferred means of maintaining regular contact with family members, especially with parents first and foremost, followed by siblings (Noh et al. 2013, 129). However, few called their more distant relatives and extended family. Another interesting, but not surprising, finding was that contacts with friends were made via the Internet rather than the telephone, and regular communication with them occurred less frequently than with family members. Across different age groups, young-age adults (twenty- to thirty-five-year-olds) called parents more regularly than middle-age or older-age adults (Noh et al. 2013, 129). Also younger and more recent Korean immigrants were more likely to retain informal transnational ties, consistent with findings by Kelly (2003) and Hiebert and Ley (2006) on length of time in the host country and transnational participation.

While not quite about immigrants and their transnational communication, the study of communication practices, specifically the use of personal web pages to connect with "home," among South Korean students in New Zealand, also revealed similar uses of international telephone calls with close family members as the Toronto survey. For example, Collins (2009, 840) found that while email, Internet messenger services, and personal homepages were used to obtain information and to communicate with friends in Korea, telephone calls were reserved for use with family and boyfriends and girlfriends (Collins 2009, 844).

In our interviews with community leaders and long-time residents, we found that multiple ICT were being utilized, including landline- and VoIP-based telephones, email, video chats, blogs, and Kakao Talk, to maintain relations with family members in Korea. While email, Kakao Talk, video chats (Skype, Facetime, MS Messenger, Facebook messenger), and/or blogs were used to communicate with distant relatives or friends, landline- and VoIP-based telephones were primarily used with close family members, especially parents, as seen in the Toronto survey. For example, Chul Ho Choi, a forty-eight-year-old member of the *Korea Central Daily* editorial staff, made regular telephone calls to family members, while with distant relatives, he used video chats and new social media for their virtually free cost. As he put it, "We usually keep in touch with family in Korea through the telephone or email. With my nieces and nephews, we use Skype and social media."

Myung Suk Oh, a seventy-four-year-old retired long-time resident, also talked on the telephone with his sister occasionally, using Skype telephone to make calls, taking advantage of the Internet technology. Soo Mi Lee (pseudonym), a thirty-eight-year-old program director of the Washington Youth Foundation, on the other hand, utilized a variety of ICT, including VoIP telephone, email, and Kakao Talk, to communicate with family members. Similar to research findings on the mundane nature of these conversations (Wilding 2006), the discussions she had with family members revolved mostly around everyday issues, although time to time Ms. Lee did have serious discussions over her faith.

As discussed earlier about ICT and their cost-saving features, in particular dramatic reductions in international telephone calls, In-Wook Hur, a fifty-nine-year-old special projects coordinator for the Circuit Court of the State of Maryland, mentioned that as international telephone calls became cheaper and email became widely available, he was able to talk to and email friends and family much more regularly than before. He was also an avid blogger, which was how he kept in touch with friends in Korea. He has yet to use Kakao Talk, however, because he did not own a smartphone.

Similar to the Toronto survey findings of calling parents regularly, Hong Jong Yoo, a forty-eight-year-old principal conductor of the Washington Youth Orchestra, also talked once a week with his parents, but hardly called his brothers, attributing it as a male thing. Although he would have liked to keep regular contacts with his friends and acquaintances in Korea, he blamed his hectic schedule and lack of peace of mind for not keeping contact with friends and distant family members. His wife, however, actively engaged in transnational communication with her friends and relatives using Kakao Talk and Skype.

Ok Chae Kim, a forty-year-old, former WKTV producer, also relied on both the telephone and email to communicate with family and friends. He pointed out that he talked more often over the telephone with his mother and close friends, but with others, depending on how close he was with them, he rarely spoke to them. He said:

> I use mostly email and telephone to keep in touch. It is mostly email, but I talk on the telephone with my mother. I do not communicate that often. It depends on how close I am with the person. With close friends, I keep in touch once or twice a week. Otherwise, it would be once or twice a month or less than that. (*What do you talk about?*) It is mostly about how things are there, whether the children are doing well. We ask about the well-being of the family, we talk about life in general, and we relay news about Korea and America.[4]

Here, Mr. Kim corroborates survey findings of using the telephone more frequently with immediate family members, especially his mother and close friends, but with others, inexpensive ICT were used.

It is clear that ICT, especially inexpensive telephone calls, help sustain ties with family, friends, and relatives compared to the days of snail mail and prohibitively expensive telephone calls (Foner 1997, 2005; Vertovec 2007). Still, because international telephone calls incur a nominal cost, they seem to be generally reserved for communicating with family members and close friends, while with distant relatives and acquaintances, inexpensive or free ICT such as Skype, Kakao Talk, and/or email are preferred. As the Toronto survey found, regular contact (once a week) via the telephone (but also other Internet-based mediums) was usually saved for close family members and friends, particularly parents.

Despite the enabling features of ICT on transnational communication, not all maintained regular contact due to factors such as strained relationships, busy schedules, absence of immediate family members in the home country, or lack of familiarity with new ICT and social media. For instance, up until his divorce in 2003, Jin Tae Kim (pseudonym), a sixty-year-old self-employed in construction, explained that he was in close and regular contact with relatives, friends, and acquaintances in Korea, but after his divorce, however, he hardly called anyone, except for a close friend once a month.

Others, especially if their relatives resided in the United States, had no compelling reasons to engage in transnational communication. For example, Jane Kim (pseudonym), a thirty-six-year-old, part-time children's pastor, noted that there was no need to call her relatives on her mother's side because all of them were living in the United States. By contrast, because her in-laws were still residing in Korea, she called them weekly via Skype and email.

The digital divide along age and class was also a factor in the frequency of ICT use for communicating with family members and friends. Corroborating studies of class divide on transnationalism in general and ICT use in particular, the divide along socioeconomic lines deprived low-income Korean transnational families from regular transnational communication. According to Yoon (2016a, 7), not only were low-income Korean transnational families unable to make frequent international telephone calls, calling mostly once a month and for brief durations, but also, due to their inability to afford laptops and smartphones, many of them had difficulties communicating regularly with their daughters living in the United States, creating loneliness for them. While smartphones and laptops have dramatically come down in price today, when they were first being introduced, they were pricey consumer items available to only middle- and upper-income families. Thus, divides along family income underscore the ability to purchase and adopt the latest and, often times, the most expensive ICT, creating challenges for sustaining transnational ties among low-income families. Similarly, the age divide, in particular, parents' ability to attain digital media literacy, also impacted the use of the popular Kakao Talk app and its features to effectively communicate with the children overseas (Yoon 2016a).

For instance, not only were there few compelling reasons for Sekwon Chong, a seventy-five-year-old retired former manager for Coca Cola, to call regularly since he had only a handful of relatives in Korea, but also the digital divide prevented senior citizens like him to easily deploy the newest ICT to communicate with relatives and acquaintances. He explained, "Unless it's for special events, I basically call to send regards, but we don't keep in touch that often. The younger generation obviously uses the Internet to keep in touch, but for us the older generation that is not usually the case. Only few of us are able to use email. Because of time differences it is actually very difficult to talk on the telephone." Here, not only does the twelve- to fourteen-hour time difference affect calling Korea regularly, but also not being well versed in the use of email prevents Mr. Chong from using ICT to engage in transnational communication.

In contrast, young adults like Andrew Noh, a twenty-six-year-old in consulting, who were well versed in the new social media, made ample use of ICT to maintain close contact with friends all over the world, including Korea. According to Andrew, he used a variety of ICT, including email, text messaging, and video calls to stay in touch with his friends, "Yes, I keep in touch with friends very often via Kakao Talk, Skype, and email. I have many friends there. When I was in New York, I had many high school friends and college friends who had returned to Korea. I keep in touch with them through Kakao Talk, Skype, email, and Facebook."

With continuous innovations in ICT, the age divide is likely to persist, creating differences in how quickly and extensively they get adopted by younger and older adults. Generally, younger adults will experiment with an assortment of the newest ICT, while older adults will adopt them more slowly, preferring to stay with ICT they have learned and find comfortable to use. Thus, bridging the age divide will certainly not be easy and will remain a challenge for Korean and other immigrants.

KOREAN MIGRANTS AND KAKAO TALK

As discussed in chapter 2, the ICT revolutionizing transnational communication, by far, has been the smartphone and the apps that go with them. In particular, Kakao Talk is changing the way Korean Americans engage with others, including family and friends on the other side of the globe. Since the introduction of Kakao Talk, email has given way to Kakao Talk as the communication tool of choice as the app allows conversing instantaneously with anyone whose devices have the Kakao Talk app installed.

The sparse literature on Kakao Talk adoption among Korean migrants finds that not only did Korean migrants to Canada all own smartphones, but also almost all of them had Kakao Talk installed on their smartphones, using the app to network with other Korean immigrants as well as to communicate with family members in the homeland (Yoon 2016b, 7). Another widely used feature of Kakao Talk among Korean migrants was its group chat function, which allowed users to send a single text message to group members to arrange, for instance, meetings (Yoon 2016b, 8).

Korean transnational families also preferred to use Kakao Talk over Facebook because parents could better monitor the children's daily routines through the app (Yoon 2016a, 10). For example, when parents send a Kakao Talk text message to the children, the app automatically sends a notification to parents (the sender) alerting them whether the message has been read by the children (recipient). This ability to check receipt of the text message is what prompts the children to respond immediately since many of them felt obligated to be timely in their responses (Yoon 2016a, 9). Moreover, unlike Facebook, which generated broad social networks, Kakao Talk was shared only with those on their telephone contact list, creating less anxiety among parents. Interestingly, Yoon (2016a) also found that children tended to use voice calls and Kakao Talk text messaging more frequently with mothers than with fathers. With fathers, they preferred written communication via Kakao Talk text messaging and email (Yoon 2016a, 11). In addition to Kakao Talk, Korean migrants were increasingly using Kakao Story, a social networking app developed by Kakao Talk which allows users to post pictures and stories (Yoon 2016b). Reminiscent of Cyworld *homepys* (Collins 2009), Korean migrants used Kakao Story to post photos and stories of their lives in Canada, but over time, as these postings became routine features, their use began to decline as there were "no new stories" to upload (Yoon 2016b, 8).

Though widely used and hugely popular today, at the time of the interview, only a handful of the interviewees, however, mentioned using Kakao Talk. It could well be that during the time of the interview, Kakao Talk was just beginning to be adopted as smartphones were slowly gaining mainstream status. Still, some respondents like Dae Sung Park (pseudonym), a fifty-three-year-old man, were using the app and explained that up until the introduction of Kakao Talk, he had relied mostly on email to communicate with his friends in Korea. But as soon as he had access to the app, he used it regularly to contact his friends in Korea, even using it on the morning before the interview. He said:

> Because we don't have any relatives in Korea, we do not have to call. With friends, I have two friends from high school with whom I Kakao Talk almost on a daily basis. I even texted with them this morning. I used to use email a lot in the past, but now with Kakao Talk, I almost always use it instead. I have been keeping in touch with friends far more frequently since it has gotten that much easier.

Here, Mr. Park aptly summarizes the far-reaching impact of Kakao Talk on his life as well as on the lives of numerous users. He notes that email had been his ICT of choice for keeping in touch with friends before Kakao Talk, but since the appearance of the app, it had become his ICT by default, conspicuously raising the volume of transnational communication compared to the old days of using conventional mediums such as letters, email, or the telephone.

To summarize, with huge declines in the cost of international telephone calls and the appearance of virtually free ICT, maintaining transnational ties with the home country through regular contact with family members and friends has become easier, faster, and common among many immigrants (Foner 2005; Vertovec 2007). Not only has it become cheaper and easier to call, email, voice and video chat than before, but also calls are getting more frequent and longer. To be sure, cost is still a factor and the incidence of making international calls or sending emails routinely among interviewees was rather low, except for family members and close friends, suggesting that the ICT used and the frequency with which parents, close friends, and distant relatives get contacted is ultimately dependent on the degree of closeness with family members and friends with whom cost and time is less of a factor.

REMITTANCES

Among the most prominent forms of regular economic transnationalism are undoubtedly remittances from migrants. With deepening globalization, the number of migrants seeking work abroad has risen sharply in recent years, prompting economists as well as sending states to recognize the value and impact of vast sums of money remitted to the home country (Irving et al. 2010; Itzigsohn 1995; Massey and Parrado 1994; Menjivar 1998; Taylor 1999). Numerous governments around the world, including the Philippines and El Salvador, have sought to actively encourage its overseas countrymen to fulfill their "national duties" of assisting foreign exchange, and building their national cash reserves by sending their money home (Foner 2005; Guarnizo 2003; Itzigsohn 2000; Levitt 2001b; Vertovec 2007).

While traditional labor migrants such as Latino immigrants are unlikely to renege on their remittance obligations given that they are target earners and families depend on them for household and educational spending[5] (Hamilton and Chincilla 1999; Levitt 2001b; Mahler 1999), remittances from middle-class immigrants such as Korean Americans have been declining in recent years. For instance, Waldinger (2007) found that among Latinos in the 2006 National Survey of Latinos, half (51%) of them regularly sent remittances. By contrast, according to the 2012 Pew Research Center's Asian American survey (2013, 8; 122), only 16% of Korean immigrants sent remittances in the past year compared to 58% of Vietnamese, 52% of Filipinos, and 12% of Japanese, a figure which was the second lowest after Japanese Americans. Remittance information from the 2010 Toronto survey, however, indicates that close to two-thirds (67%) of Koreans sent money or gifts to Korea, but an equal proportion of them also received money or gifts from the homeland. Closer analysis, however, reveals that age often determined whether Korean immigrants sent or received money. Younger-age adults were more likely to *receive* money or gifts, while older-age adults were more likely to *send* money and gifts (Noh et al. 2013, 129). More importantly though, the amount remitted was miniscule. In the 2003 D.C. Korean community survey, on the other hand, only over a third (38.3%, N=282) of Korean Washingtonians sent remittances, with most of the sums averaging less than $1000.[6]

Furthermore, according to longitudinal data from the World Bank, remittances to Korea were sizeable in the 1960s through the 1990s (as a percentage of gross domestic product) when Korea was still a struggling third world nation. For example, in 1976, $47 million was remitted (personal remittance received) to Korea, accounting for 0.15% of GDP; in 1980, $562 million was remitted, constituting 0.88% of GDP; in 1990, $2.4 billion was remitted (0.91% of GDP); in 2000, $4.8 billion was remitted (0.91% of GDP); and in 2010, $7 billion was remitted (0.69% of GDP). The peak years for remittances were from 1980 through 1990, with remittances staying around 0.9% of Korea's GDP throughout the decade (with 1986 as peak year—1.56% of GDP), but falling from 1991 through 1997 (the IMF Asian financial Crisis), but rising back up to 1.6% of GDP in 1998. With rapid economic recovery after the 1997 financial crisis, remittances began to fall and held steady at 0.9% of GDP between 1999 and 2004; it fell and climbed up to 0.7% of GDP in 2005 and to 0.62% of GDP in 2007. During the 2008 worldwide economic slump, remittances shot back up to 0.97% of GDP, but have been declining since (The World Bank 2011). Clearly, the volume of these remittances has certainly increased, underscoring the size of the remittances Korean Americans have sent home, but has, nonetheless, declined relative to Korea's GDP.

What these surveys seems to suggest is that there is a considerable drop in remittances from Korean immigrants. First and foremost, though most surveys find that few Korean Americans were sending remittances, the size of these remittances, as the World Bank data shows, has increased over time. It is likely that these remittances, however, are actually investments from Korean Americans seeking to profit from real estate, stocks, and other economic ventures in Korea. Second, if any money is remitted, the frequency and amount sent are evidently small. For example, K.Y. Park (1997, 101) found that Korean Americans in the late 1980s were sending small sums of money occasionally to parents, relatives, or friends for weddings, deaths, or illness, customary of traditions in Korea. In 2000s, K.J. Park (2009, 137) found that although Korean immigrant women were still sending clothing and food care packages to Korea, they were no longer sending remittances regularly except for birthdays or holiday celebrations.

Third, with the departure of highly educated professionals who immigrated to the United States as families and with the goals of providing greater educational opportunities for the children, along with the spectacular ascent of the Korean economy in the 1980s and 1990s, remittances are likely to have declined. For instance, according to the 2012 Pew Research Center's Asian American survey (119), while more than half (55%) of Latinos migrated for economic reasons, more than a third (37%) of Koreans were immigrating for educational reasons, suggesting that rates of remittance sending will likely be lower among Korean immigrants whose purpose of migration diverges from their Latino counterparts.

Instead, with the continuous rise in Korea's gross domestic product starting in the late 1980s, remittances have been flowing in the opposite direction to support the study of Korean students[7] abroad, or to find safe investments abroad. For example, the number of pre-college Korean students studying overseas jumped more than three times, from 7944 in 2001 to 29,511 in 2006 (Yoon 2016a, 2). As a result, many parents in Korea have been sending money to support their children's educational expenses in the United States, Canada, the United Kingdom, and Australia (Kwak and Hiebert 2010). Current trends also suggest that recent Korean immigrants receive significant monetary gifts from parents in Korea, which are often used to pay for home or business purchases in America (Park 2009).[8]

I found a similar pattern of remittance decline among the Washington-Baltimore area residents, corroborating the findings from the 2012 Pew Research Center's Asian American survey and the 2003 D.C. Korean community survey data. Among the factors cited in the sharp fall in remittances was indubitably the rise in the standard of living in Korea. According to Sekwon Chong, the former manager for Coca Cola, "There is very little of that in these days. It is because the standard of living in Korea has improved. But 20 years ago, their economic situation was much tighter. People used to send remittances back then. But in recent years as Korea got wealthier, Korean Americans are now referred to as 'beggars.'" Here, Mr. Chong notes that Korean Americans are no longer the envy of South Koreans as in the past, but are now looked down upon as Korean nationals in the homeland have gotten richer and wealthier with rapid economic development, which is a reason for the fall in remittances.

If few of the long-time residents were sending remittances regularly, by no means did this mean that they were no longer sending small sums of money occasionally to provide allowance money to parents, to mark special occasions such as birthdays, weddings, or funerals reminiscent of past practices (Park 1997; Park 2009), to help out a friend in need, or to aid a struggling church, among others. For instance, Won Sang Lee, a seventy-three-year-old former senior pastor of the Washington Central Presbyterian Church, sent small sums of money briefly to assist a struggling church in Korea, "During my early years as a foreign student, because of my support for the church, I used to make small donations to churches in Korea. But it is no longer the case now." Jiyoung Yoon (pseudonym), a fifty-seven-year-old librarian, also sent allowance money to her father every month (or several times a month), while Ok Chae Kim, the WKTV producer wired $300–500 yearly through Woori Bank, a local South Korean branch (with several branches in the Washington, D.C. area), during his mother's birthday.

The only exception to occasional but regular sums of money sent was Myung Suk Oh, a retired man, who, coming from a poor family in Korea, felt obligated to help out his siblings struggling financially by supporting the children's educational expenses. Even after his nephews had completed their studies, Mr. Oh continued to send money to support charity work in Korea, especially organizations offering scholarships to low-income students. As he explained:

> We do support various organizations such as *Heungsadan*. We have tried to do what the church does in terms of the tithe. We decided to give 20%. We donated to various places. I have about twenty sons and daughters. I support young children who bear adult responsibilities in Korea. . . . Every month I supported a student until he graduated from high school. I supported his school expenses. If I were to add them all, it would be quite a sum. As soon as we are done with one student who finished high school we would start with another. That is what I mean by having so many sons and daughters. I still do this. I send remittances to students in Korea.

In the quote above, Mr. Oh is not only sponsoring his own nephews out of family obligations, but also he is actively involved in charity work out of his Christian convictions, supporting nonprofit organizations that provide scholarships to needy students both in the United States and Korea.

Thus, with the exception of a select few, most interviewees were no longer sending frequent remittances to the home country to support family members there. All indicators, including the 2012 Pew Research Center's Asian American survey, the 2003 D.C. Korean community survey, and interviews, suggest that remittances, arguably one of the clearest expressions of economic transnationalism among migrants, no longer play the crucial role they used to perform for South Korea, namely supporting the household economies and consumption of urban and rural populations during a critical phase of Korea's swift economic ascent. Given the dramatic climb of Korea from a poor, Third World country into the thirteenth biggest economy in the world, Korean immigrants no longer need to support parents and family members as in the past. Instead, money seems to be flowing from the homeland to the United States as well-off parents (and some siblings) often send lump sum money to the emigrant children for business and home acquisitions or for other financial needs.

ASSETS AND INVESTMENTS

Portes et al. (2002) note that successful immigrant entrepreneurs often returned to the home country to expand their businesses, to purchase real estate, or to find profitable investment opportunities. Similarly, although small, even children of immigrants such as second-generation Turks there, especially among those operating Internet business in the Netherlands, sought to expand their businesses transnationally to Turkey (Rusinovic 2006, 117). Some of them also engaged in the import and export of home country products or served as intermediaries or advisers to Dutch firms seeking to expand businesses in Turkey. Second-generation Moroccan entrepreneurs also organized Moroccan concerts and brought Moroccan musicians to the Netherlands, while others invested in real estate in the home country (Rusinovic 2006, 120, 122).

In terms of assets and investments in the homeland, in the 2006 National Survey of Latinos, Waldinger (2007, 10) found that 39% of recent Latino immigrants owned property in the home country, while only 4% of long-term immigrants had any property there. Among Korean immigrants, the 2010 Toronto survey found that roughly 75% of Koreans in Toronto still held assets in Korea (home, land, cash or stock, and business), ranging from $100,000 to over $1 million (Noh et al. 2013, 130).[9] In the 2003 D.C. Korean community survey, however, the percentage of Korean Washingtonians with assets, such as real estate or investments, in Korea was 22.2%, far lower than their counterparts in Toronto, but considerable nonetheless.[10]

In our interviews with Washington-Baltimore area Korean community leaders and long-time residents, few, however, owned real estate or had investments in Korea. Some cited unfamiliarity with the local economic trends and financial markets as reasons for not investing in the home country, while others simply had no additional savings set aside to invest in Korea. This is probably because the sample consisted of community leaders and old-timers who had left Korea in the 1960s and 1970s.[11] The practice of holding on to assets or investing in the home country may be a strategy of instrumental citizenship among recent immigrants interested in maximizing their opportunities in both places.

This was corroborated by Steve Lim (pseudonym), a fifty-five-year-old accountant, whose accounting practice gave him unique insights into the instrumental citizenship of recent Korean immigrants. According to him, among his more than 100 customers, the latest cohorts were holding on to their savings accounts and assets in Korea rather than disposing them, a trend starkly different from past immigrants who had sold their properties and assets. He explained that there were, in fact, two types of customers. One consisted of long-term residents who generally had no real estate or other assets in Korea because they liquidated them after leaving the country. The other comprised of recent waves, especially the *girogi* families, who possessed many assets in Korea. According to Mr. Lim, even without steady employment in the United States, many *girogi* families were able to live comfortably from the stocks they owned in Korea or from the day trading in the Korean stock market, which helped to cover most of their expenses in the United States.[12]

Though small, among those who did seek investment opportunities in Korea, they did so because their work in immigrant small businesses was taking a heavy toll on them, prompting to look for "greener" pastures. For example, Jin Tae Kim's reasons for investing and still owning real estate in Korea had to do with his successful, but also grueling, immigrant life. While his construction business in the United States was highly profitable, the work was punishing and wearing him down, requiring putting in up to sixteen hours a day, which was why Mr. Kim started to look for another line of work, albeit in the home country. Contrary to his expectations, however, his business venture in Korea flopped, forcing him to return to the United States. This is what he had to say, "I went to Korea with $200,000 (1996 dollars) but was unable to start a business and instead, I spent the money on something else."

Others kept their bank accounts, property, and other assets in Korea to reduce the uncertainties that came with immigrating to a new country, as well as the convenience of having a savings account to draw from when visiting the home country. According to Ok Chae Kim, the WKTV producer:

> My wife and I have left open couple of accounts in Korea so that when we visit Korea, we can draw funds from those accounts. It is not a lot of money, but enough for spending money. We also have a small apartment under my wife's name. This was not done for the purposes of return migration, but since life as an immigrant is always uncertain, we wanted to set aside a safety net in case things did not work out as planned.

Here, Mr. Kim explains that their possession of an apartment and bank accounts is not for the purpose of ensuring return migration but to hedge against the uncertainties of immigration not working out as planned.

In sum, in a sharp departure from the last three decades of permanent migration, recent waves seem much more instrumental in their attitudes toward immigration and as a result, tend to hold on to their assets in the home country to safeguard against an uncertain immigration venture gone wrong, or to profit from a vibrant Korean economy making a comeback. As Steve Lim, the accountant, observes, long-time residents were hardly investing in Korea, and few had properties or assets left there. Thus, like remittances, investing in the homeland, despite the ease with which capital can flow across national borders, along with the boom in real estate values and stock markets, is not a principal goal or practice for most long-time Korean immigrants. Rather, it remains the focus of new cohorts with savings, stocks, and property in the home country. And given their desires to protect valued assets, it is safe to say that this group is likely to stay oriented toward the home country, prolonging their transnational engagement with the home country in the foreseeable future.[13]

VISITING THE HOMELAND

Research suggests that numerous immigrants seek to visit the homeland after settling down in the host country; the challenge, to be sure, is affording the cost and finding the time to make repeated travels to the home country. For immigrants who hail from countries geographically close to the United States and can be virtually "home" in a matter of hours by air travel such as Latino immigrants, home visits are more frequent (Foner 2005; Levitt 2001b). For instance, Levitt (2001b, 26) found that Dominicans made regular extended trips to the Dominican Republic. Undocumented Yucatecans in Dallas, despite the dangers of crossing the border and the uncertainty of finding jobs after home visits, also went on frequent trips to the home village during cultural and religious festivals (Adler 2004). Interestingly, what enabled both the Dominicans and Yucatecans to engage in these drawn out homeland trips was the lack of steady employment in service work in Boston and Dallas, giving them the time to travel to the home country (Levitt 2001b, 26).

In terms of the frequency of home country visits, 65% of Latino immigrants traveled at least once to their native country since immigrating to the United States (Waldinger 2007). Those with U.S. citizenship and longer time in the country were also more likely to travel to the home country. Among Latinos, Dominicans were the most likely to visit the island nation at least once, with 90% of them traveling to the Dominican Republic. Cubans, by contrast, were the least likely to visit the home country, with less than half of them being unable to visit given the political circumstances limiting travel to Cuba (Waldinger 2007, 5).[14]

For immigrants separated by vast distances such as Korean immigrants, on the other hand, despite sharp reductions in airfare and daily flights to Korea, substantial costs in airfare and time expenditure keep visits to the home country to a bi-annual (or even less frequent) affair.[15] According to Noh et al. (2013, 129), only one-third of Koreans in Toronto visited the home country, with these trips generally lasting less than a month, and only 3.6% of them visited more than once in 2009. Similarly, while fewer than a third (29.7%, N=283) of Korean Washingtonians never visited Korea, only 8.1% were able to do so on a regular basis (more than once a year). Park (2009, 137) also found that few of the Korean immigrant women in her study were able to regularly visit the homeland, visiting at most once every couple of years.[16]

I found similar patterns of home country travel among community leaders and long-time residents, with the vast majority being unable to visit Korea regularly. For example, Hong Jong Yoo, the Washington Youth Orchestra conductor, visited a total of three times during sixteen years of residence in the United States. His most recent trip was five years ago when he received his green card and traveled to the home country to celebrate the receipt of his permanent residency. Others like Sung Min Oh (pseudonym), a seventy-seven-year-old former president of the dry cleaners association and a long-time resident, went only five times since immigrating to the United States. He went to visit four years ago in order to relocate his parents' burial place to America when his mother passed away. Jane Kim, the part-time children's pastor, also managed to go only twice since immigrating to the United States, with her most recent trip being in 2009 to attend a wedding. Hyuk Kyo Suh, a fifty-one-year old publication manager for the American Bar Association, did not visit Korea until 1989 after being in the United States for more than eighteen years. Two years ago, he went to Korea to visit relatives and to attend a conference.

That said, among those who did manage to visit from time to time, they did so for a number of reasons, including deaths, weddings, or business trips. For instance, Ok Chae Kim, the WKTV producer, whose last trip to Korea was three years ago, summed up the challenges of visiting the homeland, "The last time I have been to Korea was in 2008 (in March). It has been about 3 years since I have not been back. It is not that I used to visit regularly in the past. I went to visit when there was a business matter, when my dad passed away, or when there was a wedding of a relative. Those were the reasons for the visit."

Thus, it is apparent from the responses above that visiting the home country annually or even every few years is dependent upon a number of factors and remains a challenge for most Korean Americans. Unless their work involved frequent business trips to Korea or they served as leaders of Korean American community or religious organizations, traveling repeatedly to the home country was taxing in terms of both time and cost. Because the sample included a number of religious and community leaders, many of them actually mentioned traveling to the home country frequently as part of their organizational or religious activities. For example, Myung Suk Oh, the retired long-time resident, stated that he went to Korea yearly because his work required making frequent business trips to East Asia. He explained:

> I used to go every year because we had yearly work leave. We used to go very often, sometimes two to three times a year. We went even more regularly when I was about to retire because of my work. I was in charge of the Far East and needed to monitor the progress of various constructions. I would work during the day and spend the evenings with my family. The most recent was last year. I have been to Korea a lot due to work reasons.

Here, Mr Oh's work took him to Korea on a regular basis, but he also traveled while serving as president of the Korean American Dry cleaners Association, when he was invited on several occasions by the Korean Dry cleaners Association to give seminars in Korea because of his knowledge of the industry as a former president of the association.

Former Korean Association leaders such as Jung Beom Choi and In-Wook Hur also traveled to Korea at least once a year for activities associated with the Korean Association or to attend events sponsored by the Korean government. While In-Wook Hur never made personal visits to the homeland, he went twice to Korea during his two-year tenure as president of the Maryland Korean Association, one of which was to attend an invited meeting organized by the Overseas Koreans Foundation. Jung Beom Choi, a forty-nine-year-old president of the Korean Association of Washington, also traveled to Korea several times a year for both association-related activities as well as to visit family members and conduct business.

Others like Hye Jung Cho (pseudonym), forty-seven, traveled several times to Korea on official school exchanges to meet with Korean school principals because of her job as an elementary school principal at a Maryland suburb. This is how she described her visit: "Because of my connections with them I have been to Korea several times. Through my husband I have come to meet a number of people in government positions too. . . . When I went to Korea two years ago because of my studies, I visited various schools. I met a number of principals." Here, Ms. Cho explains that her husband's as well as her own connections, along with her work experience as a school principal, are what led her to visit and meet with various government and school officials in Korea.

Finally, similar to community leaders traveling for work or on official travel, religious leaders, particularly Christian pastors in Korean immigrant churches, were active practitioners of regular transnationalism, with a number of them traveling frequently to the home country to network and to coordinate activities with churches in the homeland, including church ministries, fundraising, and missionary programs. For example, Won Sang Lee, the former senior pastor of the Washington Central Presbyterian Church in Northern Virginia, explained that although he was unable to travel to Korea for various reasons during his first nineteen years in the United States, he began to go to Korea every year within the past fifteen years. The first time he went was to attend a training seminar at Korea's Church of Love, one of the biggest churches in Korea. Later, he visited Korea to reunite with former members of the Central Presbyterian church who had returned home after completing their overseas tour as subsidiary workers or had lived in the United States as *girogi* families. He also went yearly to attend prayer meetings held annually during Easter's (in April) as part of missionary work with the Seed Mission.

As the literature on religious transnationalism finds, immigrant churches, temples, or mosques also recruit religious leaders such as pastors, monks, or imams from the home country, a common practice among many immigrant groups. For Korean Americans who have one of the highest rates of church affiliation and attendance, immigrant churches actively engage in religious transnationalism, including among other things, pastors' repeated travels to the homeland, sermons on or references to the homeland, visits and guest sermons by home country pastors in immigrant churches, and coordinated missionary and church activities with home country churches and religious organizations. While this study has not examined this aspect of transnationalism, future research should certainly consider religious transnationalism and its impact on immigrants' ties to the home country as it continues to play important and visible roles in the immigrant community.

Unless immigrants own transnational businesses, are in occupations that require frequent travels to the home country, belong to middle or upper-class split households (*girogi* or wild geese families), or serve as community or religious leaders who travel on official organizational visits, monetary and time constraints still make regular visits to the home country few and far between for scores of immigrants. Homeland visits, while easily accessible to immigrants from the Caribbean and Central America, are much more costly for immigrants coming from far-flung regions of the world such as Asia, suggesting greater reliance on ICT and consumption of home country cultural and consumer products for sustaining transnational connections.

SUMMER EDUCATIONAL PROGRAMS IN KOREA

The literature on West Indian and Central American immigrants notes that immigrant parents often sent their U.S.-raised children to the home country in order to remove them from substandard urban public schools in New York or Los Angeles. This was done to ensure, or hope, that the second generation could recover from academic and gang-related problems (Fitzgerald 2000; Foner 2005; Portes 2001; Smith 2006). For instance, Vickerman (2002, 346–347) found that West Indian parents often sent their children to the West Indies to provide them with better education. Others were forced to send children to the home country to be cared by parents, extended kin, and friends because of the high cost of child care in the United States (Brandon 2004). There were also those who sent their Americanized children to the homeland in order to expose them to the ethnic culture and language.

In the case of Korean immigrants, although most first-generation Koreans found visiting the home country prohibitively expensive in terms of cost and time, when it came to sending their own children to Korea for educational and cultural programs, they were more than willing to cover the cost of the program given the perceived benefits for children. For instance, among married Koreans in Toronto 7.5% sent their children to organized educational programs, including summer language and cultural programs in Korea in 2009 (Noh et al. 2013, 130). More than any other age group, middle-aged Korean Canadians (thirty-six to fifty-five) were the most likely to send their children for educational programs in the home country.

In our interviews with community leaders and long-time residents, more than several parents sent their second-generation children to Korea for educational and cultural purposes, including the famous Yonsei University summer study and/or the semester or year-long study abroad programs during college. These study tour programs in the homeland such as the Yonsei University program (or the Overseas Chinese Youth language and study abroad tour to Taiwan for second-generation Chinese), represent, according to Kibria (2002, 298), one of the key institutionalized forms of home country visits available to second-generation Koreans (Min 2012). Many parents, in fact, had good things to say about the program, which they viewed as helping the second generation to develop pride in and appreciation for their heritage. Thus, as long as parents were able to afford the expenses for summer programs, including airfare, tuition, room and board, and allowance money, they were more than eager to make this sacrifice.

First and foremost, a number of parents found summer programs in the homeland to be transformative for the children, instilling greater ethnic pride and understanding in the second generation. For example, In-Wook Hur, the former president of the Korean Association of Maryland, observed that before his daughter went to study at Korea University as an exchange student for a year while on leave from her graduate study in Korean Studies at the University of Hawaii, her proficiency in Korean was at what he called "kitchen conversation" level. But after the program, she was able to surpass him in her knowledgeable of Korea, landing a job with the U.S. government as a Korea expert. To Mr. Hur, the fact that his daughter came to identify more strongly with her Korean heritage after spending a year in Korea gave him a greater sense of accomplishment as a parent than his son becoming a lawyer and fulfilling his call for a career in the legal field, which was why he highly recommended it to other families.

Another effect of homeland summer programs was greater proficiencies in the mother tongue and ethnic identification. For instance, Jin Woo Seo (pseudonym), a seventy-five-year-old man, described substantial transformations on his children after attending the summer program in Korea. This is how he summed it up:

> The Korean government had a two-week program during the summer where they would bring overseas Korean children to come and visit Korea. All my children attended the program, and when they came back they were very different. For example, when we make *kimchi* or bean curd soup in a Korean style, they would complain of the smell. They went to Korea when they were in high school and when they came back they were very different. There was a 180° turn around. I think that was a good thing. . . . And my son he spent the summer school during college at Yonsei University. He did not study though. He just played there. He graduated from GWU, and he studied the Korean language. He does not speak Korean that well but he is able to understand some. He is able to read everything. That two-week program was very helpful. Our oldest has attended the program several times, and our son has attended it multiple times.

Here, Jin Woo Seo notes that summer programs had tangible benefits for the children, including improved proficiencies in Korean and pride in their Korean heritage. Furthermore, after attending summer programs in Korea, his sons, who used to dislike the smell of Korean food and hardly spoke any Korean, are now into Korean food and are more proficient in speaking and reading Korean.

Others cited an ethnic turn from the children after attending the summer program in Korea.[17] For example, Dae Sung Park, the self-employed man, attributed his daughter's ethnic turn, especially her marriage to a Korean after her positive experience with the summer program. This is how he viewed it:

> Last year, our daughter attended the Korean Language Institute at the Yonsei University for three months. My son also wants to attend the institute and we are thinking of sending him as well. My daughter loved it. The experience actually brought quite a change in her. Probably this paved the way for her marrying a Korean man because that was hardly the case in the past. Of course, she never expressed to us to whom she wanted to get married with or who she liked. But after going to Korea for three months, she seems to have learned a great deal about her roots and who she was, and she began to appreciate being Korean and wanted to be more fluent in Korean.

Here, Mr. Park credits her daughter's ethnic turn, namely pride and ethnic identification, and even co-ethnic marriage to the summer program, which is why he fully supports it.

While many parents seem to agree on the value of the summer programs for children, once the cost of the entire program is factored in, however, not everyone is able to afford to enroll children in the program. Mr. Park gave a breakdown of the total cost of the program:

> I would definitely recommend it to other parents, but it is too expensive. In the case of our daughter, it cost us $10,000 for 3 months. The cost of actual tuition was $3000, but the cost of various optional cultural programs brought the total sum to $10,000 even when, in the remaining month of her stay, she stayed with her aunt. Because the kids were not fluent in Korean, they took cabs frequently instead of using public transportation, which added to the cost. If you do not have local people who can help translate for your children, they will have some difficulty.

Though the benefits of ethnic pride and identification seem to outweigh the financial costs these incur for families, not all families, especially low-income families, will be able to actively participate in these programs, underscoring the class divide in transnational engagement (Guarnizo 1999). For example, while middle-class families are certainly likely to reap the benefits of additional investment in the children's cultural capital, working-class families, given substantial sacrifices needed to send children on homeland visits and summer cultural programs, are less likely to provide such opportunities for the children, contributing to differences in the attainment of human and cultural capital.

THE KOREAN STATE AND POLITICAL TRANSNATIONALISM

Among the factors contributing to the intensification of transnational ties has been the heavy promotion of globalization and transnationalism by the Korean state. Ranging from efforts to attract remittances and investments from overseas Koreans to providing social benefits to retirees, the Korean state has been actively seeking to broaden its influence over its overseas emigrants. Historically, the Korean state has always intervened in community affairs, including supporting language, educational, and cultural programs for its overseas population. It has also attempted to monitor and control the political activities of Korean Americans, particularly political organizing from Korean dissidents for democratic reforms during periods of authoritarian rule in Korea (Kim 1981). According to the KAFGW (2009, 159), one way the Korean government sought to influence Korean Washingtonians was by offering political office in the home country. Such transnationalism from above, however, had the regrettable effect of dividing and creating factions within the Korean Association as community leaders, who, prior to the meddling by the Korean state, had no interest in becoming officers for the association, soon began to compete for office and became entangled in charges of campaign fraud and corruption. It also led to pro- and anti-government factions in the community during a time when military dictatorships in Korea triggered democracy movements both at home and abroad. Ultimately, the surveillance of the emigrant community by military dictatorships and their efforts to gain legitimacy in the Korean community in Washington, D.C., by extending political office to overseas Korean leaders, led to increased factionalism within the community (KAFGW 2009, 185), contributing to, for example, the splitting of the Korean Association into three organizations in 1986 (KAFGW 2009, 231).

In recent years, the Korean government has also attempted to influence and maintain ties with the emigrant community by providing annual recognitions and awards to community leaders and organizations such as presidential awards to the Korean Service Center (KAFGW 2009, 233). Another has been the introduction and passing of new legislations to attract overseas Koreans. For instance, in April of 2012, Korean Americans holding Korean citizenship were for the first time allowed to vote in the Korean parliamentary elections and in the December 2012 presidential elections. Reports from Korean newspapers, however, revealed that only 4% of Korean Americans were registered for the April parliamentary elections, suggesting low levels of participation in homeland elections.

Another new legislation, which was passed recently by the Korean parliament, allows older naturalized Korean Americans to obtain dual citizenship. Indeed, a number of states around the world have been offering dual citizenship to its emigrants to court their votes, remittances, and investments (Guarnizo et al. 1998; Levitt 2001b, 205; Portes 2001; Portes and Rumbaut 2014; Vertovec 2007). Yet, it is one thing for states to seek to court them and quite another for overseas migrants to take on these initiatives. In the 2006 National Survey of Latinos, only 9% of them belonged to a civic organization, social club, or sports team in the home country, with civic engagement by long-time residents declining (Waldinger 2007). Moreover, 60% of Latinos indicated that they were more concerned with American politics and local issues than homeland politics (Waldinger 2007, 11). Similarly, transnational political participation among Koreans in Toronto was low, with few voting in the Korean parliamentary elections (3.3%) and engaging in with political parties or organizations (1%) in Korea (Noh et al. 2013, 130–131). In the 2003 D.C. Korean community survey, while three-fourths (75.5%) of Korean Washingtonians did not back a political party in Korea, a similar proportion (77%) of them, however, supported dual citizenship.

VIEWS ON GRANTING THE FRANCHISE TO OVERSEAS KOREANS

Given that immigrants often migrate for political reasons (Levitt 2001b, 7), it is no surprise that some of them actively participate in homeland politics (Portes and Rumbaut 2014). But how do community leaders and long-time residents view the transnationalism of the Korean state? What are their views on dual citizenship and voting in home country elections? Do immigrants maintain strong interest in the political affairs of the home country, neglecting their obligations to and engagement with host country politics, as feared by opponents of political transnationalism?

In order to gauge immigrant responses to political transnationalism from above, we probed our interviewees' views on voting and dual citizenship. What stood out from their responses was strong opposition to extending the franchise in home country elections, but ambivalent feelings toward dual citizenship. First and foremost, many of them argued that it was imperative for the Korean community to stake out a foothold in the adopted country rather than in the homeland. Second, they also viewed the courting of Korean American votes from Korean politicians and political parties with deep suspicion and anxiety because many were afraid the competition for emigrants' votes would set off political faction and in-fighting. For example, Jung Beom Choi, the Korean Association of Washington president, said, "They have much at stake. It can be misused for political reasons though. If all sides are given a fair chance, it's good. But I am suspicious about the current Korean government. We need to be cautious about how to implement it." Here, Mr. Choi is deeply suspicious of the Korean state and cautions against the reasons behind the Korean state's granting of the franchise to Korean Americans.

In fact, instead of granting the right to vote for overseas Koreans, most community leaders urged the Korean state to promote the integration of the diasporic community into the mainstream of receiving societies. Rather than interfering in community affairs and attempting to orient the emigrant community toward the political affairs of the home country, community leaders opined that the Korean state should support cultural and educational programs for later generations of Korean Americans. For example, Hong Jong Yoo, the Washington Youth Orchestra conductor, opposed the Korean government's efforts to extend the right to vote to Korean citizens abroad on the grounds that the decision to immigrate and seek permanent residence or naturalization was a tacit renunciation of their citizenship rights and obligations to the home country. He interpreted the Korean government's extension of the franchise as a strategy to court conservative voters to sway domestic elections and maintain political power, since overseas Koreans tended to be more conservative. Instead of these efforts, he favored state support for cultural programs for overseas Koreans.

Others argued that Korean immigrants needed to prioritize participating economically, socially, and politically in the adopted land rather than voting in the home country parliamentary elections. For example, stating the maxim of "when in Rome, do as the Romans do," Steve Lim, the accountant, contended that it was critical for Korean Americans to participate in the local PTA on behalf of the children rather than placing their energy and effort on homeland politics. Because homeland politics had little practical value for Korean Americans, and the courting from Korean politicians was merely a political ploy to gain votes, he chastised Korean politicians for using Korean immigrants for political gain. He also worried over the possible fallout from political transnationalism such as increased factionalism and disunity within the community. Jin Woo Seo, a retired man, summed up the positions of both:

> I actually do not have much interest in that. If you have that kind of energy and interest, I would want Koreans to be involved in local politics. We should instead support people to run for offices in the Maryland Senate or House. I think it is one thing to have interest in Korean politics and another to vote. If you were going to do this then you might as well live in Korea. That's my position.

Here, Mr. Seo advocates participating in local politics, especially running for office to empower the immigrant community rather than voting in home country elections, which to him did not make sense since their home was in the United States.

Echoing the positions held by these community leaders, some contended that voting in homeland elections detracted Korean Americans from participating in local politics, which impacted them deeply. For instance, Sekwon Chong, the retired, former manager for Coca Cola, viewed the Korean government's effort to court Korean Americans to participate in homeland politics as inappropriate and misguided. As he put it:

> I am opposed to it. How can you vote just like Koreans in Korea, if the way you live here is very different from the way they live over there? All we know about Korea is through the news. If you want to participate in Korean politics, then you should go and live there. I would want Korean Americans to participate in American politics instead by becoming naturalized and registering to vote. We need to show our political power by voting and presenting a unified voice. Korean Americans can also influence the course of Korea-America relations. . . . My position is that if you live here, then you should be more involved with the politics in this country.

Taking the view that residence in the host country takes precedence over homeland politics, Mr. Chong claims that immigrants should concern themselves with matters, especially politics, that affect them daily in the place of settlement rather than ones that have little bearing such as home country politics.

Others opposed the instrumentalism of voting in home country elections without meeting their citizenship duties and obligations. For example, although Myung Suk Oh, the retired man, was not opposed to temporary Korean visitors such as subsidiary workers having the right to vote through absentee ballots, he was baffled by the need to offer them to permanent residents in the United States who had no obligation to pay taxes in Korea.

Furthermore, repeating an earlier position held by one of the interviewees, Mr. Sekwon Chong contended that when individuals make decisions to immigrate to another country, this was a tacit recognition that they were also renouncing their citizenship obligations and rights to their country of origin. From this perspective, seeking instrumental citizenship, namely to wanting to have the cake and eat it too, was morally wrong and should be abandoned. Using the metaphor of the foolishness of chasing two rabbits, he argued that individuals wishing to engage in homeland politics should move back to the home country. Thus, in their opposition to extending voting rights for overseas emigrants, the common concern from all the leaders was unnecessary distraction from engaging in local life and local politics.

Others were also opposed to homeland voting rights because there was little benefit to be drawn from the ability to vote in home country elections, on top of inadequate planning and execution by the Korean parliament. For example, citing few benefits from the franchise in homeland elections, Jin Tae Kim, the self-employed man in construction, said, "I do not know why they are doing that. I think there is very little the Korean government can do for the immigrant community." Noting inadequate planning and execution by the Korean parliament, In-Wook Hur, the Korean Association of Maryland president, said, "I am opposed to the granting of voting rights for overseas Koreans. We are at a point where the basic infrastructure for voting is not set up. But as a result of their potential vote, Korean politicians are forced to pay attention to overseas Koreans and the Korean association." Here, Mr. Hur observes that a byproduct of granting the franchise, despite poor planning and execution, has been greater attention being paid to Korean emigrants by Korean politicians seeking to court their vote.

All the controversy over extending voting rights was a moot point for interviewees like Hye Jung Cho, the elementary school principal, because she doubted that green card holders, even if they were granted the right to vote, would hardly be interested in participating in homeland elections. Taking a page from the assimilationist perspective, she argued that time in the United States determined immigrants' interest in home country politics. Another reason for her skepticism was her suspicion of politics having little bearing on the lives of Korean Americans. For her, interest in homeland politics would arise if she had family members in Korea who would be affected by the outcome of political decisions.

In sum, the set of responses from interviewees suggests that fears of migrant political transnationalism, especially voting in home country elections, seem unwarranted. Clearly, given the disproportionate pool of community leaders in the sample, it is not surprising that they are all focused on local, rather than homeland, politics. But long-time residents are equally uninterested in voting in home country elections, suggesting that state efforts to court and exert influence on its emigrants by offering the franchise, dual citizenship, and other benefits are not met with much enthusiasm (see also Waldinger 2015). At least when it comes to voting in home country elections, community leaders and long-time residents are apprehensive about it, underscoring deep-seated suspicions toward the Korean government's motivations for and wary of increased factionalism that might resurface with increased meddling in community affairs by the Korean state.

VIEWS ON DUAL CITIZENSHIP

Levitt (2001b, 19–20) observes that among the various factors that were likely to continue to sustain transnational ties were dual citizenship as well as uninterrupted immigration and exclusion from full social membership. Interestingly, while there was almost unanimous opposition to extending the franchise in homeland elections, many were somewhat ambivalent toward dual citizenship. Some supported it for instrumental reasons such as wanting to offer it to family members, while others favored dual citizenship for the convenience that came with it such as being able to circumvent bureaucratic hurdles that often regulate the free movement of people and business activity. According to Dae Sung Park, the self-employed man:

> I think it is a good idea. (*In what ways*?) Probably the Korean government saw it negatively because of the compulsory military service, but I see it in a more positive light. (*Can you elaborate on it*?) For example, when you visit Korea, they give you a 30 day (although it is 3 months) stay stamp. But if you have dual citizenship, then you are no longer affected by entry requirements. That is the biggest advantage. There is no other benefit except for that. Also it does not mean I am interested in obtaining the right to vote by having dual citizenship.

Here, Mr. Park supports dual citizenship for the convenience of easing his travel, entry, and stay in Korea, but he is hardly interested in the obligations and duties that also come with citizenship such as the franchise or holding an elected position.

Others favored granting it to senior citizens, especially if they had intentions of retiring in the home country. Sung Min Oh, a retired dry cleaner, opined, "I am not sure about dual citizenship. I would be for it if it is meant for senior citizens who have plans of returning back to Korea to live."

A few argued that dual citizenship made sense for both Korean Americans, but also for the Korean state because, by recruiting skilled and talented overseas Koreans to the home country, the overall pool of the skilled would expand. According to Won Sang Lee, the former senior pastor of the Washington Central Presbyterian Church:

> One good thing about dual citizenship is that because the Korean diaspora is spread out globally and is over 7 million, the Korean government can scout for talent among that population. And this will raise the competitiveness of Korea. . . . Because we live in a global age, I am for Koreans living anywhere in the world to have an impact in the places they live.

Here, Pastor Lee shifts the tables of dual citizenship around from immigrants to the state by pointing out that the Korean state, by taking a more enlightened approach, has as much to gain from it as Korean immigrants. In other words, it would be in their best interest to grant dual citizenship since the Korean state would have a larger pool of talent to choose from, helping them to become more competitive in the global economy.

Finally, some recognized that dual citizenship would help spark interest in home country affairs even among the apolitical like Hye Jung Cho, the elementary school principal, "If I had dual citizenship I would be more interested in things that are going on in both places."

Though opposition against dual citizenship was much more muted than voting in home country elections, there were certainly those who still regarded dual citizenship and the franchise in the same light, namely the instrumentalism behind both. For example, Chul Ho Choi, the member of the *Korean Central Daily* editorial staff, said, "Dual citizenship is a form of greed where one wants to have opportunities in both places. Those who have become U.S. citizens should renounce their Korean citizenship. If they were to think hard about the type of identity they wish to pursue, then there is no need to want dual citizenship." Here, echoing earlier sentiments that naturalization symbolizes renouncing past allegiances in favor of loyalty toward the host society, Mr. Choi argues that it is selfish for immigrants to want to have both.

Arguing that immigrants' allegiance should align with the host society as soon as they renounce their home country citizenship, In-Wook Hur, the special projects coordinator, also said, "Personally, I do not think that dual citizenship will bring a lot of change to our lives or our identities. Since we have already joined our in-laws in this marriage, we need to concern ourselves with our in-laws more so than our biological family." Here, Mr. Hur uses the metaphor of the bride in traditional marriages to argue that as soon as the bride leaves for the groom's family and joins the in-laws, she needs to follow the customs and norms of the in-laws, which is how he views the franchise and dual citizenship for immigrants.

A few, although in agreement with the basic tenets of dual citizenship, placed the blame on the Korean parliament for poor execution of the voting legislation for overseas Koreans. The two media persons in the sample, for example, considered it short-sided to grant voting rights to emigrants without resolving the fundamental question of dual citizenship. Jae Won Ryu, a thirty-eight-year-old 1310 AM radio reporter, observed that it was folly to extend voting rights without addressing dual citizenship in the first place, since voting rights would have come automatically with citizenship. He contended that even if dual citizenship would not have been politically feasible, the Korean parliament should still have debated it before rushing to extend the franchise to Korean Americans.

Ok Chae Kim, the WKTV producer, equally criticized the Korean parliament's focus on the voting legislation as taking the easy way out to skirt controversies surrounding dual citizenship, pushing instead a legislation that politicians perceived to be passable and more immediate. He had this to say, "When this issue first came out, what Korean Americans actually wanted was not voting rights but dual citizenship. More than half of Koreans who live here are U.S. citizens. What they wanted for their children is the ability to retain a link with the home country, which is why they supported dual citizenship. And I am in agreement with them." Here, Mr. Kim aptly points out that with more than one-half of Korean Americans being U.S. citizens, dual citizenship is a more pressing concern for them than homeland voting rights since naturalized Korean Americans are automatically excluded from home country elections.

In sum, dual citizenship was viewed with much more ambivalence since it carried with it an instrumentalism that offered tangible benefits such as ease of entry and exit as dual nationals and health insurance and other benefits from the Korean state. It is on these grounds that dual citizenship, if granted, is likely to be sought by immigrants, while many oppose voting in home country elections. Furthermore, dual citizenship may not translate into disengagement from local politics as feared by opponents of political transnationalism. As Portes and Rumbaut (2014, 181) observe, the experience of engaging politically with the home country usually translates into more active political involvement in the country of residence, especially in a climate of general political apathy. Migrants who do not participate in homeland politics are generally less likely to participate in local politics, suggesting that dual citizenship and voting are not as closely intertwined as opponents of political transnationalism make it out to be.

CONCLUSION

This chapter examined the forms and extent of transnational activities engaged in by Korean Americans. The findings suggest that regular transnationalism is clearly the exception rather than the rule, corroborating the findings from Portes et al.'s (2002) and also Waldinger's (2007) analyses of survey data on immigrant transnationalism. From home country visits to remittances to summer programs for the children to political transnationalism, participating *regularly* in these transnational activities was much harder than expected, underscoring the significance of geography for middle-class immigrants separated by vast distances. Thus, cost and time expenditures, as well as interest, were invariably factors in Korean immigrants' ability to participate regularly with the home country.

Yet, while frequent economic and political transnational engagement with the homeland was possible for only a segment of the population, ICT were undeniably increasing the frequency and volume of contacts with the home country as demonstrated by the frequency and length of international telephone calls, emails, voice and video calls, and MIM text messaging among community leaders and long-time residents. Even though different ICT were being used (international telephone calls with parents and close friends, while email and free MIM text messaging with distant relatives and acquaintances), the sheer quantity and accessibility of these instantaneous ICT was without doubt breaking down the barriers of space and time.

This suggests that for middle-class immigrants like Koreans, encumbered by the weight of distance, they will be even more pressed to rely on ICT to maintain regular transnationalism. Stated differently, compared to the transnational practices found among Caribbean and Central American immigrants,[18] such as sending remittances and visiting the home country, these play a minor role for Korean Americans. And although most Korean Americans engage in occasional economic and political transnationalism, this should not lead us to dismiss it as unimportant, or that other forms of transnational activities such as cultural transnationalism are not being practiced. Furthermore, not only is the Korean state actively courting the votes and investments of overseas Koreans, but also Korean conglomerates have sought to capture global and co-ethnic markets as they search for new investment opportunities and markets both within and outside the immigrant community in America. In this context, the fusing of the ethnic with the transnational is taking apace through the consumption of transnational media/television and home country consumer goods, establishing the foundation for synchronization with the homeland. Clearly, the scope and intensity of these cultural transnational activities have to be further examined empirically, but the sum total of mostly occasional transnational engagements, mixed with some regular transnational participation, can have profound impacts on the latest cohorts for sure, and possibly on long-time residents as well. It is to this aspect of transnationalism, namely cultural transnationalism, that chapter 4 will examine to assess the role that transnational media may increasingly play for sustaining transnational connections with the home country.

NOTES

1. Their study focuses on informal social ties, contacts, and organizational participation as indicators or measures of transnational engagement (1). In the survey, more than three-fourths (77.4%) of participants immigrated to Canada before 2000.

2. The more prominent transnationalism of Korean Canadians may be due to the fact that 60% of Koreans in Canada as of 2006 were recent immigrants who had arrived in the past 10 years (Yoon 2016b, 2). As Yoon observes, Korean Canadians exhibit adhesive adaptation (Hurh and Kim 1984), or high ethnic attachment and low assimilation. These were also obviously the effects of high self-employment and co-ethnic church attendance, which are two salient features of the Korean community both in Canada and the United States.

3. The 2012 Pew Research Center's Asian American survey found that 63% of Korean Americans still had close family living in Korea, a figure which was the third highest after Asian Indians and Vietnamese.

4. It should be kept in mind that as smartphones become more ubiquitous and cellular service providers offer fewer "dumb" phones for purchase, it is likely that Kakao Talk and other smartphone apps will be extensively adopted by late smartphone adopters.

5. For migrant families in the home country, remittances represent one of the few, often the only, sources of income, which serve to pay for home improvements or to purchase appliances, among other items of daily household consumption (Levitt 2001b, 2). In other cases such as Filipino families, remittances from Filipina mothers support the children's education and enable households to maintain middle-class status (Parrenas 2001, 385).

6. In light of the significant plunge in remittances from first-generation Koreans, it should be expected that the second generation will be even less likely to engage in such practices. According to the 2004 IIMMLA, only 15.7% (N=395) of second-generation Korean Angelenos ever sent any money to Korea, with the vast majority (84.3%) abstaining from it. In addition, among those who had ever sent any money to Korea, two-thirds (66.1%) had sent only once or twice, and close to half (47.6%) had sent less than $500.

7. Globalization and increasing neoliberalization of Korean society have forced growing numbers of Korean families to voluntarily create split or *girogi* households for the purpose of pursuing authentic English as families struggle to sustain their class standing, especially after the 1997 IMF Asian financial crisis (Kwak and Hiebert 2010).

8. Behind Korean immigrants' efforts to maintain transnational ties with the home country, the contributions Korean immigrant women have made should be properly acknowledged and highlighted. For instance, married Korean women, as Park (1997, 101) notes, were the main agents of transnational communication through the letters they wrote to parents and in-laws. Another was the role played by women's parents, usually the mothers, who came and stayed with the immigrant family for extended periods of time to help with housework and childcare, which, as Park (2009, 88) observes, enabled the women to work in the family business as unpaid labor. Similarly, transnational support, including emotional and material support such as remittances, clothing, food, and care packages from the home country, was critical in easing Korean immigrants' adjustment in the United States (Park 2009, 86).

9. The breakdown is as follows: one-third (33%) of respondents had assets worth between $100,000 and $500,000; 14% had assets worth between $500,000 and $1,000,000; and 10% owned assets over a $1 million.

10. Another rough proxy of transnational investments by Korean immigrants can be gleaned from online forums on legal matters pertaining assets abroad. After the American government announced mandatory declaration of assets abroad from foreign nationals and immigrants, MissyUSA.com, a popular website among Korean American women, was flooded with numerous questions and responses concerning assets in the home country.

11. It could also be the case that the sample did not include wealthy Korean Americans who invest in Korean property and stock markets.

12. A recent *Korea Times* article reported that some *girogi* families, in order to cover their living expenses in the United States, were purchasing desirable commercial property (in the millions) in America as a means of drawing rental income from the leasing of rental, store front units.

13. The same is true among Korean nationals who seek to invest and park their assets abroad. The *Korea Times* (Ryu 2015) reported recently that Korean nationals were buying up commercial and residential properties in Los Angeles and in other major cities.

14. This may change as relations between the United States and Cuba get normalized and flights from the United States to Cuba get started.

15. Oh (2016, 2233) found that many posting related to transnational ties on Missy USA centered around home visits. Among these, the top question was on the cost of airplane tickets (price, travel agencies), followed by places to stay or visit in Korea, and gifts to take while visiting family and relatives in Korea. Dhingra (2012, 178) also found that Asian Indian motel owners engaged in a range of transnational activities, including transnational communication, homeland visits, remittances, and consumption of transnational media.

16. The latest admission statistics from Korea Immigration Service found that 47,181 Korean American men and 36,367 women visited Korea in 2016.

17. For second-generation Koreans and Chinese who visit their parents' home country on these study tour programs, many of them also report that they were better able to appreciate and understand their parents' parenting practices after the trip, which, in their view, contrasted sharply from the rearing practices of their fellow American students during childhood (Kibria 2002, 305).

18. This does not mean that immigrants from the Caribbean and Latin America are not utilizing the latest ICT; they certainly are as immigrants tend to be the earliest adopters and heaviest users of new ICT.

Chapter 4

Cultural Transnational Activities

The Consumption of Transnational Media With Young A. Jung and Gyu Tag Lee

Soonjoo Kim (pseudonym, female, fifty-eight years old) has been living in the United States for more than eighteen years and operates a convenience store with her husband in the Washington-Baltimore metropolitan area.[1] Ms. Kim resides in a typical suburban bedroom community of single-family homes, large backyards, and well-maintained sidewalks. She works from late afternoon till 11 pm every day, and her nightly ritual before going to bed consists of preparing the midnight meal and watching Korean dramas for an hour or two. While she is busy fixing up the couple's late night dinner, Mr. Kim is tidying up the living room and previews Korean news for ten minutes from the local Korean American channel before he hands over the remote control to his wife. Ms. Kim is a regular viewer of Korean dramas, which she watches religiously after coming home from work.[2] This is how she described her reasons for watching Korean dramas:

> I am sure it is true for other Korean immigrants, but running a convenience store is hard work. You have to be at the store seven days a week, 365 days a year. Even if we were to hire help during mornings and lunchtime, it is almost impossible to hire someone for the whole day in these hard times. My husband and I are there in the evenings, but during the day I hardly have any time to relax because of household chores and grocery shopping. How do you expect us to have any joy with our lives? Our only down time after a long day at work is to take a little break by watching dramas as soon as we are done eating dinner with my husband. Yes, these days we enjoy watching *Please Laugh Donghae* (*Wooseora Donghae*, 2011). My daughter tells me I keep watching the same dramas with predictable stories. But I still like them even though they are the same ones. You see, the main character may be from a seemingly humble origin, but finds out later that there is a twist to his class background and is able to regain his original upper-class position. Donghae as well as Anna end up getting

rewarded through their own effort and live a model life. I really like that kind of story. I was really happy to see that Donghae and Anna turned out successful. . . . Well, although our work lives are hard, we still have a nice house, and our children made it to a good college. I am sure that we can reap much reward after all the hardship. I think we have a pretty decent life. I just wish I had more down time to relax.

Jisook Goh (pseudonym, female, forty-seven years old) has also been in America for twenty-four years and operates a dry cleaner with her husband in a busy Korean strip mall in Northern Virginia. In addition to the dry cleaners, the Gohs also own a coin laundromat in a suburban shopping mall. During the frenzied Saturday afternoon when the interview was conducted, the dry cleaners was filled with office workers dropping off their shirts and pants, while housewives were looking to do minor alterations. Mrs. Goh's facial expression appeared relaxed while serving customers in front of the cash register. Behind the counter and far inside the large and open interior of the store, two Latino employees were speedily and adeptly steam ironing the clothes. Another Latino worker was skillfully sorting the clothes and hanging them onto a machine that resembled a large conveyor belt. The store, however, seemed cramped with thousands of clothing items cluttering every inch of the open space. A twenty-four-inch television set, on top of Mrs. Goh's alteration workbench, was on all the time. When asked if working at the dry cleaners was grueling, this is how Mrs. Goh replied:

Well, the work is a little hard but I like this business. I work as much as my husband does and we earn considerably. I don't understand why women in Korea live so extravagantly and mooch off their husbands. . . . I don't understand why women stay at home after having graduated from college. I like the fact that I don't have any guilt since I come and work as hard as my husband does. Yes, I leave the television on all the time because it is boring in the store. Alterations are pretty simple to do, so I can watch the dramas time to time while sewing. Plus, the stories are pretty much the same with these dramas so it is easy to follow them. These days I am watching *Baby Face Beauty* (*Dong An Minyeo*, 2011), and I like those characters such as Soyoung who works really hard. Like the drama I saw last time in *Queen of Reversals* (*Yeokjeon ae Yeowang*, 2010), they now feature many working women. It is true that children of conglomerate owners still appear and the storyline involves women dreaming of Cinderella-like stories, but at least because they have their own work they come across better. I think Korean women are changing. That is certainly the case, because how can you live your life relying only on your husband? You've got to have your own work.

Jin Soo Kim (pseudonym, male, twenty-five years old), a typical second-generation Korean American raised in the suburbs, reluctantly came to terms with his ethnic identity when his coworkers assumed he would speak Korean and "behave" culturally Korean simply because of his ethnicity. He recalls growing up, he was forced by his parents to go to Saturday Korean-language schools, but it was not until after college and after moving out of his parents' home and working at his new job that Jin Soo began to seriously take interest in his identity and attend Korean-language classes. When asked about his efforts to improve his Korean, including taking Korean classes, this is what he had to say:

> I watch a lot of Korean historical dramas that my dad likes. He used to tell me that Korean history is very interesting and is filled with a lot of educational content. I like the fact that we have something in common to talk about by watching these historical dramas. I usually watch it through dramafever.com. These days I am watching *Dongyi* (2010). Dongyi is King Sookjong's concubine who later gives birth to King Yeongjo, one of the greatest kings during the Joseon Dynasty. When I watch historical dramas featuring kings or queens, it is true that they tend to be very melodramatic. But I still like the fact that this drama puts much emphasis on Dongyi's compassion for the commoners. In that sense, I actually prefer to watch *The Duo* (*Jjakpae*, 2010) rather than *Dongyi*. *Jjakpae* is really special. Although it is very similar to other Korean dramas that usually hide their class origins or birth secrets, what I like about the story is that the hero is not interested in finding out about his past, but dedicates his life to fighting for the lives of the masses. I am tired of heroes that you get from American Hollywood movies. I find that dramas like *Jjakpae* capture very nicely the predicaments of modern Korean society. It really speaks to issues facing the average person. There are times when you are immersed in the story and it is really hard to catch up with the English subtitles. But perhaps because I have seen so many of them, I am now able to understand simple Korean expressions. By watching these historical dramas, I have become more proud to be a descendant of a long tradition and history. But if I want to understand these dramas better, I should put more effort into learning Korean history.

The three vignettes presented above illustrate practices which are becoming increasingly common in the wider Korean community. As many Korean immigrants would attest, spending their evenings glued to Korean television after a long day in the family business to catch the latest news and the hottest dramas, is one of the few forms of entertainment and relaxation for many. As discussed in chapter 2, revolutions in ICT are shrinking the constraints of time and space, enabling immigrants to live simultaneously in the United States and in the home country. In particular, the ease, speed, and magnitude with which cultural products from the homeland can be consumed sets today's cultural transnational practices apart from past engagements (Duany 2011; Foner 1997, 2005; Vertovec 2007).

Since much of the literature on transnationalism has focused on migrants' economic and political transnational activities and less on their cultural transnational practices, this chapter considers the consumption of transnational media/television as a salient but neglected feature of immigrant lives in general, but more particularly those of Korean Americans. How prevalent is the consumption of transnational media/television among Korean Americans in the Washington-Baltimore area? How does such consumption shape the contours of work and private life? What are the implications of growing cultural transnationalism as it becomes a regular and taken-for-granted feature of immigrants' everyday lives? These questions are addressed by analyzing the cultural transnational activities among the area's community leaders and long-time residents. The chapter begins with an overview of the evolution of Korean transnational media/television, including the impact of the *Hallyu* or the Korean Wave on the Korean community and beyond. Following this, we discuss the cultural transnational activities of the community, including the impact of ethnicity and transnationalism on the lives of Korean Americans. We conclude with a discussion on the short and long-term implications of cultural transnational practices for the Korean community.

KOREAN TRANSNATIONAL MEDIA BEFORE 1990S

During the 1960s and 1970s when the Korean population was still small and the community was just being established, there was little to speak of transnational or ethnic media. Nonetheless, the first ethnic dailies to appear in the United States and in the Washington-Baltimore region was the *Dong-A Ilbo* in 1967, the *Korea Times* in 1970, the *Korea Central Daily* in 1978, and the *Chosun Ilbo* in 1984.[3] Weeklies such as *Hanmi Shinbo* also appeared in 1973, along with *Korea News* in 1977, *Hanmi Times* in 1981, and *Mijoo Times* in 1987, to name a few (KAGFW 2006, 202–203). Other weeklies also turned up in the 1980s, 1990s, 2000s, 2010s, but due to intense competition, most either went out of business or reappeared under different names or management.

With the explosion of the Korean population in the 1980s and 1990s, transnational media began to diversify from ethnic dailies to include other forms of media such as radio and television stations, filling the informational and entertainment needs of the community. The first radio station to debut in the area was Washington Korean Radio in 1970 (KAGFW 2006, 203–205), which broadcast on WHFS-FM for one hour on Sunday mornings. In the 1980s, Korean radio gained some ground with two new stations—WLMD-AM and WABS-AM (Korean Christian programming). Around 1984, WPKX-AM began to expand its programming, bringing news, entertainment, and gossip, along with direct broadcasts of KBS news from South Korea. Other Korean radio stations also appeared later, increasing both the length and scope of programming offered, with some stations running for as long as seventeen hours per day. By bringing news at regular intervals and providing practical information to immigrants, Korean-language radio stations, as Min (1996, 44) observes, enabled Korean immigrants to listen to Korean news, music, and entertainment "anywhere anytime." Yet, intense competition and financial losses drove many of them to close, leaving only Radio Washington AM 1310 to operate in the area today (KAFGW 2006, 208–209).

Korean television stations also appeared around 1986 with Korean Cable Television (KCW) (KAFGW 2006, 210–212). Broadcasting daily KBS news via satellite, the station offered three hours of Korean programming, especially Korean dramas and variety shows. But like other ethnic media outlets struggling to stay afloat, the station changed hands soon after and was renamed the Washington Korean TV (WKTV). In the 2000s, WKTV became available on Cox Cable, expanding the number of Korean viewers. Another Korean television to debut in the area was the Korean Broadcasting Network, Inc. (KBT-TV) in 1999 (KAFGW 2006, 211). As part of the Cox Cable channel (channel 13) in Northern Virginia and Comcast Cable (channel 667) in Maryland, KBN-TV brought Korean programming for four hours (7:30–11:30PM) in Virginia and twenty-four hours in Maryland (KAFGW 2006, 211).[4]

But with the advent of the digital revolution ushered in by the Internet in 2000s, television broadcasts from the Korean airwaves can now be viewed either live or streamed immediately after they have been broadcast in the home country, significantly speeding up the viewing time as well as broadening the choices of programs available to consumers. All in all, the evolution of transnational media suggests that the ease and speed with which television programming, among others, can now be viewed, as viewers can watch Korean television in real time or close to it, is qualitatively transforming the consumption of transnational cultural products, not only helping to integrate the geographically dispersed Korean community and bringing Korean immigrants much closer to Seoul than before (Min 1996, 45), but also making synchronized lives a feature of immigration in the digital age.

THE KOREAN WAVE, THE *HALLYU*

Another significant change besides the ease, speed, and volume in the consumption of transnational media before 1990s and consumption afterward is the increasing salience of *Hallyu*, or the Korean Wave. Since the 1990s, the *Hallyu*, epitomized by Korean films, dramas, and K-Pop, has taken East and Southeast Asia by storm, and is now spreading globally (Hong 2014; Jung 2011; Shim 2008). From highly acclaimed Korean films such as *Shiri* (1999) and *Oldboy* (2003), to immensely popular Korean dramas such as *Winter Sonata* (2003) and *Jewel in the Palace* (2003–4), to K-Pop sensations Wonder Girls, Girls' Generation, and Big Bang, these three genres in Korean popular culture have spearheaded the Korean Wave regionally and now globally. For example, with the meteoric success of Psy's popular music video, *Gangnam Style*, on YouTube (1.5 billion views), K-Pop and the Korean Wave are becoming more popular than ever, appearing to even make inroads into the most competitive and lucrative media market in the world—the United States.[5]

Because these three genres constitute the backbone of Korean transnational media today, they merit special attention since their rising popularity offers even more reasons for first-, and especially second-generation Korean Americans to seek, consume, and identify with transnational media (see Oh 2012). In the following sections, we provide a general overview of each genre that comprises the Korean Wave, focusing on their evolution and reception.

Korean Feature Films

The first Korean feature films that can be said to have given rise to the Hallyu phenomenon were undoubtedly *Shiri* (1999), *My Sassy Girl* (*Yeopgi-jeogin Geunyeo*, 2001), and *My Wife is a Gangster* (*Jopok Manura*, 2001). Subsequent Korean blockbusters such as *Oldboy* (2003), *Memories of Murder* (*Sarin-ui Chueok*, 2003), and *The Brotherhood of War* (*Taegukgi Hwinallimyo*, 2004), after becoming number one box office hits in several Asian countries and also earning critical and commercial acclaim in prestigious film festivals in Cannes, Berlin, and Venice (Shim 2008), brought even further outside interest into Korean feature films, spreading their popularity regionally and globally (Jung 2011).

What accounts for the sudden commercial success of Korean feature films domestically, but especially internationally? First, one of the major factors in precipitating innovation and commercial success of Korean films has been the liberalization of the film industry which began in the late 1980s and early 1990s (Hong 2014; Jung 2011). For instance, the 1997 IMF Asian financial crisis in Korea set off several decisive reforms, including the restructuring of the economy and the liberalization of protectionist policies from the Korean state. The entry of foreign distributors and competitors, especially Hollywood blockbusters, was heavily resisted by domestic movie producers for the fear of a global movie industry takeover of the local film market. Competition from global cinema, however, had the opposite effect, forcing Korean cinema to innovate and raise the quality and appeal of its feature films. Second, the Korean state also pushed Korean conglomerates (*chaebols*) to invest in Korean film and television industries when they themselves were seeking new profitable places, infusing capital and management know-how to the production of commercial films and spurring the birth of new Korean blockbusters (Huang 2011, 7; Jung 2011; Shim 2008). Finally, the Korean state's policy of globalization or *segyewha* helped to promote the export of Korean popular culture regionally and globally, resulting in the expansion of the Korean media industry (Chua and Iwabuchi 2008; Hong 2014; Jung 2011; Park 2004; Shim 2008). For example, the Korean government played an active role in increasing the visibility of Korean television, in effect subsidizing the industry, by buying the rights to popular dramas and distributing them for free to many countries (Huang 2011, 8).

While these reforms and investments from the state were critical in enhancing the quality and competitiveness of Korean feature films, why have Korean films also appealed to audiences in Asia and in other parts of the world? According to Jung (2011), a major reason for their success stemmed from the hybridized character of Korean films, or what she calls transcultural hybridity (see also G. Lee 2013). For example, Korean cinemas were marked by a mixture of local and foreign influences, appealing to non-Korean audiences because they offered the familiar, but also the unfamiliar. In other words, Korean blockbusters offered the familiar through their big-budget, Hollywood-style entertainment formats, but they also capitalized on elements of unfamiliar Korean culture, which clearly differentiated them from Hollywood blockbusters. Another significant trait of Korean films was its lack of nationality, which arose because nothing was entirely foreign or native in Korean feature films, creating what Jung (2011) refers to as "cultural odorlessness" in these films. In other words, similar to the success of Japanese cultural exports which borrowed heavily from the United States but also added their distinct Japanese flavor, leading to a blending of Western culture with Asian values (Iwabuchi 2002), Korean cinemas took on a hybridized and tempered cultural character which softened the markers associated with race, ethnicity, and culture (Huang 2011, 4; Jung 2011; Shim 2008).

Korean Dramas

Another key piece to the *Hallyu* phenomenon is without doubt Korean dramas. The *Hallyu* made its first appearance in China in 1997 through broadcasts of televised Korean dramas (G. Lee 2013). Spearheading this flow and achieving its first major success in East Asia, particularly in Chinese-speaking regions such as Mainland China, Taiwan, and Hong Kong, was the drama, *What is Love All About?* (1991). Following on the heels of this hit, the next series of Korean dramas, including *Winter Sonata* (2003), *Full House*

(2004), and *Jewel in the Palace* (*The Great Jang Geum*, 2003–4), topped off the charts in China and in other Chinese-speaking regions and Southeast Asian countries, including Vietnam, Thailand, the Philippines, Singapore, Malaysia, and Indonesia. Dramas like *Full House* (2004), which drew upon the popularity of K-Pop sensation Rain, who, in 2006, was selected by *Time* magazine as one of the world's 100 most influential people, became immensely successful. Another drama, *Jewel in the Palace* (*The Great Jang-Gum*, 2003–4), achieved even more fame and was broadcast in more than sixty countries around the world (Jung 2011).

Despite being considered one of the most difficult media markets to penetrate, Japan was also swept by the *Hallyu* in the mid-2000 following the monumental success of *Winter Sonata* (2003) starring Bae Yong-Joon. When the male star of this popular drama appeared in Japan to promote the drama, he was greeted by a crowd of five thousand adoring female fans at Narita airport, launching the "Yonsama Syndrome" among middle-aged Japanese housewives. Thus, as Shim (1998) notes, inroads made by Korean dramas were decisive in attracting Japanese audiences to other types of Korean popular culture, especially K-Pop and Korean films.

Again, several factors were important in raising the profile of Korean dramas throughout Asia. First, the entry of new television networks on public airwaves, in particular the Seoul Broadcasting System (SBS), gave much needed jolt to the Korean drama industry, bringing greater competition to the sector and pushing the networks to enhance the quality (and quantity) of dramas produced in Korea (Shim 2008). According to Shim (2008), the three major television networks in Korea—KBS, MBC, and SBS—were airing more than thirty television dramas per week. Second, Korean dramas profited from exceptionally good timing as they (with the Korean Wave) rode the wave of economic development and democratization sweeping East Asia since the early 1990s (Chua and Iwabuchi 2008). Before 1990s, many countries in Asia maintained strong protectionist policies against foreign cultural imports, but with globalization and the 1997 IMF Asian financial crisis, local media markets loosened barriers against foreign imports, providing rare opportunities for Korean media products to gain significant ground there (Shim 2008). Furthermore, economic growth and political liberalization in the region spurred the expansion of local and satellite television channels (such as Rupert Murdoch's Star TV), creating huge demand for inexpensive, but high-quality, television programming.

The Korean media industry, which had been forced to export Korean popular culture abroad, benefited in particular from the pent-up demand since Japanese dramas were too expensive for many television stations there (Chua and Iwabuchi 2008). In the past, Japanese dramas, although more expensive but highly popular, used to fill the airwaves in a number of Asian countries

(Huang 2011).[6] But now cheaper, but well-made, Korean dramas and music television programs were well suited to satisfy both the quality and cost-end of programming needs, filling a void throughout East and Southeast Asia.[7] Aired several times during the week and sometimes daily in the free-to-air and satellite television, Korean dramas became regular fixtures, becoming, in the process, hugely popular with local audiences (Chua 2008; Iwabuchi 2001; Pease 2009; Sung 2006).

For example, when Korean dramas took off especially in places like Taiwan, they benefited from Taiwan's strategic location as the center of dubbing, subtitling, and distribution of foreign media to the overseas Chinese diaspora, helping to spread Korean dramas to Hong Kong and other Chinese markets in Singapore and Malaysia (Chua 2008). Furthermore, in Taiwan, middle classes' appetite for novel media products, cable television's demand for new programming, and local newspapers' need for stories also contributed to greater reception of Korean television (Huang 2011, 7). Another was Taiwanese news media's positive coverage of Korean dramas, along with pop music writers' promotion of romantic images of Korea, which helped to widen the appeal of Korean cultural products there (Huang 2011, 10).

Finally, similar to Korean feature films, Korean dramas struck the right chord with Asian audiences with their emphasis on Asian cultural values, including family values, respect for elders, and aspirations for modernity and material comfort. For example, Korean dramas were popular in Vietnam due to cultural proximity, different portrayals of masculinity, emphasis on romantic love and emotion, and modern consumerism (Vu and Lee 2013, 309).[8] In China and Vietnam, Korean dramas were also better received than Japanese or American ones because they retained traditional values but also expressed modern ambition and sophistication. Korean dramas, which played on themes of nostalgia for a less capitalistic past with desires for a modern, consumerist future, resonated well with Asian audiences seeking lifestyles embodying material well-being and upward mobility and also preservation of family values and cultural traditions (Chua 2008; Shim 2008).

K-Pop

If Korean films and dramas were the two pillars behind the Korean Wave, they also rested on the popularity and success of K-Pop. The term K-Pop refers to specific music genres created and circulated after the late 1990s.[9] It implies a new, modern, and global Koreanness which is distinctive from the *gayo ballad* or popular Korean ballads. Although some music critics, taking a nationalistic stance, have attributed K-Pop to be a 'uniquely Korean' form of music (see Chohan 2005), there are actually few elements of traditional Korean instrumentation, melodic modes, or compound rhythms in K-Pop.

Instead, K-Pop as well as *gayo ballad* are marked by hybridity and localization. From the onset, K-Pop was heavily influenced by Western music, especially Western electronic club dance music, often dubbed "electronica," that incorporates a machine-like electronic sound with repetitive rhythmic patterns based on digital technologies.[10] Second, K-Pop vocalists and rappers draw upon and make references to mostly contemporary American R'n'B and hip-hop musicians (see Kang 2011). Third, K-Pop's radio-friendly melodies, vocal harmonies, and relatively simple and easily accepted rhythms are patterned after those of Europop. Elements of J-Pop have also influenced K-Pop, such as its style of stage performances, costumes, and group-composition.

Although K-Pop has drawn from a wide range of global popular music styles and sources, it is still construed as "authentically Korean" because of the visibility of Korean producers, performers, and audiences in the articulation of this genre.[11] More importantly, both Korean and East Asian audiences, despite their awareness of K-Pop's transnational and fused elements, perceive a distinctive Koreanness in K-Pop, rendering it uniquely Korean (see Chua and Iwabuchi 2008; Pease 2009).

Among the factors behind K-Pop's success are, first and foremost, their low cost. For example, royalties paid to the K-Pop industry are much lower than those paid to the global (Western) music industry and it is far less expensive to host K-Pop musicians and hold K-Pop concerts than Western musicians.[12] In addition, although some cultural boundaries are more difficult to bridge than others (e.g., comedies; see F. Lee 2006, 264), popular music has fewer barriers than other mediums. Not only are melodies and rhythmic patterns in popular music already highly standardized globally, but also despite differences in language, which can hinder the consumption of foreign culture, they are relatively unimportant in most popular music genres (see Frith 1991). This is, in fact, a major reason why global popular music products, usually produced by Anglo-American corporations, have been able to easily penetrate local markets, and it is the same logic which allows non-hegemonic (semi-peripheral or peripheral) media products to enter other markets if they have the capital and the know-how to produce quality music, as has been the case with K-Pop.

CONSUMPTION OF TRANSNATIONAL MEDIA/TELEVISION

The discussion above was intended to briefly review and discuss the impact of the Korean Wave regionally and globally. Yet, an important question related to cultural transnationalism that should be raised is the extent to which transnational media, in particular Korean television, is consumed by Korean Americans. To date, there have been few studies on the consumption of transnational media/television among Korean Americans. In one of the handful studies of Korean immigrant transnationalism, Noh et al. (2013, 130) found that over 89% of Koreans in Toronto watched Korean television programming or movies *often or daily*, and about 90% of respondents read news about Korea from newspapers, magazines, or Internet websites *often or daily*.[13] In the 2003 D.C. Korean community survey, over three-fourths (76.4%) of Korean Washingtonians indicated that they watched Korean programming regularly.[14] A 2003 Fairfax County commissioned survey of 130 Korean families also found that 71.3% of Koreans obtained their news and information from Korean newspapers, while 46.5% watched Korean programs on television, and 50.4% listened to Korean radio (KAFGW 2009, 52).

According to the 2003 D.C. Korean community survey, Korean Americans, on an average, spent from a low of fewer than two hours to a maximum of ten hours per day on Korean television. In another study, C. Lee (2004) found that respondents were watching Korean programming for two to four hours per day, mostly in the evenings. Yoon (2016) also found that some Korean migrants in Canada were even aware of daily and weekly television schedules, suggesting deep incursions and hold of transnational media/television on Korean immigrants' daily lives.[15]

With widespread consumption of transnational media, how are innovations in ICT, especially the Internet and new digital technologies, impacting the television viewing habits of the Korean community? In the past, before the advent of cable and satellite television, ethnic video shops were the primary means by which transnational television was consumed. With the expansion of cable and satellite television in the late 1990s and onwards, the old method of receiving videos from South Korean broadcasters, then copying them and renting them to customers, gave way to ethnic programming on local cable television. At first, most video shops were able to compete against cable and satellite television because it took several weeks to broadcast Korean dramas and variety shows on local cable channels (Min 1996, 44). The only advantage cable television had over video stores was its broadcasts of daily Korean news via satellite.

With the arrival of the Internet, however, Korean immigrants were certainly incorporating the latest digital technologies to consume Korean television, shifting from traditional mediums to Internet-based ones. For example, Yoon (2016, 7) found that Korean migrants in Canada generally used the Internet, including hard-based downloading and streaming services, to view Korean transnational media. Park (2009, 137) and Son (2015, 388) also found that many Korean immigrant women were relying on the Internet to watch Korean news, movies, and television. The same was true among Korean women foreign students in Britain who were not only downloading movies and music but also watching Korean dramas on the Internet (Y. Kim 2011, 94).

Reasons for Consuming Transnational Media/Television

Among the various factors influencing migrants' use of transnational television in chapter 2 were unresponsiveness from host media, language and cultural barriers, sense of identity and community, need for entertainment and information, and escapism, to name a few. Studies examining the consumption of Korean transnational media found similar reasons for turning to transnational television, including indifference from host media, language barriers, cultural unfamiliarity, sense of community, nostalgia toward the homeland, and need for entertainment and information, among others. For example, a major reason why Korean migrants in Canada were attracted to Korean television was because the host media offered little to no ethnic programming relevant to their lives (Yoon 2006). Among Korean, Chinese, and Japanese women foreign students in Britain, many of whom had turned to British television to learn English and British culture, a principal reason why many of them stopped watching the host media after the first year was because hardly any minorities were represented in UK television (Y. Kim 2011, 93). Furthermore, what is interesting about Korean women foreign students' transnational turn was that in Korea, scarcely few of them had actually tuned in to Korean television because of their busy social lives, but in Britain they became avid consumers of transnational media (Y. Kim 2011, 94).

In conjunction with host media's indifference to migrants' programming needs, language and cultural barriers were, not surprisingly, key reasons for choosing transnational over host media. For instance, Lee (2004) found that many Korean Americans watched Korean television because of their unfamiliarity with American culture and difficulties with English. Park (2009, 154) also found that many Korean immigrant women in her study obtained their U.S. news through Korean media because of language barriers. The same was true among Korean transnational families in Son's (2015) study, with lower-to-intermediate English speakers more likely to turn to Korean transnational media than more proficient English speakers, attesting to the role of language barriers in transnational media consumption (Son 2015; Yin 2015). In short, cultural, linguistic, and socioeconomic barriers pushed Korean migrants in Canada away from the host media (Yoon 2016, 10).

Among a segment of Korean migrants in Canada, cost, namely the inability to afford cable television package subscriptions, was also a factor for not using the host media (Yoon 2016, 11). Moreover, corroborating some studies linking decreased use of host media with increased use of transnational media, Korean migrants who did not regard cultural integration to be important also tended to disregard Canadian media as essential for integration, reducing their consumption of host broadcast media (Yoon 2016, 12).

While the above discussion zeroed in on the host media's unresponsiveness that pushed migrants away from the host media, the reasons for consuming transnational media also had to do with the various benefits that Korean media/television brought for Korean immigrants, including sense of community, nostalgia toward the homeland, and need for entertainment and information, to name a few. For instance, in a study of television viewing habits among Korean Americans, a major reason for watching Korean programming was to keep up with current events in Korea without having to visit the home country (C. Lee 2004). For others, consumption of home country cultural products such as television shows, films, and magazines gave continuity to their immigrant lives, making it possible to extend the lifestyles these women had enjoyed prior to migrating to the host country (Park 2009, 88).

Among older Korean immigrants, transnational television, especially shows featuring songs they grew up with, helped to rekindle nostalgia for the home country (C. Lee 2004). Especially after witnessing the transformations of the homeland from a poor and economically backward country into a modern, bustling nation, with their fellow countrymen enjoying improved standards of living that included a host of amenities such as fancy kitchens, stylish cars, and new buildings, some viewers became nostalgic and developed strong desires to visit the homeland (C. Lee 2004). Others indicated that Korean television was useful for teaching the Korean language and culture to the children, with a few noting that the children developed interest in visiting Korea after watching Korean dramas (C. Lee 2004). Some, however, watched transnational television for mundane reasons such as to reduce stress, to find entertainment, or to kill time.

Korean television also served to demarcate boundary lines between ethnically invested second-generation Koreans and their more assimilated counterparts. For example, similar to Panagakos's findings among Greek Canadians, Oh (2012, 261; 2015) found that the more second-generation Koreans identified ethnically as racialized ethnics, the more they were likely to use transnational media to express their identities. This was a conscious and active choice made since transnational media was not readily accessible and was usually discouraged by their white peers (Oh 2012, 263). Furthermore, for those in the immersion and integration identity positions, Korean dramas and movies represented unique assets since it was they, unlike their uninterested white peers with little to no understanding of Korean media, who had the interest in and knowledge of Korean popular culture (Oh 2012, 266). By invoking moral superiority or ethnic authenticity through evaluations of cultural competence, which rested primarily not on historical or social knowledge or cultural norms of Korea but on knowledge of Korean popular culture, Korean transnational television helped to establish social closure within the second generation (Oh 2012, 267). Thus, among the ethnically invested second-generation Koreans, markers of ethnic authenticity and identity were predicated on Korean-language proficiency, but more importantly, on knowledge of Korean popular culture, drawing boundaries against those who either lacked cultural competence or whose Koreanness was questioned (the "twinkies") (Oh 2012, 267).

Though not quite about Korean immigrants, the media consumption of Korean Chinese in Japan also offers some clues about their motivations for consuming Korean television. For example, in their online study, Lee and Lee (2015, 28) found that Korean Chinese in Japan had many options in terms of media choices after migrating to Japan: Chinese, Korean Chinese, South Korean, and Japanese media. Interestingly, however, most Korean Chinese preferred to watch Korean television such as Korean dramas and variety shows because first, many of them grew up with Korean transnational media in China; second, the quality of Chinese television was mediocre compared to Korean television; third, linguistic and cultural differences pushed Korean Chinese away from Japanese television; and finally, the Korean Chinese were interested in keeping up with current trends in Korea (Lee and Lee 2015, 33). Additionally, their being viewed as Korean, rather than Chinese, in Japan also pushed them to favor Korean transnational media.

Thus, the few studies on transnational media consumption suggest that Korean television not only assist immigrants to follow the latest sociocultural trends and issues, but also reinforce and engender greater connections among viewers as they acquire common tastes, preferences, and knowledge (Park 2004). By consuming homeland popular culture, even second-generation Korean Americans adopt shared tastes and interests, not only helping them to reconnect with the parents' home country (Park 2004) but also serving to demarcate the boundaries of ethnic authenticity and identity (Oh 2012, 2015). In sum, transnational media not only provide entertainment and information that help Korean immigrants keep abreast of the latest trends and events in Korea, but they also help to preserve ethnicity, serving as vehicles of cultural transmission and identity for immigrant children (Lee 2004). Whether these practices translate into other forms of transnational and ethnic participation remains to be seen.

Korean Washingtonians' Consumption of Transnational Media/Television

In this section, we examine the television viewing habits of community leaders and long-time residents in the Greater Washington, D.C. area. We explore their reasons for viewing Korean television programming and the implications of these cultural transnational activities on the immigrant community. We also consider the impact of the *Hallyu* on the first and second generations and the extent to which a more Americanized or Koreanized way of life emerges with growing cultural transnational participation.

Among community leaders and long-time residents, a handful of them did, in fact, tune in to Korean television programming fairly regularly. For example, both In-Wook Hur, a fifty-nine-year-old special projects coordinator for the Circuit Court of the State of Maryland, and Jin Tae Kim (pseudonym), a sixty-year-old self-employed in construction, were frequent viewers of Korean television. While Mr. Hur subscribed to NTV, a new Korean Internet streaming service, to watch Korean news, Mr. Kim was a huge fan of historical dramas and viewed them on the Internet. Due to the zero-sum nature of viewership, both of them reported that the more they spent their evenings watching Korean television, the less they watched American television.

Others also read the news and watched Korean television through ethnic dailies and satellite television. For instance, Sekwon Chong, a retired, former manager for Coca Cola in his mid-seventies, started his day by reading all the major Korean newspapers, including the *Korean Central Daily* and the *Korea Times* and occasionally watching Korean dramas in the evenings, particularly historical dramas such as *Isan* through DirecTV.

Among the reasons for watching Korean television included language barriers, cultural familiarity, nostalgia for the homeland, entertainment, transnational political commitment, interest in learning Korean, inertia, and maintenance of current social and cultural trends in Korea. In the case of Jiyoung Yoon (pseudonym), a fifty-seven-year-old librarian, cultural unfamiliarity was a primary reason why she tended to watch mostly Korean rather than American television. Although Ms. Yoon had no difficulties following the plots in American sitcoms, she still struggled to understand the culturally specific puns, which was why she preferred to watch Korean television because of her familiarity with Korean cultural references.

For a few, deep political commitment to the homeland and active involvement in community affairs pushed interviewees like Hyuk Kyo Suh, a fifty-one-year-old, 1.5-generation working as a publication manager at the American Bar Association, to watch Korean television. In addition, Mr. Suh's television viewing habits were influenced by his wife's programming choices, which were mostly Korean dramas.[16] Not surprisingly, the more he and his wife watched Korean television, the less they got to watch American television. This is how he described his and his wife's consumption of transnational media:

> Because of my interest, I monitor the Korean news daily in Korean and English, the developments and what is going on (in Korea). We watch Korean movies and Korean soap operas. My wife more so. Once in a while if it's interesting, we will watch it together. That's part of our cultural activity. I read Korean books

and I read Korean newspapers everyday and through that stay in touch culturally with what is happening in Korea and with Koreans around the world, I guess. (*Do you find Korean dramas and films to be more appealing*?) Not particularly. I mean my personal interest is in different independent films and international films. So I am not particularly saying that Korean films are the best or most interesting. But we see more because my wife sees more than me. And because for television programs (that) I get is pretty much more Korean TV shows than American TV shows, so (Korean TV shows are) culturally more appealing to me or (I feel) more connected (to it) I guess than just seeing American comedies or reality shows. That's not what holds my attention. Korean shows that sometimes touch upon current events or current cultural situations, societal issues, those that have more connections to us are appealing [*sic*].

Here, Mr. Suh explains that in terms of his own media inclinations, however, he actually prefers to watch independent and foreign films rather than Korean television. Moreover, rather than television, Mr. Suh keeps up with homeland affairs by reading Korean newspapers and books.

For some, inertia or difficulties in resetting channels from American to Korean channels on Direct TV was their explanation for watching mostly Korean television. According to Teak C. Chung, a fifty-eight-year-old pastor and president of American Wheat Mission, because he found it cumbersome to change channels each time from American to Korean, he simply left the Korean channels on for most of the time.

Others noted that Korean television helped to alleviate feelings of nostalgia toward the homeland. For instance, what drove Mi Jung Jeon (pseudonym), a fifty-seven-year-old woman, to view mostly Korean television was feelings of homesickness that often came with the uprooting process. As a result, she was fond of and drew much inspiration from reality television shows like *Human Drama* (KBS documentary) because it made her realize that there were many people who were less fortunate than her.

A few watched Korean television to keep up with current trends in Korea. Especially among those working for the Korean media, keeping close tabs of the news and current trends was critical part of their work. For example, both Jae Won Ryu, a thirty-eight-year-old 1310 AM radio reporter, and Ok Chae Kim, a forty-year-old WKTV producer, were avid consumers of transnational media products since their line of work pushed them to be attentive to events in the homeland. While Mr. Ryu read Korean news daily on the Internet, Mr. Kim consumed a variety of media products from the homeland, including dramas, news, variety shows, and documentaries, in order to keep up with the latest cultural, social, economic, and political trends there. Ok Chae Kim explained, "Because I work for the local Korean cable television, I always watch it. Every program out there. Because I am involved in news making, I always tune in to the news at work or on the Internet. Since my job requires keeping abreast of American and local news, which is connected with Korean news, I keep attentive to Korean news as well."

Because it had been some time since Mr. Kim had been back to Korea, it was primarily through transnational media that he was able to keep abreast of the rapid changes in the home country. By keeping tabs on new television programs, including the topics they covered, Mr. Kim was able to discern the changes in the focus and emphasis from current media products. An example he gave was differences in the coverage of news in Korea, including the mad cow disease and the treatment of the economic crisis between the past administration and the current one.[17] He also explained that he followed American news more closely than Korean news because it was his job to relay important national and local news to the Korean community.

As observed by Lee (2004), Korean television also helped to spark interest in learning Korean, especially among the second generation. Andrew Noh, a consultant in his mid-twenties, indicated that he was a fan of Korean variety shows but not Korean dramas. As he put it:

> I don't watch Korean dramas, but I watch a lot of Korean TV shows such as *Infinity Challenge*. Whenever I have time, I go to redspot.com to see them. I watch it without English subtitles. I also watch the news. I watch the news because I am taking Korean language classes. Since I don't have cable, I watch it after downloading the videos. (*Which do you watch more, Korean or American TV?*) I still watch more American TV.

Here, Andrew's motivations for watching Korean television, as hinted in the vignettes that opened the chapter, is due to his interest in learning to speak Korean. He watches mostly Korean variety shows without English subtitles to practice his listening comprehension of the Korean language.

The responses above suggest that many first-generation Koreans have made viewing Korean television a highly routinized nightly ritual. To be sure, not everyone was interested in or cared for Korean television or for that matter, television in general. For some, the reason for not watching Korean television was general disinterest in television. For example, Jin Woo Seo (pseudonym), a seventy-five-year-old in consulting work, hardly watched any Korean television because he was uninterested in television generally, whether Korean or American, although he read Korean newspapers faithfully via the Internet. He said, "I read the Korean news on a daily basis. I read the *Washington Post* and also the *Korean Central Daily*. Regarding TV, I'm not accustomed to watching television."

Others found Korean television, especially the news from the homeland, unhelpful. For example, Dae Sung Park (pseudonym), a small business owner in his early fifties, was not fond of Korean news or Korean dramas although he did occasionally watch Korean television. He was especially averse to keeping up with Korean news because he found them to be irrelevant to his life in the United States. As he put it, "I don't watch the Korean news that often, but I do occasionally watch Korean television shows through the Internet. I hardly watch any Korean dramas. The reason why I don't watch Korean news is because I find them to be of different nature. And taking interest in political matters does not add anything of value to our lives." As discussed earlier about his antipathy or indifference to Korean politics, Mr. Park's aversion to Korean news stems from the coverage of Korean politics in the news, which he considers it unhelpful in his life.

Just like inertia was keeping Pastor Chung's Direct TV to be set on Korean channels, inertia also affected the viewing habits of some respondents, in this case staying away from Korean dramas. According to Jane Kim (pseudonym), a thirty-six-year-old part-time children's pastor, after stopping to watch it during graduate school, she gradually lost interest in Korean television altogether although she did monitor the Korean news on a regular basis through Korean television and the Internet. She remarked:

> I regularly get the news through the Internet and television. In the case of dramas, when I first came to the United States and until college, I made an effort to watch it. But since attending graduate school for my Master's, I have not been able to watch any. Once you start watching these dramas, I had the feeling that too much time was spent on it, and especially in graduate school, given I had very little time to study, I consciously made an effort to avoid it. Ever since graduate school, I lost interest in it. I do not watch other Korean television shows either.

Here, since taking a long break from Korean dramas to devote to her graduate studies, Ms. Kim is unable to resume her television viewing habits when she completes her degree and starts working. Seeing it as "wasteful" and unproductive, Ms. Kim does not seem to have sought it for entertainment nor for information. Yet, as discussed earlier in the book, what is interesting to note here is that despite Ms. Kim's thick ethnicity in the private domain, Korean television is not a big part of her transnational cultural activity although she does keep abreast of Korean news. This suggests that the forms and levels of transnational media consumed will vary according to media preferences and interests, and these distinctions in media consumption should be examined more carefully in future research.

Some interviewees, especially among religious leaders, avoided Korean television and television in general altogether because of their worldly (read negative) content. For instance, Won Sang Lee, the former senior pastor of the Washington Central Presbyterian Church, the largest Korean church in

Northern Virginia, objected to watching popular Korean dramas for its negative content. During his tenure as pastor, he had very little time and interest in Korean television, but after retiring from the pastorship of the mega church, he began to watch more Korean television, particularly historical dramas which he found to be less offensive. Pastor Lee, who was in his early seventies, gave a description of his viewing habits:

> When I was serving as pastor, I rarely watched it, but I watch some now. But they are all similar, and because of their unhealthy content, I have lost interest in it. But I do watch Korean historical dramas such as *Jewel in the Palace*. I view them through cable TV, specifically Direct TV. I don't watch dramas through the Internet; I read newspapers. I only watch the news such as ABC and NBC from American TV.

Here, Pastor Lee notes that Korean television has not only objectionable content but also most of the story lines, after a while, tend to very similar, which is why he does not watch them.

In sum, it is clear that with several exceptions, most watch Korean television to satisfy their need for entertainment and news. Language and cultural familiarity are also important reasons for viewing Korean television. Some second-generation members seek to learn Korean by watching Korean dramas and variety shows. Others, especially those who work in the media, are voracious consumers of Korean media to keep up with the latest developments in the home country. As one of the only forms of entertainment after immigrants' daily toil in the family business, transnational television not only enable viewers to enjoy and consume cultural content in their own language, but also relieve stress, creating a common culture that can be shared with others. In short, transnational media serves to fill the entertainment and information void of immigrants, and more importantly, they enable the sharing of a common culture and identity among viewers, critical functions which need to be explored more carefully in future research.

THE *HALLYU* AND ITS IMPACT ON FIRST- AND SECOND-GENERATION KOREAN AMERICANS

Even before Psy's spectacular launch into the U.S. music scene, Korean popular culture, especially the *Hallyu* or the Korean Wave, was captivating audiences regionally and globally. Given the discernible influence it had on putting Korea and the Korean culture on the mental map of audiences worldwide, we were curious to examine what impact the *Hallyu* was having on the Korean community, both on the first and second generations. When queried on their views about the *Hallyu*, and whether the phenomenon was affecting them or the children, most, however, noted that the *Hallyu*, especially K-Pop, had minimal impact on the first generation, while its influence on the children was more substantial.[18]

While acknowledging that the *Hallyu* and Korea's economic standing in the global economy positively affected the identities of the second generation, some remarked that Korea's improved image and the *Hallyu* had no direct bearing on their identities. For example, Jae Won Ryu, the 1310 AM radio reporter, was unconvinced of the *Hallyu*'s influence as he was not personally affected by it. He did, however, notice that with Korea's prominence in global affairs, it was no longer necessary to explain to members of the Congress where Korea was on the map when he was reporting from Capitol Hill. What still caught him off guard was the inability of many in the Congress to distinguish between North and South Korea.

Similarly, contrary to expectations, Andrew, a second-generation Korean American working in consulting, explained that he derived more pride as a Korean American from the visibility of Korean conglomerates and rapid advances of the Korean economy than from the *Hallyu*. Though he followed and listened to K-Pop, he drew negligible interest in and pride from it:

> I have a sense of pride from it, but I am not that interested in the *Hallyu*. I will listen to the music (K-pop), but I do not have pride from the *Hallyu*. I have more interest in the economy. I feel more pride from the fact that Hyundai, Samsung, and LG are doing well. . . . My identity is that of an American. It (*Hallyu*) does not affect or influence greatly my identity as a Korean American.

In the quote above, Andrew seems to be following K-Pop like other Korean Americans in his age. However, this has not translated into deep involvement with it. Instead, he drew pride in his heritage from the increased name recognition of well-known, global Korean companies.

Others also had skeptical views of the *Hallyu*, especially its alleged popularity beyond the Korean fan base. For example, Dae Sung Park, although he conceded that Korea's dramatic economic rise significantly boosted its image abroad, suspected that the Korean media was exaggerating the prominence of K-Pop among Americans to create a false sense of national pride. He countered:

> It is true that the image of Korea has improved through Samsung and Hyundai, and as a result, there are more places one can travel with a Korean passport. It looks as though the majority of K-pop fans are Koreans, and few Americans are actually interested in it. It seems that Korean broadcasters are exaggerating the phenomenon, giving the impression that more people are interested in it than it

> actually is. I think it was the intensive lobbying from the industry to CNN and other American broadcasters that made possible their coverage on CNN. We will certainly find out the outcome of K-pop's initial inroads in ten or twenty years. These events have no real relevance on my identity at the moment.

Here, Mr. Park argues that K-Pop is hardly popular outside the Korean American fan base, failing to reach the larger American audiences. He actually subscribes to a conspiracy theory that K-Pop's coverage on CNN is the result of intensive lobbying from the Korean music industry as he cannot fathom the idea that American fans would be attracted to K-Pop.

Jane Kim was equally skeptical of the *Hallyu's* popularity beyond the immediate Korean and Asian American circles. She observed:

> I feel that the renewed image is slightly helpful for the standing of the majority of Korean Americans and Koreans. In the case of K-pop or Korean popular culture though, it is not only Korean Americans but also Chinese Americans and other East Asian Americans who express much interest in it and are fond of it. But I have never felt that just because that culture is popular and visible, my stature as Korean American has risen. I don't believe that identity is influenced greatly by external factors but is rather a personal matter. With the exception of East Asians, I have not noticed a change in Americans' views of Koreans with the popularity of K-Pop.

As a 1.25-generation Korean, Ms. Kim agrees that the improved standing of Korea benefits Korean Americans by shifting their perception in the mainstream of American society. Yet, she is doubtful that K-Pop's visibility, which appeals to mostly East Asians, is helping to break down cultural barriers and increasing understanding among Americans. Furthermore, she has yet to see the *Hallyu* translate into tangible benefits such as raising the status of Korean Americans or the Korean community, which is why she doubts ethnic identity is shaped by external events such as the *Hallyu*.

Instead, some claimed that college was more important in youths' identity formation than the *Hallyu* or K-Pop since it was during this time when the younger generation struggled with ethnic identity and developed interest in Korea and on the Korean culture. Dae Sung Park quipped, "It is not K-pop that is affecting their identity, but up until 18, children grow up thinking they are Americans. As they reach college age though, they begin to reflect on their roots and identity. It is through their questioning of their identity that they develop an interest in Korea or the Korean culture and not because of K-pop." Here, Mr. Park argues that identity questions would still loom large for second-generation Korean Americans during college even if the K-Pop and *Hallyu* phenomenon had not appeared, hinting at the significance of race and ethnicity on identity formation.

Others like Hong Jong Yoo, the Korean orchestra conductor, while acknowledging the broad influence of the *Hallyu* on his children and the younger generation, was troubled by the younger generation's narrow view of the Korean culture as being synonymous with Korean popular culture. As he explained it:

> I can hardly feel the impact of *Hallyu*. But it is probably different with my son's generation. Because I have studied classical music, my wish is that other types of Korean culture are also recognized. All they get is Korean popular culture. Also I am opposed to getting too deeply wrapped up in *Hallyu* because their academics will be impacted. I wish that they would enjoy it to the extent of relieving their stress.

Here, what really worries Mr. Yoo with extensive involvement in K-Pop, more than a narrow understanding of Korean culture, is that his children's academic standing would suffer, which is why he dissuaded them from getting too deeply involved in it.

Finally, rejecting the false premise that the mainstream's view of Korean Americans was being transformed because of positive images of Korea and the popularity of the *Hallyu*, some like Min Jee Lee, a health education specialist in her mid-thirties, argued that changes in Korean Americans' reception and acceptance in the mainstream of American society came with power and visibility of the Korean population in Fairfax County (VA) and their contributions to American society than changed depictions in the media. According to her, it was the numerical strength and visibility of Korean Americans in places like Fairfax County, VA that forced county leaders to recognize and pay attention to the community, offering numerous programs to help preserve ethnic traditions and identity. By contrast, when she lived in rural areas with few Koreans, there was hardly any effort to promote diversity, pushing immigrants instead to acculturate into the local culture.

Ok Chae Kim, a WKTV producer, also disputed the impact of the *Hallyu* or Korea's ascent in country rankings as factors in the improved image of Korean Americans. He said:

> I don't find the improved image of Korea or the *Hallyu* to have made an impact on how Americans see the local Korean community. Changes in the image or perception of the Korean community do not come at all from the *Hallyu* or a favorable image of Korea. Instead, these come from increased number of Koreans, occupational changes of the community, and the successes of certain individuals from the community. Even if the *Hallyu* brings a positive image of Korea, Americans are not affected directly as much by it.

Like Ms. Lee, Mr. Kim attributes Korean Americans' visibility in the mainstream of American society as reasons for the improved image of the community, helping to change Americans' views of Korean Americans and the community. To him, power and visibility of the community come with numbers and increasing prominence of Korean Americans in well-known fields.

Notwithstanding most respondents' objections to *Hallyu*'s influence, there was some recognition of the growing influence of the new social media and the Internet as well as the *Hallyu* on second-generation identity formation. For example, Hyuk Kyo Suh, the 1.5-generation officer at NAKA, claimed that the *Hallyu* and the new social media helped to bring a shared sense of culture and identity to the second generation, keeping ethnic attachments and identities alive and salient. As he put it:

> I guess each family is different, each children [sic] is different. But generally when I see children of my peers of my generation, I think there's a positive impact, the sense of interactivity of the Korean *Hallyu*, being Korean, I think there is more interaction now, Youtube and all the social media, so I guess the children here are more perceptive to cultural happenings in Korea and I guess maybe they share some common ground. That way is a positive development I guess. But I think one aspect I see in my children is that, and maybe some other children too is that, they see more pan-Asian cultural awareness, not just Korean but being more pan-Asian perspective, respecting other cultures, like my son's friends are Indian friends and Vietnamese friends, Chinese friends, so it's not just Korean but pan-Asian, Asian American experience I guess how they identify, not just as Korean American but Asian American.

Here, Mr. Suh sees and predicts a marked rise in pan-ethnic (pan-Asian) identities for his children and their peers through increased contact and interaction via the new social media. This is perhaps where the new social media and the *Hallyu* will have the most impact in the making and remaking of pan-Asian identities in the future. But as Mr. Suh observes, the demographic diversity of the place, that is, the mix of Asian American peers in the school and neighborhood settings, is also a significant factor in creating opportunities for meaningful social interactions first and foremost, followed and aided by the use of the new social media that reinforce those social ties.

Though it is still too early to come to reliable conclusions about the impact of K-pop and the *Hallyu* on second-generation identities given the limitations of the data, one of the possible benefits of K-pop and the *Hallyu* may be in breaking down intergenerational barriers between parents and the children by fostering dialogue and understanding. According to Ok Chae Kim, the WKTV producer, by triggering second-generation interest in Korean culture and language through K-pop and the *Hallyu*, a common ground was being forged between the generations, reducing misunderstanding and distrust. He summed up the benefits of the *Hallyu*:

> Yes, the second generation has developed an interest in Korean popular culture through K-pop and the *Hallyu*, and now it has spread to other areas. I do find these to be very positive. Because many second-generation Koreans also encounter the Korean language at home, they are likely to absorb the *Hallyu* faster and much easier than non-Koreans. In the past, there were few things that second generation and first-generation Koreans could share with each other, but given that many second generation now know the names of these musicians and entertainers, through the *Hallyu*, they have an opportunity to share and communicate with each other. I am able to see firsthand how the second generation is now making an effort to understand Korea and also view Korea in higher light than in the past. . . . Through Korean dramas, music, and movies, they have greater opportunities to understand Korea, and to expand their sense of commonality with their parents or the first generation. These are the potentials of the *Hallyu* for reducing the generational gaps that exist.

In the quote above, by knowing the names of the musicians and entertainers, the children are able to find common reference points with which they can use to strike conversations with parents. Through dramas, music, and movies, children also have greater opportunities than before to learn about Korea and the Korean culture, increasing their understanding and narrowing the generation gap that they may have felt toward the parents. This is perhaps the biggest promise of the *Hallyu*, especially K-Pop and Korean dramas, in promoting greater second-generation interest in the Korean language, culture, and history.

This point was precisely driven home by the transformations Hye Chung Cho (pseudonym), a forty-seven-year-old elementary school principal, observed with her two sons. Growing up, her children, typical of many second-generation Koreans raised in the United States, were seldom interested in attending the Korean-language schools and learning Korean. But since attending college, her sons developed marked interest in exploring their heritage and also learning the Korean language. In fact, she inadvertently discovered that her son's computer screensaver was not only adorned with photos of popular female K-Pop artists, but he also knew and could sing the latest K-Pop songs. To her, these were clear indications that K-Pop and the *Hallyu* were becoming salient and had made significant inroads into the lives of the next generation. She said:

> I have two children. One is at Georgetown (University) and the other one is in his third year at (the University of) Maryland. They attended the Korean school at church. They used to write and be able to read especially the menus when they went to a restaurant. I don't think they had a special desire to learn Korean. They also did not find Korean to be too useful. That's probably why they had little desire to learn. Now that they are all grown up and are attending college,

> however, when you look at their screensaver, I actually don't know who they are, but there are these female K-pop artists. That's the screensaver and I think when they listen to the music I think it's K-pop. He actually knows a lot of Korean songs and is able to sing them.

Here, attending the Korean-language school at church and learning Korean growing up was, according to Ms. Cho, of little value to the second generation. But in college, K-Pop, in particular female K-Pop artists, seems to have peaked keen interest in Korean popular culture among second-generation males (or vice versa for second-generation females), often times pushing them beyond K-Pop and *Hallyu* to other aspects of Korean culture, including Korean language, food, and cultural traditions (see Oh 2012).

In sum, despite the immense success of Psy and growing popularity of Korean films, dramas, and music globally, many first-generation Koreans remain highly skeptical of *Hallyu's* popularity beyond the Korean and East Asian fan base, questioning Korean media reports about the globalization of Korean popular culture. Furthermore, many had problems with how the children narrowly linked Korean culture with K-Pop and wished they would broaden their understanding of Korean culture. Nonetheless, there was recognition that the *Hallyu* had the potential to bridge the generational gap between the first and the second generations as second-generation interest in Korean culture and identity rose substantially by listening to K-Pop and watching Korean television. In this sense, the *Hallyu* and consumption of Korean transnational media are not only bridging the generation gap, but also are serving as conduits for ethnic preservation as the ease, speed, and volume with which members of the community are able to participate in these activities are picking up, making cultural transnationalism more common in years to come.

KOREANIZED VERSUS AMERICANIZED WAYS OF LIFE

The narratives from the community leaders and long-time residents underscore a perception that the *Hallyu* scarcely affected them, although many do recognize that it may have had greater impact on their children. Another question asked to ascertain the impact of transnationalism was lifestyles, namely Koreanized versus Americanized ways of life in the private domain. Whether Korean Americans lived an ethnic versus non-ethnic lifestyle in their everyday lives is meaningful and reveals a great deal about the institutional completeness of the immigrant community, as ethnicity becomes comprehensive and organizes ever more parts of daily life (Cornell and Hartmann 1998).

Our focus centered on how extensively transnationalism had managed to creep into the lives of Korean immigrants. A common theme that emerged was the extent to which first-generation Korean immigrants led an ethnic life, while also undergoing assimilation. Though their responses went beyond specific questions related to food, home country consumer goods, and transnational media to include cultural and social activities that created a "thick" ethnicity, the picture that emerges is one of a comprehensive role of ethnicity in the lives of the immigrant generation (Cornell and Hartmann 1998). Even the lives of the 1.5-generation were seen to be highly organized by ethnicity despite their acculturation and linguistic and cultural abilities.

Findings from the 2012 Pew Research Center's Asian American survey, for example, suggest that ethnic life in the private domain, specifically co-ethnic friendships, was highly salient for Korean Americans, with more than half (58%) of them having all or mostly Korean friends, which was the highest of all Asian groups (52).[19] This is also corroborated by Park (2009, 92–93), who found that Korean immigrant women hardly interacted with their neighbors because of language barriers and cultural/racial differences, preferring to form friendships with co-ethnics. Korean immigrant women also preferred to shop at Korean groceries and Korean-owned businesses and relied upon Korean professionals such as doctors, lawyers, accountants, and bankers for many personal services (Park 2009, 93). While these can handicap immigrant adjustment, they, nonetheless, help to sustain ethnic identity and cultural continuity (Park 2009, 93).

In her focus group study of Korean immigrant women in Wisconsin, Son (2013, 385) also found that Korean women behaved more American at work, while at home they acted in a more Korean way by watching Korean television shows, speaking Korean, and eating Korean food, which were considered markers of ethnicity. Son (2015, 386) observes that these women made distinctions between their lifestyles and those of their counterparts in South Korea, noting that they, as emigrants, were going to have a harder time keeping up with a rapidly changing Korea.

In our interviews, an apt illustration of ethnicity still shaping meaningful relationships such as friendships was provided by In-Wook Hur. For instance, although he worked at a predominantly American (read white) work setting, Mr. Hur struggled to establish meaningful relationships with his coworkers, forming friendships instead with mostly other Korean Americans. He explained that perhaps this was a matter of language and cultural comfort, but he also contended that his fast-paced lifestyle, namely lack of time, prevented him from socializing with Americans. Besides his job at the court, he led a busy, private life engaged in church and Korean Association-related activities. Thus, outside of work, his private life was organized heavily by ethnicity and ethnic institutions, and he contended that most first-generation Koreans also led an ethnic life similar to his.

A different explanation as to why they lived ethnic lives was offered by Hong Jong Yoo, the orchestra conductor, who regarded "thick" ethnicity being the predicament of first-generation immigrants generally. Mr. Yoo's response on what it meant to lead a Koreanized lifestyle also had a different connotation since he made an explicit distinction between the lifestyles of overseas Koreans (Korean Americans) and their counterparts in Korea. In other words, Korean Americans generally led an ethnic lifestyle relative to an American one, but this lifestyle was still poles apart from typical Korean lifestyles led by Korean nationals. This is how he described it:

> There are times when we enjoy eating American food, but since the language and way of thinking is Korean, it is closer to a Koreanized lifestyle. No, it is actually more accurate to say that we live an overseas Korean lifestyle. We cannot say it is the same as a South Korean lifestyle. Because if I were in Korea, I would be smoking in the living room and drinking more alcohol. But because we live in America, we are more careful. We also attend a Korean church. . . . (*Whether his Korean friends lived a Koreanized lifestyle*) 90% of my friends live a Koreanized or overseas Korean lifestyle. Those who are younger seem to prefer an Americanized lifestyle, but I would bet that most 1.5 and first-generation Koreans live a Koreanized lifestyle. No matter how well they may speak English, as long as they eat Korean food and their family members are Korean, they will be Korean. I am first generation and have little choice but to live a Koreanized lifestyle.

In the quote above, Mr. Yoo distinguishes the lifestyles of Korean Americans from Korean nationals by the degree of cigarettes and alcohol consumed in Korea. Furthermore, he also notes that his Korean friends carry a Korean American lifestyle, namely speaking Korean, eating Korean food, and attending Korean church. Although he recognizes that the younger generation is going to be much more assimilated, he counters that even the 1.5 generation, despite their English proficiency, as long as they prefer to eat Korean food and grow up in a Korean milieu, are likely to maintain a thick ethnicity in the private domain. It is not clear here whether he is referring to the 1.5-generation's identification as Korean, namely symbolic ethnicity that persists in the later generations, or maintaining practices that help to retain the ethnic culture (Vasquez 2011).

For others, similar to findings on food, language spoken at home, and other cultural practices as markers of ethnic life in the private domain (Son 2013), thick ethnicity in the private domain was marked by speaking Korean and eating Korean meals at home. For instance, Sekwon Chong, the retired, former manager for Coca Cola, explained that he rarely went out to dine in American restaurants. As he put it, "In my case when it comes to food I still eat Korean food most of the time. In terms of eating American meals it would only be during special occasion when we go out to eat in an American restaurant." To respondents like Mr. Chong, ethnic meals and traditional cultural practices and values such as showing respect to elders and celebrating New Year's Day with traditional bows such as the *saebae* were what they hoped to preserve and pass on to the next generation.

However, not everyone fit into or sought a thick ethnic life; instead, they sought to preserve some ethnic practices while also undergoing acculturation and assimilation. For example, Dae Sung Park, although he ate mostly Korean meals at home and attended a Korean church, had mostly non-Korean (white American) friends because he found them to be more trustworthy. He stated:

> I believe it is mostly an Americanized lifestyle. (*In what ways?*) When you consider the style of raising children, in Korea parents are fixated on their children such as how much education they would like their children to have and the careers they should be pursuing. I have no such expectations from my children. My parents raised me without any of those expectations. Although I tend to eat a lot of Korean food, I can do without eating Korean food. When our children reached 18 and 19, they began to eat more Korean food, so we now eat Korean food along with hamburgers and pizza. When it comes to friendships, most of my friends are non-Korean. Except for church, most of my friends at work and from school are American. I still have a number of friends from work that I keep in touch with regularly. They are mostly white. I have a number of friends around the country, and I still keep regular contact with them. I find Americans to be much more honest, and when there are times of need, they are much sure to help.

Here, unlike other traditional Korean American parents who believe parents know what is best for children, Mr. Park scales down his educational expectations from his children, reflecting his own acculturation of mainstream values and attitudes. Yet, when asked about his Korean American friends, Mr. Park seems to be fully aware of their limited acculturation and continued significance of ethnicity in their lives. What is also interesting in Mr. Park's remarks is that all the salient features of thick ethnicity are not present in his life except for church. Yet, it could also be that as influential as ethnic churches are in ethnic preservation, they do not seem to have produced an ethnic turn marked by Korean food, Korean friendships and social circles, and expectations of status schools and careers for Mr. Park's children.

As predicted by the assimilation theory, long-term residence and greater English proficiency also led to the thinning of ethnicity among some. For example, Jin Woo Seo, a long-time resident in his mid-seventies, explained that acculturation came naturally to him because both he and his wife had left Korea as teenagers and had lived most of their adult lives in the United States. He said:

> For us, it is more American than Korean. Maybe it's because we got here when we're young. My wife came to New York in the 1960s. Her family went to

> Japan right after the outbreak of the Korean War. They lived there for more than 13 years. She attended and completed school there. Then she came to study at FIT in New York. So it is the same for my wife who has not lived in Korea that long. We have a neighbor who is Korean. But most recent immigrants tend to attend a Korean church and socialize with other Koreans. But this is true for other immigrant groups as well. . . . It is easier for us to mingle with Americans than with Koreans.

Not surprisingly, they attribute both his and his wife's assimilation and ability to easily interact with Americans to their entry into the United States as young adults in the 1960s and their residence here for more than half a century.

Assimilation literature also suggests that intermarriage, as opposed to co-ethnic marriage, is likely to dilute the impact of ethnicity in the lives of immigrants and subsequent generations. As Vasquez's research (2011) shows, marriage is an important site for keeping ethnic traditions and practices alive, or vice versa, loosening them depending on whom they marry. Mexican Americans who married out were the most likely to carry symbolic ethnicity, while those who married co-ethnics, especially those who spoke Spanish and practiced many of the Catholic (Mexican) holidays and rituals, were more likely to preserve ethnic traditions (Vazquez 2011). Following this logic, whether interviewees lived with in-laws or with the extended family may also affect their degree of cultural assimilation.

For example, Jiyoung Yoon, the librarian mentioned earlier, in part due to her husband's rapid acculturation and assimilation, took on a similar lifestyle as that of her spouse, including befriending mostly non-Korean friends. She said, "Relative to other Koreans, we are an exception. I have few Korean friends as well. . . . There are rather bad things when we are together with other Koreans. They like to show off and look down upon when they go to church or Korean community activities." Here, Ms. Yoon's distancing from other Korean Americans is motivated in part by her husband's acculturation but also because she is turned off by the excessive status-seeking among Koreans at church and other social settings.

By contrast, while her workplace was completely Americanized, at home, Hye Jung Cho, the 1.5-generation school principal, cooked and ate mostly traditional Korean dishes, making a conscious choice to let ethnicity shape her life in the private domain. Ms. Cho made a deliberate decision to attend the Korean-language ministry instead of the English-language ministry at the Korean church despite the fact she was fluent in English, she herself was quite acculturated, and the church also offered a separate English-language service. As she explained:

> At school it's all American-style. As soon as I go home, it's all Korean food. It's because my in-laws live with us. And my husband does not like American food. We eat mostly Korean food at home. Also when I was growing up, my

mom, who was raised in the countryside, would cook traditional Korean dishes such as *namul* (vegetable side dishes). My friends would comment that I was old-fashioned despite my looks. . . . At home it's primarily a Korean lifestyle. It is very different from school. I attend a Korean church. Even at church I am involved in the Korean-language ministry instead of the English-language ministry. I teach children there.

Although it is not clear whether her husband is a first- or 1.5-generation Korean American, the fact that her spouse prefers to eat Korean food and that his parents are living with them suggests that her ethnic preferences at home are being strongly influenced by her spouse and her in-laws. Had she married a highly acculturated Korean American or non-Korean spouse, she would likely have carried a more symbolic ethnicity and be far less committed to preserving the Korean traditions and practices given her high degree of acculturation.

Notwithstanding these reservations from a few, in light of the challenges of learning a new language and adapting to a different culture, it should not be too surprising to find that most first-generation Koreans preferred to lead ethnic lives in the private domain. What is also remarkable, however, is that several 1.5- and 1.25-generation Koreans in the sample, despite their acculturation and English and cultural proficiencies, were also choosing to prioritize ethnicity in the private sphere. Besides their interactions with non-Koreans (mostly white Americans) in the workplace and in other public places, ethnicity wielded tangible influences in the day-to-day lives of some of these 1.5-generation Koreans. For instance, Jane Kim, the part-time children's pastor, chose to live a life where almost all aspects of her private and work life were marked by thick ethnicity, including the meals she cooked and ate, the language she spoke at home, the church she attended, the friends with whom she socialized, and the coworkers with whom she interacted daily. She aptly put it:

I think I am living a completely Koreanized lifestyle. I speak only Korean at home, eat Korean food for every meal (It is because my husband does not like to eat sandwiches or eat American food and prefers to eat Korean food), attend and work at a Korean church, and have only Korean American and Chinese American friends. I do not have any white friends. I used to work at the Korean Counseling organization.

Here, Ms. Kim observes that it was the Korean upbringing and language that helped to preserve ethnic traditions and practices. But she also admits that perhaps she is pushing the ethnic side farther than others. She said, "My friends, those who are 1.5 generation like me, they all maintain a Korean way of life (I am probably the worst). Because we were raised by first-generation parents, we tend to preserve a Koreanized lifestyle. The way I see it, the more comfortable you are with the Korean language, you tend to live a way of life strongly colored by Korean culture." It could well be that her preference for speaking Korean at home is shaped by her choice of food, friendships, and church, leading to a thickened ethnic life. But as hinted earlier in the book, it could also be that her experience with discrimination and the realization that full inclusion was out of reach produces a reactive ethnicity (D. Kim 2013). These ethnic choices and practices in the private domain are reinforced even further by her full-time work in the ethnic enclave, further increasing the significance of ethnicity despite the fact she is a 1.25-generation adult.

Finally, the institutional completeness of the immigrant community, made possible in many ways by growing cultural transnational connections, is aptly illustrated by Mr. Suh's poignant observations of the stark separation between the public and private domains in the lives of many Korean Americans, including those of 1.5 and second-generation immigrants. As many researchers increasingly recognize, assimilation can coexist with ethnic life and transnationalism (Foner 2005; Levitt 2001b; Portes and Rumbaut 2014), as the divide between them does not seem to weaken, but actually enhance, the quality of immigrant lives. Mr. Suh, the 1.5-generation staff at NAKA, remarked:

> I guess the experience is similar to many Koreans living here. They sort of compartmentalize I guess because during the day time people work what would be regular American work place or small business that interacts with Americans, not Koreans, so they would deal with Americans, so called mainstream society through American colleagues or customers. That's one component of their daily experience, which I do daily through my colleagues at work. That's American all the way. I guess when you go home it's different story (laughter) because *you eat Korean food, you hear Korean music, watch Korean soap operas*, so that's another kind of lifestyle or mindset when you go home. It's sort of Korean package or packaged Korean lifestyle for you, and then when you go to church, you go to Korean church, that's another realm where you stay with your Korean contacts. So we all live in two worlds I guess—one mainstream American society, one Korean community, and for most of us, I think the Korean community component is larger than the American component because you tend to interact more with Koreans than Americans. In that aspect I guess our lifestyle and mindset is more Korean per se than American. [*sic*]

Here, Mr. Suh speaks vividly of the role that assimilation, ethnicity, and transnationalism play in the lives of Korean Americans, including the 1.5 generations. Perhaps this may be an effect of a small sample, but the ethnic and transnational choices made by select 1.5 and second-generation Koreans point to experiences with discrimination and racialization as well as the ease with which transnational media and home country consumer goods can be consumed in the digital age. Furthermore, the increasing ethnoburbanization (ethnic suburbs) of the Korean and Asian populations, that is, the changing demographics of major metropolitan areas, also means that an ethnic and transnational turn is more possible and easier than before (see D. Kim 2013).

In sum, for scores of first- and select 1.5-generation Koreans, an ethnic and transnational life seems to dominate and define their lives in the private sphere. From the food they eat to the media they consume, ethnic lives are increasingly marked by growing cultural transnational activities, especially in the private domain. To be sure, the ethnic institutional completeness of the immigrant community, including attending Korean churches, befriending Korean friends, joining Korean organizations, to name a few, is what also enables the continued penetration of ethnicity into the private sphere. The compartmentalization of the public (working in the mainstream and assimilating) with the private (preserving ethnicity) domain suggests that assimilation and transnationalism need not be incompatible (Foner 2005; Levitt 2001b, 5–6; Levitt and Schiller 2004; Portes and Rumbaut 2014), but rather both will continue to influence the lives of first-, but also perhaps those of select 1.5- and second-generation Korean Americans.

CONCLUSION

The lives of Korean Americans in large metropolitan areas, including the Greater Washington-Baltimore area, are marked by increased flows of cultural products from the homeland, which are not only enabling but also intensifying the Koreanization of private life. Even before the critical advances of the *Hallyu*, or the Korean Wave, into the mainstream, consuming transnational media, particularly Korean television, was one of the few recognizable, leisurely activities available to Korean Americans. Nowadays, viewing Korean news, variety shows, and dramas has become unquestionably easier and faster, furthering the scope and intensity of cultural transnational activities. Even 1.5-generation Korean Americans, whose linguistic abilities and cultural competency differentiate them sharply from the first generation, are increasingly seeking to have and enjoy lives characterized by assimilation at work, on the one hand, and ethnic/transnational life at home, on the other.

Unlike the past when home country cultural products and consumer goods took weeks to arrive to the immigrant community, creating noticeable differences in the consumption practices between the immigrant community and homeland nationals, with innovations in ICT and transportation technologies, today's immigrants are able to not only conduct more institutionally complete ethnic lives than before, but also to experience lives that are *in greater sync* with home country cultural and consumer practices. In other words, there is very little lag time between the consumption trends between the home country and the immigrant community as both can consume transnational media and homeland consumer goods almost simultaneously. In some ways, this suggests that there is increasing convergence between the ethnic and transnational, producing a more uniform culture although there is likely to be some divergence between immigrant culture and their counterparts in the home country. Furthermore, though a two-way street, with the ethnic also influencing cultural and consumer trends in the home country, the transnational may increasingly have greater impact on the immigrant community, given the power of transnational media and Korean conglomerates' (and Korean state's) globalization efforts.

Yet, as more Korean Americans incorporate ethnic and transnational practices into their private lives, the specter of dissimilation looms large. Although an inherent tension exists between transnationalism and assimilation, most research finds that immigrant lives are enriched by pursuing both (Foner 2005; Levitt 2001b; Portes 2014; Vertovec 2007). In this scenario of selective assimilation, an ethnic lifestyle in the private domain is fully compatible with integration into the mainstream. Certainly, this ability to enjoy the best of both worlds has been facilitated by greater tolerance and acceptance of diversity and multiculturalism in mainstream American society (Alba and Nee 2003; Foner 1997, 2005; Jimenez 2010; Kasinitz et al. 2008; Levitt 2001b; Vertovec 2007). Moreover, cultural transnationalism is seen as more benign and less threatening than economic or political transnationalism, which is often frowned upon due to fears of immigrant ambivalence and disloyalty. Thus, the transmission of ethnic culture through transnational cultural practices is likely to continue in light of their greater acceptance by mainstream society, on the one hand, and immigrants' need for cultural familiarity and identity, on the other, exerting a strong pull on immigrants and possibly remaining salient in later generations.

In an increasingly interconnected world, the ease and speed with which home country cultural products can be acquired means that Korean immigrants will continue to consume transnational media, in particular Korean television, for the various functions they provide: entertainment and information. By consuming Korean television (and other forms of transnational media), homeland cultural practices (latest fashion, music, and cultural trends) and consumption habits will also be promoted, including the marketing of home country consumer goods through Korean dramas and films. For example, the recent popularization of Korean spas (*Spa World* in Centreville, VA and elsewhere) among Korean Americans can be attributed to its popularity and exposure in Korean dramas. Consequently, the newest and latest home country cultural practices and values will be transmitted to Korean Americans through transnational media, helping to reinvigorate and shape what it means to be Korean in the immigrant community. Ultimately, these cultural transnational practices, because of their ease, regularity, and taken-for-granted nature, may have greater impact on and shape immigrants' sense of home and identity than occasional or even regular forms of economic and political transnationalism (Shuttika 2011), which is the subject matter of chapter 5.

NOTES

1. Young A. Jung and Gyu Tag Lee have completed their doctoral degrees from the Department of Cultural Studies at George Mason University. Young A. Jung conducted a dissertation study of Korean wild-geese or *girogi* families and their sense of belonging in the Washington-Baltimore region, while Gyu Tag Lee examined the K-Pop phenomenon in Korea and East Asia, including its history, diffusion, and reception domestically and regionally in his dissertation.

2. The second author of this chapter conducted the three observations/interviews and provided the vignettes on television viewership.

3. According to KAGFW (2006, 201–203), these dailies started out by importing newspapers printed in Korea (via air) and then distributing them to community members. This was how many operated in the 1970s, directly importing newspapers from Korea, copying them in bulk in the United States, and then mailing them to paying readers. Later, with the growth of the Korean population, local branches were established in the 1980s and 1990s, enabling them to expand coverage of local community news, in addition to news from the homeland.

4. The third Korean television station started in the area was WBS Washington Mission Network, Inc. (WBS) in 1994 (KAFGW 2006, 212). WBS-TV was broadcast every Wednesdays, Thursdays, and Fridays (9–11PM) on Cox Cable (channel 30), offering Korean Christian programming, along with educational and cultural programs.

5. For instance, a number of K-Pop musicians such as BoA, Wonder Girls, and Big Bang reached the top spots in the Billboard's main album chart "Billboard 200" in 2011, prompting Billboard to introduce a wholly new weekly K-Pop chart in July of that year. Soon after their impressive debut in the music charts, Girls Generation, one of the most popular K-Pop girl bands, also appeared as featured guests on the popular David Letterman Show (01/31/2012).

6. The popularity of Japanese dramas had multiplier effects for Japanese brands and products, including greater recognition and increased sales (Huang 2011, 8).

7. After the 1997 IMF Asian financial crisis, the Korean media industry had no other choice but to look abroad given their smaller and weaker domestic market, while the reverse was true for the Japanese drama industry, which, with bigger and wealthier audiences, had no urgent need to export its products overseas (Chua and Iwabuchi 2008).

8. Vu and Lee (2013, 317–318) also found in their survey of Vietnamese women, that after taking age and education into account, women who tended to watch Korean

dramas more frequently had a more favorable impression of Korea and Korean men, even increasing their willingness to marry Korean men.

9. The term "K-Pop" has its origins from the term "J-Pop." Ugaya (2005, 2–7) notes that J-Pop was created by a FM radio station "J-Wave" in the late 1980s when it was looking for a new musical category that distinguished Western-sounding Japanese music from those which were exclusively Euro-American music (see also Mori 2009, 225).

10. These are digital audiotape recorders (DAT), multitrack recorders (MTR), sampling synthesizers (sampler), sequencers, auto-tune, and musical instruments digital interface (MIDI).

11. K-Pop's unique hybrid and transnational style also comes from producers' and musicians' international and cosmopolitan backgrounds. American, European, and Japanese composers and producers have written some of K-Pop's biggest hit songs, and considerable numbers of producers and musicians are 1.5- and second-generation Koreans from the United States, Canada, and Australia. Industry insiders have also studied music production and entertainment management abroad, most notably in the United States and Japan.

12. K-pop is distinguished by a hierarchical music production often referred to as the idol-agency system, or agencies. The vast majority of those performing K-Pop are boy or girl bands called "idol groups" or "idols." The idol group is usually composed of four to six members, each of whom is charged with specific tasks and roles such as singing, rapping, dancing, modeling, and narrating. On stage, wearing matching, flamboyant costumes, groups perform rhythmic and acrobatic group dances. K-Pop agencies also engage in what can be termed "total management," which implies micromanaging all aspects of the music and entertainment business, including training musicians, marketing and promoting music, creating and producing songs, recording engineering, choreographing group dances, and coordinating fashion and costumes. The four agencies that dominate the industry are SM Entertainment, JYP Entertainment, YG Entertainment, and DSP Media. In order to continuously produce successful idol groups, agencies have developed a unique recruiting and training system called "*yunsupseng*" academy. On the condition of accepting applicants with uncertain futures, agencies agree to provide housing, food, and training to new talents, forcing them into exclusive contracts which bind them to particular agencies for a minimum of five to a maximum of eleven years. After *yunsupsengs* complete their intensive training for three to five years, a few of them get selected and join an idol group, getting their break to become *idols*.

13. The sample size of survey respondents was 274.

14. Even among second-generation Koreans in the 2004 IIMMLA, 48.9% close to one-half (48%) were watching Korean programming once a week or more, while 10.6% tuned in once or twice a month, and 17.9% watched it only a few times a year. Only less than a quarter (22.6%, N=358) of second-generation Angelenos indicated that they never viewed or listened to Korean programming. This suggests that the growing popularity of the Korean Wave, or *Hallyu*, including K-Pop and Korean dramas and films, as they become widespread and gain in popularity among high school and college circles in the largest Korean communities in Los Angeles, New York, and Washington, D.C., is attracting not only first-generation Korean audiences

but also their second-generation counterparts. This may foster ethnic renewal and transnationalism in the second generation as more of them engage in the consumption of transnational media and home country consumer goods.

15. According to Oh's (2016, 2235) content analysis of postings on MissyUSA, some of which capture the transnational activities conducted in the United States, questions regarding Korean television came in the most, followed by wire transfers to Korea, and consumer items, respectively. Many of these postings on Korean television inquired about specific websites to stream/download and view Korean television. For example, "(I) want to watch Korean TV dramas . . . in a legal way by paying a membership fee. Can you introduce me one of its legal websites?" (February 28, 2012) (Quoted in Oh 2016, 2235).

16. Similar to Georgiou's (2012, 7) findings of men choosing to watch the news among Arab speakers, there was some variation in television viewing by gender, with men generally favoring the news, while women preferring to watch Korean dramas. Occasionally, some men watched Korean dramas with their wives, but they indicated that they preferred to watch historical dramas over romantic ones. However, given the small sample size, we are unable to generalize beyond the limited patterns observed.

17. Here, the past administration refers to Roh Moo-hyun's administration, while the current administration refers to Lee Myung-bak's.

18. Anecdotally, among Korean American teenagers, following K-Pop has become an unstated norm when making friends with other Korean Americans, corroborating the rising popularity of K-Pop among 1.5 and second-generation Korean Americans. Thus, more than any other genre in the Korean Wave, K-Pop seems to have become a significant cultural icon for Korean American adolescents.

19. Among the factors behind the salience of co-ethnic friendships is probably Koreans' limited English fluency, jobs in the ethnic economy, and most importantly, regular attendance of and participation in co-ethnic congregations. The 2012 Pew Research Center's Asian American survey (94) found that after the Vietnamese (21%), only less than a third (30%) of Koreans indicated that they could carry on a conversation in English "very well," the second-lowest of all Asian groups.

Chapter 5

Where Is Home?

Identity and Belonging in the Digital Age

The previous chapter considered the cultural transnational activities promoting the synchronization of the ethnic with the transnational. In this chapter, I examine whether increased transnational connections bring about changes to Korean Americans' sense of home, belonging, and identity. Do immigrants identify and develop a sense of home and belonging with their adopted country? Or do they continue to maintain an enduring attachment to and identification with the home country? Or do they selectively choose and mix practices that reflect both the assimilationist and transnationalist tendencies?

In the 2006 survey of Latinos, Waldinger (2007) found that despite holding favorable views of and remaining strongly attached toward the home country among those who were more transnational, when it came to their children's future, most regarded the United States as a better place for them. Contrary to fears of disloyalty and dissimilation, transnational linkages and involvement did not prevent immigrants from establishing more permanent roots in the host country. For example, two-thirds (66%) of Latino immigrants planned to live permanently in the United States, and such feelings rose substantially among those who had been in the United States for more than thirty years (Waldinger 2007, iii). Additionally, when asked about where they considered their "real" home to be or where they felt most at home, one-half (49%) of Latinos chose their country of birth as their real home, while 38% selected their adopted country. But, in terms of identifying with the host country, less than a third of them identified as Americans, although identification with America did increase among long-time residents. Moreover, the proportion identifying with the home country was higher among recent arrivals.

However, when years of residence and citizenship are taken into account, migrants engaging in transnational activities had weaker attachments and identification with the host country (Waldinger 2007, 21). Still, these did not translate into returning back to the country of origin as two-thirds (67%) of respondents planned to stay permanently in the United States, suggesting that attachments and identifications were mostly symbolic. In practice, most expected to live in the United States indefinitely instead of returning to the home country. Especially when asked about the best place to raise and provide a brighter future for the children, the United States was viewed as a much better place than the home country. As Waldinger (2007, 22) put it, "A significant minority severs all ties to their home countries; at the other side of the spectrum, a significant minority continues to engage in frequent travel and communication, even after many years of residence in the United States. However, the best way to characterize the immigrants' 'here-there' connection is to describe them as 'in between.'"

TRANSNATIONALISM AND SENSE OF HOME AND BELONGING

A key debate with increasing globalization, transnationalism, and innovations in ICT is whether belonging, identity, and loyalty, which were seen to be tied to the nation-state, are ever more being eroded by mobility, multiple allegiances, and transnational and cosmopolitan affiliations (Nedelcu 2012, 4). For example, while Beck (2003) sees globalization as leading to increased denationalization, transnationalism, and re-ethnification, others observe that states still play critical roles in international affairs and national identity, with strong states wielding greater influence than weaker ones. Furthermore, unlike some proponents of globalization who see a "flat world" (Friedman 2005), Dunn (2010, 5) points out that the idea of a frictionless world was being overstated since nation states and borders still had the power to limit the movement of people and goods and services.

In light of increasing interactions and exchanges between the home and host countries, how are migrants' sense of home, identity, and belonging being impacted by the intensification of transnational engagements? First and foremost, transmigrants, Basch et al. (1994, 6) write, "use the term 'home' for their society of origin, even when they clearly have also made a home in their country of settlement." The condition of being at home in multiple places may produce ambiguous identities among migrants, since in their effort to have and enjoy dual lives, one by assimilating into their place of settlement and the other by maintaining links and identities with the homeland, they may not be fully integrated in either places. According to Kearney (1991, 52), "people that span national borders are ambiguous in that they in some ways partake of both nations and in other ways partake of neither." Yet, it is this dual frame of reference, or migrant bifocality (Vertovec 2007, 67–68), that binds migrants to both the home country and the place of settlement, helping to successfully navigate between the pressures of assimilation and transnationalism for a truly dual life.

For example, among professionals who relocate abroad for work, like highly mobile Australian transnational professionals, a strong orientation and sense of home, not surprisingly, toward the home country was pervasive (Butcher 2010). Consequently, not only were efforts made to create familiar Australian cultural spaces in Singapore, but also social activities revolved around other Australians. But for Chinese Australian expats holding Australian citizenship, because of their experience with marginalization in Australia, many held a more subdued sense of home toward Australia compared to their white Australian counterparts. Instead, because of their physical similarities with Singaporeans, they held a greater sense of home and belonging to Singapore (Butcher 2010). Still, due to the fact that they could leave any time, given their Australian citizenship, their commitment to the current place of residence was also a lot weaker. By contrast, as a privileged group of mobile IT professionals, Romanian migrants in Canada felt at home both in Canada and also anywhere they settled, since it was relatively easy for them to adapt and make home in different parts of the world (Nedelcu 2012, 11).

Among Korean immigrant women whose sense of belonging to the United States tended to be much more instrumental because of strong emotional identification with the home country, a transnational orientation, however, did not preclude seeking belonging in multiple places, as many realized that their stake was also in the United States (Park 2009, 156). Park (2009, 137) writes, "These imagined communities included variously the South Korean society back home, the larger U.S. society, Korean immigrant communities in the U.S., and the Korean Diasporas outside the U.S." Furthermore, because Korean immigrants were regular churchgoers and spent most of their religious and social activities there, it was through the church that these women also found their sense of belonging to the immigrant community (Park 2009, 103).

Korean migrants to Canada also developed a multiple sense of belonging into the host society, the ethnic community, and the home country, holding a strong sense of belonging to the local and transnational Korean community, but a more muted one to the host community as not everyone was interested in or made efforts to seek belonging to the host society given their marginalization (Yoon 2016, 13–14). By contrast, in her study of Korean women students in Britain, Y. Kim (2011, 143) found that while students' mobility and desires to be mobile were facilitated by transnational media, their transnational lives, nonetheless, created imperfect belonging since many felt stuck between the receiving and sending societies.

WHERE IS HOME? KOREA, THE UNITED STATES, OR BOTH?

In our interviews with community leaders and long-time residents, an apt metaphor captures the relationship between the home country and their adopted land. Korea was often depicted as the "mother" or the birth family, while the United States was described as the "father" or the in-laws. For example, In-Wook Hur, a fifty-nine-year-old Special Projects Coordinator for the Circuit Court of the State of Maryland, referred to Korea as their "biological family, while the metaphor of 'in-laws'" was used to depict the United States. Wishing that his biological family (Korea) got along well with the in-laws (America), Mr. Hur said, "I feel like Korea is *chinjongjip* (my birth family) and America is *sijib* (my in-laws). So, I always hope that *chinjongjip* and *sijib* live in harmony with each other."

When asked about a hypothetical scenario where he had to take sides such as a sporting event or war, this is how Mr. Hur spoke about his loyalty toward the host country: "If I have to choose sides, I think I should side with the *sijib* (in-laws) because I am living here now. However, when it comes to my emotions, my heart is always with Korea. Watching the 2002 World Cup game between Korea and the U.S. national team, I was cheering for the Korean team. But my children cheered for the U.S. team."

By contrast, Hyuk Kyo Suh, a fifty-one-year-old publication manager for the American Bar Association, considered Centreville, VA as his "physical home," but regarded Korea to be his "spiritual home." For him, his passion for and concern toward the home country stemmed from both his birth and childhood in Korea as well as his transnational political activism. He said, "I was born and raised there. I feel strongly about what's happening in Korea. It is a divided nation and (unification) remains an unfinished business in the peninsula. Korean Diaspora. Korean history. We need some 'closure' to what happened in recent history, maybe through unification." Here, Mr. Suh's sense of Korea as his home seems to be associated with his transnational political activities, which activate and sustain his deep interest and involvement in homeland affairs, helping to maintain a resilient ethnic identity.

United States as Real Home

A common sentiment among many immigrants is deep-seated nostalgia toward the homeland. Such sentiments endure even with migration, but over time, as assimilation theory would predict, immigrants also develop a sense of home and belonging toward the place of settlement. Because nostalgia for the homeland is a common emotional response, often it is through homeland visits that immigrants come to realize the substantial disconnect between their idealized views of the home country, which were formed during their teenage years, and the transformations these places have experienced during their absence. For instance, Myung Suk Oh's taken-for-granted understanding of Korea as his hometown or home was utterly shattered after visiting Korea and family members. During the trip, it dawned on him that his real home was in America, a place he was inevitably familiar with and well adapted to compared to a changed Korea that was foreign and distant. According to Mr. Oh, a seventy-four-year-old retired man:

> Since I have lived here for about 40 years, I get a certain feeling. When I used to visit Korea in the past, it felt like my hometown. But couple of weeks later there, I feel the urge to go back to my real hometown. This is irrespective of the problems with Korean economy and politics. Probably this is because of having been accustomed to a life that is very structured in America, which feels quite unfamiliar when you stay in Korea. You do get used to American culture after all after 40 years in the country.

In the quote above, although feeling comfortable for couple of weeks, Mr. Oh soon realizes that he is itching to go back "home" to America once the initial sense of comfort begins to quickly wear off and the reality of living in Korea sinks in. In the end, the power of assimilation, that is, having lived for more than forty years in the United States, makes it self-evident to long-timers where their true home is.

For others like Jin Woo Seo (pseudonym), a retired seventy-five-year-old in consulting work, though still nostalgic toward the homeland, visits to South Korea did not elicit the same emotional responses as the above respondent because they were originally from the North. In others words, having fled the North during the Korean War and immigrating immediately after, Koreans from the North tend to have a weaker sense of attachment to South Korea given their brief residence and shallower roots. Research indicates that Koreans who had fled the North and migrated to the South during the Korean War were more likely to immigrate relative to those with permanent roots and connections in the South (Kim 1981). As a result, Jin Woo Seo's trip to Korea helped him to see more clearly than those born in the South that the homeland was no longer his home, revealing again the disconnect between migrants' general longing for eventual return to the home country and the reality of extended residence abroad. In short, both Mr. Seo and Mr. Oh have come to understand that Korea is no longer their home, that is, the country of birth. Rather, the United States is their home, a place where they had spent most of their productive years, confirming assimilationist views that time in the United States does matter and strongly influences immigrants' sense of home.

Another factor shaping their sense of home was immigrants' attitudes toward immigration, namely coming to accept migration as a formal break with the home country. For example, Sekwon Chong, a seventy-five-year-old retired, former manager for Coca Cola, distinguished between the homeland and sense of home. In other words, although Mr. Chong saw Korea as his homeland, a fact which was self-evident to him given his birth and well-established roots there, his home, however, was the United States because of his life-changing decision to immigrate and devote to building permanent roots in the new country. He explained:

> Although I have left Korea, I have never lost the idea that Korea is my homeland or motherland. No matter how well I may live here, I have tried to instill this idea to my grandchildren as well as the future generations. But my argument is that since you live here, it is imperative for Korean Americans to contribute to American society. They may be interested in Korean politics, but I don't think about going back to live in Korea.

Here, Mr. Chong sees the United States as his real home and argues that immigrants owe an immeasurable debt to the host country for the opportunities afforded to them, which they must repay with hard work and loyalty. This in no way, as he saw it, contradicts seeing the home country as his homeland. Perhaps this may simply be semantics, a quibble over the distinction between home and homeland, but the decisive criteria for sense of home is loyalty and gratitude to the host country. He also argues that immigrants must accept the decision to immigrate as a form of voluntary separation with the home country, which advocates for establishing long-lasting roots in and commitment to the receiving country rather than trying to lead dual lives. The power of long-term residence thus resonates unequivocally for a segment of the interviewees.

Others cited time in the United States, along with acquisition of citizenship and legal status and presence of immediate family members, as factors affecting the sense of home and belonging. Whether long-time residents had family members in the home or in the host country had an effect on the sense of home and belonging. Given that immigrants seldom migrate alone and sponsor immediate family members as soon as they are well established, it is not surprising that the sense of home and belonging is linked with chain migration. For instance, home, for Min Jee Lee (pseudonym), a thirty-six-year-old health education specialist for the county and owner of a *hagwon*, was strongly associated with family and personal investments in the place of long-term settlement. Noting that the United States was her home since it was here where members of her immediate family, except for her brother, currently resided, she aptly put it, "Korea is my country. Home is where I am currently living in."

Some also considered the act of acquiring citizenship in the host country, which symbolizes establishing a sense of home with the adopted country, as being synonymous with rupturing ties with the home country. For example, Dae Sung Park, a fifty-three-year-old man, contended that it was less his desire for American citizenship than Korean government's unwillingness to grant him dual citizenship which forced him to sever emotional ties with the home country. He explained, "America is my country. When I got U.S. citizenship, I gave up my Korean nationality. At that time, America allowed dual citizenship, but Korea did not. Exactly speaking, Korea abandoned me, not that I abandoned Korea. (*Interviewer: How about emotionally?*) I feel the same way. America is still my country." In the quote above, Mr. Park signals disappointment at the Korean government for precluding keeping dual citizenship with the United States, a reason he cites for surrendering his Korean citizenship in the process of becoming a U.S. citizen.

In sum, the consensus from long-time residents seems to be that although Korea was viewed as the homeland or motherland, or it conjured up strong emotions, "home" was still tied closely with long-term residence.[1]

Homeland as Real Home

Though most long-term residents came to identify and developed a sense of home with the place of settlement, there were a few who stuck to a position that birthplace, nationalism, and inclusion/exclusion were integral to sense of home and belonging, deeming the home country as home. According to Chul Ho Choi, a forty-eight-year-old member of the *Korean Central Daily* editorial staff, because he was born, raised, and spent most of his adult life in Korea, home was indisputably associated with birthplace, childhood, and young adulthood. He said, "Because I have lived in Korea until I was 40 years old, what people would typically consider as their home would for me be Korea. My character and values were all established in Korea."

In this context, legal citizenship and long-term residence were not enough to view the United States as home. For example, Jane Kim, a thirty-six-year-old children's pastor (part-time) and 1.25 generation, remained steadfast in her distinction among citizenship, residence, and birthplace, deeming Korea as her real home although she remained a U.S. citizen and resided in America. According to her, "I currently hold U.S. citizenship and live in America, but I always regard Korea as my true home."

Others put the matter both in terms of instrumentalist views of citizenship and residence and racial marginalization and discrimination. For instance,

Hong Jong Yoo, a forty-eight-year-old principal conductor of the Washington Youth Orchestra, while putting forward a nationalistic understanding of home, cited racism and discrimination as reasons for regarding the homeland as home. He explained:

> I came to the United States because I wanted to continue to study music. . . . I am Korean . . . Because I had received stipends from the government (referring to his days as a conductor in the military orchestra), I feel indebted to the Korean government. If there is a war in Korea, I will return to Korea right away. I am very worried about the current situation in Korea. I came to the United States when I was over 30. That means my emotional roots and beliefs are based in Korea. America is not my country. I am living here for convenience sake only. I may die here and my remains will get buried here, but my motherland is still Korea. . . . My identity is Korean since I am living in America for convenience. Although Korea has become quite globalized, Koreans are still a minority in the United States. Even if America is a nation of different states and people, it is still a country dominated by whites. We are just like visiting here. Lately I have been feeling like we are "guests" in this country. The fact that the image of Korea has been improving is a good thing for immigrants like us.

Here, Mr. Yoo does not associate legal citizenship with the sense of home and belonging because despite notions of the United States as a nation of immigrants, immigrants still struggle to gain full acceptance and integration due to racial and cultural differences. Thus, in line with the views of Ms. Kim, whose reactive ethnicity was discussed in chapter 3 and whose ethnic turn was marked by her inability to achieve full inclusion, the larger society's treatment of immigrants as, what Mr. Yoo calls, "guests" in their country of residence and citizenship is what impels a sense of home and belonging with the home country.

Another was whether immigrants held a sojourning orientation toward the host society. Given that sojourners, by definition, are those who migrate temporarily for the purpose of returning home with more wealth and status, it should come as no surprise that they generally gravitate toward the home country. For instance, Jin Tae Kim, a sixty-year-old, self-employed man in construction, who adhered to a sojourning orientation toward immigration, viewed long-term residence in the United States as still being unable to stamp out immigrants' sense of home toward the home country. Interestingly in Mr. Kim's case, although he wished to go back to live in Korea, his fear of going back unsuccessful and being labeled a failure also kept him back in America. As a result, he was stuck in limbo because he could not imagine going back to live in Korea even though he owned a house and land there, nor could he start a new business in the United States because he also imagined returning to the home country in the near future. Lamenting at the predicament he was in, he quipped, "I am Korean. I am only living here so that I can make money. . . . I never had this idea to stay here on a permanent basis."

Finally, just like those who regarded the United States as home because of the presence of immediate family members here, those with family members residing in Korea associated home with birthplace, upbringing, and kinship ties. For example, because Ok Chae Kim, forty-year-old WKTV producer, has been in the United States for less than five years and his immediately family still resided in Korea, not surprisingly, he tended to link home with the home country. Ok Chae Kim said, "Home is the homeland. That is the place where I was born and raised. My family and my friends are there. It is not simply a place where I was born, but the meaning is broader."

This suggests that immigrants' reception and treatment, whether favorable or negative, in the place of settlement, along with whether they hold a sojourning orientation and have immediate family in the home country, may be critical variables in developing a strong sense of home and belonging toward the host society.

SENSE OF HOME AND PERCEPTIONS OF ECONOMIC, SOCIAL OPPORTUNITY AND POLITICAL FREEDOMS

The section above discussed where Korean Americans felt most at home—the United States or the home country—and the reasons behind them. In this section, I consider other factors that impinge upon the sense of home and belonging such as perceptions of opportunities, including economic, social, and political, and social citizenship, that is, full inclusion, in the country of settlement. The 2012 Pew Research Center's Asian American survey (124) offers some clues on Korean Americans' perceptions and expectations of opportunities which may impact their goals of establishing permanent roots in the receiving country, returning back to the sending country, or maintaining dual lives. According to the Pew survey, 69% of Korean Americans agreed that opportunities to get ahead were better in the United States; only 7% replied that conditions were better in the country of origin, but this figure was still the second highest after the Chinese (8%) whose views of economic opportunity are without doubt influenced by China's phenomenal economic growth.

Similarly, perceptions of political freedom or the lack thereof may also impact immigrants' desire to see the host country as home as opposed to the sending country. Two-thirds (66%) of Korean Americans in the 2012 Pew Research Center's Asian American survey (125), for example, agreed that they had greater freedom to express their political views in the United States than in the country of origin. This figure was the third highest after the

Vietnamese (94%) and the Chinese (77%), a proportion which is not surprising given the Communist rule in both nations. The 2012 Pew Research Center's Asian American survey also covered other questions such as the freedom to practice one's religion, moral values of society, and strength of family ties. While these questions help us to understand Asian immigrants' experiences and perceptions of life in America compared to the home country, the conditions for raising children, a major question for families entertaining to stay for an indefinite period, may be a better indicator for establishing deeper roots between the host country and the home country. Two-thirds (67%) of Koreans in the survey agreed that conditions for raising children were better in the United States than in the home country (Pew Research Center 2012, 129), suggesting that many Korean families were likely to put more lasting roots in and come to regard the United States as home.

The 2012 Pew Research Center's Asian American survey showed that in key measures of economic, social, and political opportunity, Korean immigrants viewed the United States as a better place for getting ahead, for expressing political views, and for raising children. In this regard, the degree of satisfaction with the lives established in the new country, namely a productive life filled with material abundance, intergenerational mobility, and success, will bring greater satisfaction and identification with the host country, while a life of hardship and material scarcity will bring regrets and dissatisfaction with immigration.

In our interviews, economic opportunity and success were cited as reasons for a more positive view, and in turn, greater sense of home and belonging to the host country. For example, Dae Sung Park, the self-employed man, recounted that although he had a financially stable life in Korea, because of his productive immigrant life in the United States, he did not regret immigrating to the United States. He said, "Although I do not know personally how well I would have done had I stayed in Korea, I do not regret coming to America. I am a special case. I lived very well in Korea. Could I have maintained such a lifestyle? I am not sure. I worked very hard in the United States. I worked for one company for 16 years, then I switched jobs, and later I had my own business." Here, while Mr. Park is not certain if he could have sustained his comfortable premigration lifestyle, he still has no regrets immigrating to America because of his financial accomplishments. Nevertheless, given his prosperous family background, he may have done equally well in Korea had he stayed there.

If financial success brought greater attachment and identification with the host country, then the reverse, including financial hardships and maladjustment, could also cause misgivings about immigration, loosening sense of home with the receiving country. For instance, Teak C. Chung, the fifty-eight-year-old president of American Wheat Mission, came to doubt his decision to encourage his brother, a high-profile branch manager for Kookmin Bank in Korea, to immigrate after suffering downward mobility and status loss in the United States. Though Mr. Chung was saddened by the toll the grueling life of working as a dry cleaner took on his brother, he was comforted by the spiritual gains made by his brother, as he now lived an exemplary Christian life. This is what Pastor Chung had to say, "He came to live here because I encouraged him to. The reason why I invited him was because of his high status in Korea, he was not a devout Christian, and smoked and drank a lot there. I invited him so that he would regain his faith. Also the other reason was because in Korea, many are forced to retire when they reach 50 and older". While Mr. Chung himself did not regret his decision to take up his calling to serve the immigrant community and reside in the United States, he does regret inviting his brother to immigrate since although his spiritual life had improved, he also suffered hardship and lowered social status in America.

As hinted earlier in the chapter about the relationship between social citizenship and sense of home and belonging, difficulties integrating into the broader American culture and identity, namely the view of Korean and Asian Americans as "forever foreigners," were cited as factors in developing a sense of home toward the homeland. For example, encounters with discrimination and racialization, just like her ethnic turn, seem to have shaped Ms. Kim's identification with Korea as her true home despite her U.S. citizenship and residence. According to Jane Kim, the part-time children's pastor, a major reason why she identified more closely with her ethnicity was because of the prejudice and discrimination she, as a minority woman, encountered in the United States. During a trip to Iraq as a volunteer, not only did she realize she was culturally more Korean as she craved for Korean food while her American peers yearned for hamburgers and French fries, but also more importantly, her treatment as an ethnic outsider by fellow American soldiers during the tour reminded her of her outsider status, compelling her to identify ethnically. Despite her American citizenship and cultural dexterity, what was noticed was her race and ethnicity, that is, physical and cultural differences, which marked her as a racial other and cultural outsider. She explained:

> I came to America when I was in high school and sought to be a "real American." There was a particular incident that basically reminded me I could never be fully American. When I was in college, I went to Iraq for volunteer work. About twenty of us went there, and except for the three of us (me, another Korean, and one Chinese American), the rest were all white Americans. Because of the restrictions against women there, it was getting to be quite frustrating, and we could only eat Middle Eastern food and kebab. While the Americans who were with us would constantly tell us they missed the hamburgers, French fries, and coke, I was yearning for rice and *kimchi*. This is despite the fact that back in

> the States I seldom had a picky taste bud and for that matter, I hardly craved for Korean food. I realized then that no matter how much I wanted to become an American, I was inevitably Korean. . . . It was not only food, but whenever Americans were meeting Iraqis or other foreigners and they were introducing me and other East Asian Americans, they would never introduce me as an American but always as a Korean. It was the same for the Chinese Americans who were always introduced as Chinese. To them it did not matter that I lived in America and held an American citizenship. Regardless of how much I wanted to be an American, I realized that to them I will always be a Korean.

Here, what shapes Ms. Kim's understanding of sense of home and belonging is her interactions with fellow American soldiers who, instead of finding commonalities in their American citizenship, zero in on her race and culture, marking her as a racial other and cultural outsider, which underscores the power of race and cultural differences in gaining full acceptance into the mainstream of American society. Racial microaggressions (Solorzano et al. 2000), namely assumptions of being foreigners or aliens in their own land, continue to shape questions of minority inclusion, reminding that legal citizenship, which confers citizenship rights, has yet to translate into social citizenship (see Kim 2013). In short, attempts to assert and claim an American identity (i.e., social citizenship) are still ineffective when the power of ascribing or assigning identities based on racial markers continues and is taken for granted in American society. It is precisely for these reasons that Ms. Kim makes the ethnic turn, a choice made involuntarily from the cumulative impact of racializations from childhood to adulthood.

Consequently, rather than trying to become what she could not, Ms. Kim sought to focus on her ethnic side by passing on the ethnic traditions and culture to her children.[2] She said:

> Because we are a minority, even if we do not want to recognize and accept it, we are forced to live that way. As a result, I will be teaching my daughter the Korean language, culture, and etiquette. She will be absolutely speaking Korean at home, and from now on she will become more familiarized with the Korean language by video chatting (Skyping) with her grandparents. And if there is opportunity and my daughter is older, I am thinking of sending her to Korea during the summer vacations to learn the Korean language and culture.

Clearly, the predicament of being a racial minority forces 1.25-generation immigrants like her to find support from her ethnic culture, becoming, in turn, more ethnic. It is for these reasons that she also plans to transmit ethnicity to her children, teaching them the Korean language, values, and traditions, including sending her daughter to summer heritage programs in the home country. Thus, as discussed earlier, despite her acculturation and legal citizenship, her involuntary ethnic turn resulted in a thicker ethnicity in the private domain, further reinforcing a sense of being culturally more Korean. In short, the inability to gain acceptance as fully American pushed her to seek out and embrace the ethnic culture and identity, contributing to her weakened sense of home and belonging toward the country of settlement. Against this backdrop, it is not surprising that Ms. Kim seeks to pass on the ethnic identity and culture to her daughter, including the Korean-only rule at home and summer programs in Korea to help preserve the language and culture.

PLANS TO RETURN TO THE HOME COUNTRY

Historically, many immigrants have returned back to the home country to find a spouse, to reestablish family relations, or to retire in the home country. According to one study, as many as one-third to one-half of Italian immigrants to the United States returned back to Italy after a period of sojourn (Foner 1997, 2005). Among Italian and German immigrants, Levitt (2001b, 17) notes that many of them went back to Italy and Germany to get married, to provide an education for their children, or to retire in the home country. In the contemporary period, although statistics on return migration are scarce and imprecise, today's immigrants continue to engage in this practice, suggesting that returning back home is a consideration for many.[3] Thus, examining immigrants' attitudes and plans toward return migration will help gauge their sense of home and belonging to the host country. To be sure, a general feeling of wishing to go back is very different from actual return migration. Yet, those sentiments could be linked with weakened sense of home and belonging toward the host society. Whether migrants intend to or make specific plans to return hint at the possibility of transnational orientations in the future and where they consider their real home to be.

In her study of Korean immigrants in the 1980s, K.Y. Park (1997, 97) found that Korean immigrant men were more likely to return to the homeland, while women were more likely to become naturalized and to sponsor family members, similar to other immigrants where men tended to orient themselves toward the home country, while women sought to establish more durable roots in the host country (Foner 2005). In a later study of Korean immigrant women in 2000s, K.J. Park (2009, 137) also found that many women had no expectations of returning back to the home country. In the 2003 D.C. Korean community survey, almost three-fourths (71.6%) of Korean Washingtonians had no intentions of returning to Korea, while only 6.6% were certain of going back and one-fifths (21.8%) were undecided/unsure of their future plans. By contrast, Noh et al. (2013) found that one-half (50%) of Koreans in the Toronto survey responded affirmatively to wanting to return to Korea, while the other half also wished they were living there.[4]

Data from the Korean Ministry of Foreign Affairs and Trade provides actual return migration statistics of Korean immigrants. According to KAFGW (2009, 40), there were about 1,000 Koreans returning annually to Korea on a permanent basis in the early 1980s, although the number of returnees began to decline in the mid-1990s. By 1986, there were 2,060 returnees, 3,813 in 1987, 4,667 in 1989, 4,882 in 1990, 6,687 in 1992, and 2,612 in 2000, putting the total number of returnees at 42,000 between 1980 and 1993 (KAFGW 2009, 40). The latest statistics on Korean Americans (U.S. citizenship holders) residing in Korea from the Korea Immigration Service show slight increases from 2012 through 2016, rising from 44,567 in 2012 to 45,253 in 2013, 46,426 in 2014, 46,737 in 2015, and 46,050 in 2016 (Korea Immigration Service 2016, 70).

Among the most important reasons for returning to Korea for a quarter were difficulties in adapting to life in America (see also Belluck 1995). In terms of the profile of returnees, a third of them were senior citizens seeking to retire in the home country (KAFGW 2009, 40). Some of the returnees were also those who had left Korea during the 1997 IMF Asian financial crisis. Faced with stricter restrictions after overstaying their visas and going out of status, these migrants had a harder time readjusting their status or finding appropriate employment in the United States, giving them no other choice but to go back (KAFGW 2009, 41). Interestingly, one-fifth (19.5%) of returnees were also 1.5- and second-generation Koreans looking for job opportunities in Korea.[5]

While not quite the same as return migration, another useful measure for ascertaining sense of home and belonging is whether immigrants, if given the chance, would immigrate again. According to the 2012 Pew Research Center's Asian American survey (120), more than two-thirds (68%) of Koreans agreed that they would come again to the United States, while close to a quarter (23%), a figure which is the highest of all Asian groups, answered they would have stayed. These figures suggest that close to a quarter of Koreans did not find living in the United States meeting their expectations as they disagreed about immigrating again.

We also asked our interviewees concerning their plans to return to Korea, particularly their reasons for wanting to go back. One of the most important reasons for wanting to retire in Korea for a segment of the first generation, not surprisingly, was language barriers and difficulties in fully assimilating into the mainstream of American society. Some also contended that they would be in a position to fully retire and return to Korea as soon as their obligations to the children, in particular paying for children's college expenses, were fulfilled. For instance, Chul Ho Choi, member of the *Korea Central Daily* editorial staff, observed, "I have no plans of going back. I have not made any specific preparations, but I will probably start preparing for it. I am finding that full assimilation into American society will be impossible. I think it will be easier to live in Korea when I get older. After sending my second child to college I will return back to Korea."

Here, Mr. Choi speaks of a desire to go back because of his difficulties in achieving full inclusion, but whether many first-generation parents actually act upon them is a different matter as plans do not materialize or change. Also he has not made any specific arrangements that would raise his chances of going back, but simply engages in wishful thinking of returning back when his children complete college.

A few, especially those with grandchildren, seemed to settle on the idea that going back and forth, perhaps one-half of the year in Korea and the other half in America, would solve both their desires to retire in the homeland, on the one hand, and their sense of duty to help raise and care for the grandchildren, on the other.

Several community and religious leaders, who voiced strong Christian convictions, echoed a sentiment of wanting to engage in volunteer and missionary work abroad, with some returning back to Korea, while others looking to spread the Gospel in developing countries. For example, Jin Tae Kim, a self-employed man in construction, explained that he was still hesitant to become naturalized because of his desire to return to Korea in the distant future. Yet, because he feared going back empty handed and unsuccessful, instead of returning to his hometown, he claimed he wanted to work with an organization in Korea that did volunteer work in India and the Philippines to spend the rest of his productive years there. In-Wook Hur, a special projects coordinator for the Circuit Court of the State of Maryland, also stated that after retiring from his current work in a couple of years, he wanted to spend the rest of his productive life doing community or missionary work in developing countries such as Manchuria, Mongolia, or Sakhalin where many Korean Chinese resided.

As much as immigrants may engage in wishful thinking of going back to retire in the homeland, leaving everything behind, especially full-time jobs, was a lot easier said than done. Especially for couples, spousal relocations abroad were especially difficult when one of the spouses held well-paying and promising jobs in the United States. This was certainly the dilemma Ms. Cho faced whose prospects for relocation to Korea were the most viable among interviewees, but also the most difficult to reconcile. For example, Hye Jung Cho (pseudonym), whose husband traveled regularly to Korea as part of his work, was seriously considering returning back to live after retirement. However, quitting her current job as elementary school principal to join her husband was an unrealistic option at the time of the interview. She said:

> We are still thinking about it. When my husband retires he does want to go to Korea. He's currently going back and forth due to his job. He has a lot of acquaintances there. We are actually thinking about moving there in a couple of years. For me I would have to take a sabbatical and go there. For me it's a question of how to apply what I have studied and learned here over there. I wonder if I can use the knowledge that I have here and apply it there.

In the quote above, despite the fact that the Chos are seriously contemplating relocating to Korea because her husband's work involves going back and forth, still leaving her full-time job as a principal of an elementary school is impractical for Ms. Cho because finding comparable work in Korea was going to be not only difficult, but also highly improbable. Instead, a more realistic scenario is to move back when both of them retire from their current jobs. Yet, as touched upon earlier, even after retirement, the prospects of wanting to or having to help to raise the grandchildren will complicate plans to return and retire in the home country.

The prospects of return migration, therefore, were much more likely among those who immigrated during the late 1990s and 2000s, who not only held more instrumental views of immigration, but also retained property, bank accounts, and other assets in the home country. For instance, Ok Chae Kim, the former WKTV producer, still owned a small apartment and maintained several bank accounts in Korea, keeping his options of staying in the United States as well as returning back open. As he put it, "I am actually okay with it (return migration). Many people try out life here and in Korea. If the conditions for living in Korea are suitable, I am ready to move back. . . . I have not made specific preparations for it, but it is a general feeling of wanting to return to Korea."

Here, even with an apartment and bank accounts in the home country, which hints at greater prospects of return migration, Mr. Kim still contends that he has not made any specific arrangements to go back. Instead, returning back is a general outlook that he, along with many others in his shoes, harbors. Whether he acts upon them, to be sure, is contingent on job and economic opportunities in the home country vis-à-vis current economic situation as well as children's educational considerations in the host country.

No Desire and Plans to Return to the Homeland

The previous section examined the expectations of and motivations for return migration. But with the exception of a few cases, the vast majority had no particular plans to return to Korea, let alone thinking about doing so, contradicting the Toronto survey, but corroborating the findings from the 2003 D.C. Korean community survey. Although there was unwavering nostalgia for and attachment to their hometown, many long-timers did not regard Korea as their "home" since all of their children, siblings, and extended family were residing in the United States.

Among the various factors mitigating against return migration were pragmatic reasons such as helping to raise the grandchildren as discussed earlier and having a rent-free place to live, which would not be readily available in Korea. For example, Teak C. Chung, president of American Wheat Mission, replied that he had no plans to return to Korea for the simple fact that all of his children were residing in the United States and he had a mortgage-free home. Teak Chung explained:

> I have not given much thought about returning back to Korea. First and foremost, all of my children reside in America. I need to live close by my children to take care of the grandchildren when my children get married and have kids. Also, I have been paying taxes in the United States, and when I retire, I have a place to live here. However, in Korea, I do not have anything. I have not paid any taxes there or own assets.

As the quote illustrates, Pastor Chung is certainly homesick and wishes to go back, but in practice, his hometown is no longer his home, namely the Korea he left as an adult and for all purposes and intents, has nothing waiting for him. Instead, home is his current place of residence, namely the place where he devoted his entire adult life and upon retirement, will be entitled to retirement and social security benefits that will cover his minimum living expenses. Home for him is also where his adult children reside close by and, if needed, can easily offer a hand to help raise his grandchildren.

Others cited children's education and political freedom as reasons for not wanting to go back, corroborating the 2012 Pew Research Center's Asian American survey. For example, Steve Lim, fifty-five-year-old accountant, doubted there was as much return migration as reported on the news. He did concede that return migration would be an option for those experiencing difficulties in America due to language and cultural barriers. It would also appeal to those with immediate family members still residing in Korea, but since all of his siblings were living in the United States, he had no compelling reasons to go back. His basic premise was that if the reason for immigrating to the United States was to provide better educational opportunities for children, return migration was not a serious option.

A number of interviewees contended that return migration should not even be part of immigrants' vocabulary since the act of immigrating, echoing earlier views that stressed on demonstrating gratitude and loyalty to the host country, was itself a form of voluntary break from the homeland. In other words, even if immigrants came thinking that they would in some distant future go back to the homeland, in practice, they had to come to terms with the fact that their settlement was going to be much more permanent as their lives became securely planted in their adopted country. For instance, Sekwon Chong, a retired former manager for Coca Cola, claimed that return migration was inconceivable to him and his acquaintances.

He elaborated:

> I do go visit Korea once or twice a year. But the place where I live is the United States. I have never thought of returning back. I have ten grandchildren, and since my children and grandchildren live here, I actually have never thought about retiring and moving back to Korea and live there by myself. If you have decided to immigrate to the United States, you should look toward 100, 200, 300 years of putting your roots here. If you were to take a genealogical approach, I would be the source of my family roots. Our children were all born here and are U.S. citizens. . . . My thinking is that we have lived here and will be buried here. My mother passed away in Korea. Although my grandfather's burial place is in Korea, we seldom visit. We used to go to Korea every couple of years to visit my father's burial place. There are many Koreans who go to Korea to bring back their parents' grave.

Here, Mr. Chong takes the position that theirs and their children's and grandchildren's lives will be firmly rooted in the country of settlement. This is fundamentally an assimilationist position that rejects transnationalist claims of dual life. It asks for loyalty and identification with the country of settlement as transnational ties lose salience for immigrants and especially among subsequent generations. In addition, it is also impractical to be separated from his children and grandchildren.

For others, the realities of readjusting back in the home country after years of life abroad proved to be deciding factors against going back. Just like home visits earlier in the chapter helped to bring into sharp relief the disconnect between Korean immigrants' nostalgia for the homeland and the reality of living there, return migration would exact significant financial, emotional, and social costs on respondents, but especially on the children. For example, Jane Kim's apprehension in moving back to Korea was her fear of readjusting to an unfamiliar place after years of living in America as an immigrant child, a reaction bolstered by feelings of being out of place when she visited Korea. Jane Kim, the children's pastor, explained, "I don't think I have the courage to go back and live there. Even my parents who went to visit their birthplace in *Gohyang* (Buchon) said that it seemed too foreign to them as the place had changed so much. The sense of unfamiliarity would be even greater for me since I have lived less than 10 years in Korea." As Ms. Kim observes, if her parents, who had been raised in Korea, felt out of place in a changed Korea, imagine how much more difficult it was going to be for someone like her raised in the United States.

Min Jee Lee, the health education specialist, also agreed that her reason for not wanting to go back to live in Korea was because of the fact that she was much more used to life in the United States than in the home country. Not only did she find the overcrowding and the traffic jams distressing and irritating, but also she was afraid that her Americanized children would have a harder time reintegrating to life in Korea. What is notable about these two responses is the realization that it is almost impossible to readjust back into the home country after years of living abroad. Not only have they changed, but also the home country has undergone transformations that exact significant costs in readapting to the home country.

Corroborating the observations above, the impracticality of starting all over again was succinctly captured in more practical terms of economics, social networks, and job security. According to Dae Sung Park, the self-employed man, not only would he have to start from scratch, such as purchasing a house and a vehicle, but also he would have to establish new connections to secure job and economic stability, which he obviously lacked. As he put it:

> I have given some thought. But I believe it is practically impossible to return back. First, I do not have the school connections which are very important in Korean society. Next, there is couple of basic things that is needed in order to live in Korea such as a house and a car. If you have a house and a car, it is pretty nice to live over there because there is no mortgage to pay for. But I have none of these. I have been to Korea regularly for travel, but it will no longer be easy to live there. Not only for economic reasons but also cultural.

In the quote above, Mr. Park has a much more realistic assessment of what it takes to move back compared to general wishful thinking, citing lack of school connections, job security, and mortgage-free homes and cars. In addition, there is a changed culture that he will have to adapt to on top of starting anew economically and socially.

Related to these practical considerations of having to start fresh was the recognition that plans did not go as intended. The two responses below show how even temporary sojourns, whether as students or H1B workers, can turn into permanent settlement as political and economic conditions in the home country alter their initial goals, prolonging their stay and in the process, making return migration much protracted than anticipated. In others words, as the experience of many sojourning migrant workers attest, even when students come with the goals of studying and returning back to the home country, in practice, various mitigating circumstances lead to extended stays that often turn into permanent immigration.

For example, Jin Woo Seo's short-term goals of furthering his education in the United States ended up in a drawn-out stay following the political and economic upheaval in Korea in the 1960s and 1970s. Jin Woo Seo came to the United States in the late 1950s to pursue additional education, and his plan was to return to Korea after obtaining his degree. But when the April 19 student movement for democratic reforms broke out in 1960, which forced Syngman Rhee to resign from the presidency, going home became untenable. Advised by his parents to remain in America even though he was offered several jobs in Korea, Mr. Seo's temporary sojourn turned indefinite and protracted. This is how he, a retired old-timer, saw his situation in the 1960s:

> When I was active in the community, most of the leaders at the time were not immigrants but students that had come to study but ended up staying. Why did they stay? When I graduated from Georgetown, I could have obtained a government position in Korea since I had received a few offers. I was supposed to go back after graduating in 1961. But there was the 4.19 (the student movement). But my parents who were affected by the event told me not to return back. . . . My parents have passed away. Only my youngest brother still lives there. I have been living in the United States for more than 60 years. As I said before, the place where I am currently living is my home. If I went back, I still have a few high school friends. If I were to go back, it would be just to visit and stay for only couple of months.

After organizing rallies and protests against Park Chung Hee's authoritarian regime during his leadership of the Korean Association, Jin Woo Seo's prospects of returning home are completely shattered. Hence, what starts out as an initial sojourn for the purpose of advancing his education ends up in more than sixty years of immigrant life in the United States, foreclosing any possibilities of going back to Korea. Furthermore, with the recent passing away of his parents, any remaining possibility of returning back is closed. After more than one-half century of living abroad and with few in his immediate family still residing in Korea, going back to live no longer makes much sense.

By the same token, changing economic conditions in the home country, especially the unraveling of the Korean economy during the 1997 Asian IMF financial crisis, forestalled Hong Jong Yoo, the Washington Youth Orchestra conductor, from returning back, forcing him to take his chances in the United States although it was never his intention to stay here permanently. Like many student-turned-immigrants who saw their stay as provisional, Mr. Yoo's stay in America was also supposed to be temporary until he finished his graduate studies and obtained his degree. But after successfully adjusting his legal status to that of a permanent resident, going back had to be weighed against his options in the United States, including job prospects and quality of life for him and his family. He said:

> I had initially planned to return to Korea after completing my degree in 1999. But it was bad timing because even the Korean army was facing cuts and restructuring due to the IMF Asian financial crisis in Korea. Now though I am beginning to feel that I need to spend the rest of my life here. The children may get bullied in Korea. In many ways, obtaining a green card means that one is ready to become naturalized and become a U.S. citizen. Because I am a green card holder, I believe my place of residence is the United States.

Here, not only is Mr. Yoo coming to accept the idea that his long-term future and life lies in the United States, but he also understands that he and his family, especially his children, are going to have difficulties readapting to a changed home country after years of residence in a linguistically and culturally different country. Consequently, any decisions to return back are predicated upon the burdens that parents wish their children can avoid, especially sparing unnecessary adjustment hardships to the children.

Others seeking home and identity with the country of settlement were in a serious bind since not only did they recognize that returning to the home country was impractical given their long-term residence abroad, but also they were unable to fully be accepted because of their minority status. For instance, as much as Ms. Kim considered the homeland as her real home because of the prejudice and discrimination she experienced in the United States, in practice, however, she had no plans of going back for fears of encountering difficulties in reintegrating to the home country. While her U.S. citizenship signaled where her real home was, which was in America, she also found that she did not fully belong there. It was this lack of social citizenship that captured the predicament of those seeking home and identity with the country of settlement but have yet to attain full belonging.

In sum, the two quotes above show the power of contingency in immigrants' lives and point to migrants' plans that do not go as intended. As Waldinger (2007, 2015) observes, migration never works out as migrants had planned, but are contingent upon a number of factors and circumstances. It is clear from the responses of long-time residents that while some may imagine going back, few actually make the leap and return to Korea to live there permanently. Though growing number of states offer incentives to attract emigrants such as dual citizenship, voting rights, and access to health care, whether immigrants choose to go back is never as straightforward as it seems.

CONCLUSION

This chapter examined the sense of home, belonging, and identity in light of globalization, transnationalism, and advances in ICT. While a few associated the sense of home with birthplace and nationalism, the power of assimilation, that is, time in the place of settlement, had a profound impact on sense of home. In this regard, homeland visits made it crystal clear to many that deep-seated nostalgia toward the home country was at odds with their own personal transformations, including adjustments in their lifestyles and preferences, after spending years living abroad.

Moreover, with the exception of a few, most saw it impractical to return back as return migration would exact significant financial, emotional, and social costs on them and their children. This general desire to go back had to be weighed against pragmatic questions of mortgage-free homes, pensions, and separation from the children, especially grandchildren. While retiring in the home country made sense for some senior citizens, even for this group, the better option was to spend one-half of the year in the home country and the other half in the United States, as the latter allows them to maintain family intimacy and provide help with child care needs. Thus, except for retirees, return migration was undoubtedly more difficult to put into action not only for those without homes, bank accounts, and other assets in the home country, but even for those with property and assets, as not only their own economic opportunities in the home country but also their children's educational and social needs had to be considered. This suggests that long-term residence in the place of settlement invariably shapes sense of home, identity, and belonging toward the host society (Waldinger 2015). Though some may engage in "ways of belonging," expressing continued identification and attachment with the home country, this is most likely to be symbolic, raising doubts about their implementation beyond transnational activities that require little effort and commitment.

In future research, scholars need to tease out how sense of home, identity, and belonging are affected by the scope and intensity of transnational activities, including those that are effortless and costless to ones that exact significant time and monetary costs. Research also needs to examine more carefully and systematically how different types of transnational activities, including political, economic, and cultural, affect the sense of home, identity, and belonging.

NOTES

1. Concerning questions on the sense of home, a whopping 95.0% (N=401) of second-generation Korean Angelenos regarded the United States as their home, suggesting that interest in the home country is one thing and sense of home is another. While interest in homeland affairs persists across generations, where one feels at home does switch to the place of birth and upbringing. But given that there is very

little data on these trends over time, it is unclear whether such interest is rising or declining as sending states seek to court its emigrants.

2. Discrimination and racialization can trigger not only ethnic turns, but also other responses such as ethnic rejection or biculturalism (see D. Kim 2013).

3. Though first-generation immigrants have periodically engaged in return migration, most second-generation immigrants, including Koreans, consider their parents' country of origin as a nice place to visit but not to live on a permanent basis (Kasinitz et al. 2008). For example, Espiritu and Tran (2002) found that the overwhelming majority of 1.5- and second-generation Vietnamese did not want to return to Vietnam. In fact, 87% of them saw the United States as their home. Kibria (2002, 304) also observed that though many second-generation Koreans reported feelings of deep connection with Korea when they first arrived, the longer they stayed there, the more they also came to realize how Americanized and culturally different they were from Korean nationals (see also Tsuda 2003).

4. It should be noted that the Canadian figure shows higher rates of return migration because there are more international students, in relative terms, studying in Canada.

5. Andrew Noh, a twenty-six-year-old in consulting, was open to the idea of living in Korea, although it was clear to him that it was not going to be on a permanent basis. He said, "They sent me to work in Google Korea from Google Hong Kong in the beginning of June. I spent three weeks working for Google Korea. While working there, I felt that I could actually live here. (*Would you want to live in Korea then*?) Yes I would like to. (*Why*?) Because everything is convenient here. The metro is convenient. I have lots of relatives and friends here. My Korean is pretty decent. Work is not that different from America since I need to work 80 hours a week."

Chapter 6

Compatibility of Assimilation with Ethnic Preservation and Transnationalism

With deepening globalization, it no longer seems imperative to be physically present in the home country as migrants can lead simultaneous lives with their countrymen through ICT and consumption of homeland goods and cultural products. In other words, unlike the 1970s and 1980s when emigration to the United States generally meant a permanent break from Korea, home country assets were sold off, and returning home was put on hold indefinitely (Park 2009), today, it is no longer necessary, and in many ways disadvantageous, to break off completely from the homeland as cross-border contacts and exchanges enable immigrants to enjoy the best of both worlds.

In fact, when asked about the direction of the community, selective assimilation was preferred, recognizing that assimilation and ethnic preservation (and transnationalism) can indeed be compatible and also made more sense in a shrinking world. For example, according to several community leaders and long-time residents, transmitting ethnicity across generations was a lot harder in the 1960s and 1970s since pressures to assimilate were more intense during that time, pushing the children to learn English instead of retaining the Korean language and culture. To be sure, notwithstanding the melting pot ideology of the times, in light of their small numbers and dispersal into the suburbs, it was also much more difficult to preserve ethnicity since outside the home, there were few opportunities to practice the Korean language and culture. Recalling the prevailing norms and practices of the times, Jin Woo Seo (pseudonym), a seventy-five-year-old in consulting work, discussed the challenges of preserving ethnicity:

> I don't know if this is true for all of us in that generation, when we came to the United States in the 1950s and 1960s, American policy or society, when immigrants came, they wanted immigrants to completely assimilate into American

> culture and society. It was called the melting pot. We wanted our children to grow up as an Asian American and they were raised as such. We could not even imagine identifying as a Korean and not as an American. . . . As they grew up, we did have to instill a sense that their heritage was Korean. It's different now. But in the past, there were not a lot of opportunities.

Here, Mr. Seo observes how normative Americanization and the melting pot ideology had been in the early phase of Korean immigration in the 1950s and 1960s, noting that pressures to Americanize left immigrants with few other options. This was also corroborated by Andrew Noh, a twenty-six-year-old second generation, who explained how, growing up in the suburbs, he had been barred from speaking Korean at home. He recalled, "My parents came to the U.S. as college students. They never used Korean at home."

What changed all of this, of course, were demographic changes following the explosion of the immigrant population after the enactment of the Immigration and Nationality Act of 1965. As a result, not only did the Korean population surge in the area over a fifty-year period, but also the American society began to come to recognize and accept the increasing diversity of its residents. For instance, while it was common for Korean Americans like Sekwon Chong, a seventy-five-year-old retired former manager for Coca Cola, to be mistaken for Chinese in the past, with the rapid influx of Korean (and Asian) populations to the region, he was no longer mistaken for them nor was he asked questions about his ethnicity. He said, "They would ask me this question 'where are you from?' I would tell them I am from Virginia, and they would ask again." Here, Mr. Chong is the victim of the ethnicity guessing game (see D. Kim 2013; O'Brien 2008), a pervasive microaggression (assumption of forever-foreigner) affecting Asian and Latino immigrants, but which seems to have diminished with growing numbers and changing racial and ethnic make-up of the metropolitan area.

Moreover, the racial taunting and teasing prevalent during this time period has gone down considerably with increasing diversity of the area. This did not mean, however, that Korean (and Asian) Americans were fully being embraced and accepted as "moral equals" as Hye Jung Cho (pseudonym), a forty-seven-year-old school principal explained:

> When I was younger when we first immigrated in 1973, there were few Asians. Many people did not know about Korea so we were seen as Chinese. We did get taunted and teased by other children which affected our identity. It was quite harsh at the time. Kids today in school, instead of saying that they're Koreans, they seem to say they are Asian. As a principal of the school, many people when they come to visit the school they would often ask me whether I work as a teacher, or in the kitchen. I would tell them no, and my secretary would tell them that I am the principal. "Oh, is that right?" they would say. . . . The kids

seem to have pride when they find out that I am the principal. Many Korean parents also come by often.

Recounting her struggles with interpersonal racism against Korean (and Asian) Americans such as racial lumping, teasing, and taunting growing up, Ms. Cho describes how Korean American students in her school today increasingly take on a pan-Asian identity. But despite racial progress, many parents and visitors to her school are still unable to fathom the idea that an Asian American woman can be the principal of the elementary school as they assume she is either a school teacher or cafeteria worker. But for the Korean American students who learn she is the school principal, they are more than thrilled and filled with pride and joy.

In contrast to the past when immigrants had been forcibly pressured to relinquish their ethnic traditions and identities, the national climate in recent years has come to acknowledge and accept the increasing diversity of the nation (Alba and Foner 2015; Foner 2005, 74; Waldinger 2015), producing in turn, an awareness of and a desire for bilingualism and biculturalism among immigrants, including those of Korean Americans.

SELF-SEGREGATION OR RACIALIZATION?

The previous section examined shifts in mainstream American society's attitudes from melting pot toward multiculturalism and diversity, and in turn, Korean immigrants' emphasis from assimilation toward biculturalism and bilingualism. This, by no means, suggests that pressures to assimilate have altogether disappeared or that multiculturalism and diversity have been fully embraced in American society. In fact, in public discussions of immigrant acculturation and integration, media and political commentators as well as immigrants alike, including Korean immigrants, often criticize immigrants' unwillingness to assimilate as principal reasons for their continued segregation. For example, contending that many Korean immigrants had no interest and made little effort to blend in with the larger society, Dae Sung Park, a fifty-three-year-old man, citing an article he read, characterized Koreans as clannish, extravagant, and uninterested in assimilating. He said:

> I see it as separating. For example, there was an *L.A.Times* article while back asking Americans why they did not like Koreans. There were three reasons. First, they were seen to be clannish and wanted to do things with their own kind. Second, they seemed to have homes beyond their means and were picky about the school districts. Third, they did not want to learn English and if possible, were adamant in speaking Korean amongst themselves. They were not

> interested in blending. This is what the paper had reported. (*Do you feel this is a language issue*?) I do not think it is a language issue. I feel Koreans do not want to understand and blend in to the culture and values of the American people.

In the quote above, Mr. Park blames Korean immigrants for their lack of assimilation and integration, attributing their segregation from the mainstream to their clannishness and stubborn ways and desires to speak Korean.

Others, however, were more sympathetic to the plight of first-generation immigrants' difficulties in learning a new language and culture. For example, Jane Kim, a thirty-six-year-old children's pastor (part-time), contended that what was actually delaying Korean immigrants' assimilation was less their unwillingness to blend in than their difficulties in developing proficiencies in English, which did not come as readily to first-generation immigrants compared to their U.S.-raised children. Hence, the first generation's propensity to self-segregate had more to do with their inability to overcome language barriers and cultural differences than general hostility toward assimilation. She said, "I think they lead separate lives. The biggest reason is probably language barrier. My parents are like that, and most first-generation Koreans have difficulties with English and they are unable to resolve this issue. There is also the problem of cultural difference and also discrimination against non-whites." Here, Ms. Kim points to what is familiar and common knowledge regarding language difficulties and cultural barriers, which affect Korean American assimilation and integration into American society. She also brings up the role of racial discrimination in their exclusion from the mainstream of American society in contrast to simplistic notions of immigrant indifference and reluctance toward acculturation and assimilation.

Along these lines, some also took issues with the blaming-of-the-victim discourse on Korean immigrants' obstacles in blending into the larger society by explaining the community's separation as an outcome of the institutional completeness or self-sufficiency of the immigrant community, especially the continued replenishment of the first generation through immigration. According to Jae Won Ryu, a thirty-eight-year-old 1310 AM radio reporter, the Korean community was actually on track to generational changes from the first to the second generation with the aging of the 1960–1980 cohorts. But the 1997 IMF Asian financial crisis in Korea brought in a new pool of first-generation immigrants to the community, which replenished the aging, immigrant population. The outcome has been delayed assimilation of the immigrant community, leading to not only the retention of ethnic identity and language among later cohorts, but also transnational ties, which according to Mr. Ryu seems to border on separatism.[1]

Likewise, while acknowledging the increased salience of transnational influences on the immigrant community, Myung Suk Oh, a seventy-four-year-old retired man, had more negative views of the impact of cohort shifts on Korean American assimilation. Not only were later cohorts adopting home country values and practices, but also they were paying undue attention to trends in Korea, seeking to derive status and recognition from past homeland social arrangements. Contending that transnational orientations and activities, therefore, were incompatible with assimilation, Mr. Oh said:

> Many Korean-Americans are assimilating and at the same time retaining their ethnic traditions. My thing is to tell people that since you are here, you should leave your business card behind. But whenever there is a gathering many people would say I used to be such and such person back then. That's all useless. I really feel this when I go to LA where there are many Koreans. They keep practicing the same bad habits which they should have left them back in Korea. When you are in LA, which is very big, they insist on eating Korean food. Even with clothes they all want the fancy brand names and this type of culture travels very rapidly. Whatever is trendy in Korea they try to emulate it right away. Women are more into that. What is the famous bakery? *Shilla* bakery. When you go there it's very much like in Korea. You can get everything that you get in Korea, especially in places like LA.

In the quote above, Mr. Oh is critical of the practice of following the trends and lifestyles of the home country, including holding on to homeland values, attitudes, and practices, because these detract the assimilation of the immigrant community. Not only are Korean immigrants following the fashion trends in Korea but they are also seeking to derive status from their premigration relations and identities. Yet, the ready availability of Korean consumer goods, including Korean restaurants, bakeries, and clothing stores, was making dual life more possible and widespread than before, leading to ethnic preservation, on the one hand, but also separation, on the other.[2]

By contrast, a few argued that assimilation had less to do with whether immigrants sought to blend in or not, but how the broader American society treated and received them, which ultimately decided their full inclusion. Consistent with her reasons for an ethnic turn, Jane Kim, the children's pastor, faulted the media for creating and spreading stereotypical images of Korean Americans, which had a negative impact on Korean American integration into the mainstream of American society. She explained:

> Instead of the disadvantage of keeping two cultures, American society is one that looks down upon and ignores Asian Americans, but prefers descendants of Europeans who have also immigrated. This is why I have few white friends, and it has been rare for a white person to come and make friends with me. When I was working as a counselor, there was a time when a white man came to see me. As soon as he found out that the person who was counseling him was an Asian,

> he said to me "I am a redneck. I am forced to counsel with you this time, but this will be the last time." And indeed, he never came back to see me again. This is a disadvantage of what it means to be an Asian American.

As noted above, Ms. Kim disputes some of the claims made by members of the community and the larger society on Korean immigrants' penchant for self-segregation. Instead, she argues that discrimination against Korean and Asian Americans, rather than a propensity to avoid assimilation, is a primary reason. Ultimately, it is their lived experience with discrimination and exclusion that compel an ethnic turn.

Though a view of the Korean community as insular was pervasive, there was also an acknowledgment that the immigrant community was becoming more outward-looking than before, pointing to efforts to accommodate non-Koreans with bilingual signs and menus in restaurants and supermarkets. For example, Min Jee Lee, a thirty-six-year-old health education specialist (Fairfax County Health Department), owner of *hagwon*, nineteen years in the United States, noted, "In the past the Korean community was notorious for being exclusive due to language issues. These days, there is more effort to accept non-Koreans such as many non-Koreans in Korean restaurants, signs in Korean and English. Even during the KORUS festival it was run in Korean and English and many young people were involved. They seem to be assimilating."

Here, Ms. Lee points to the visibility of English signs in Korean restaurants and yearly cultural festivals such as the KORUS festival as indicators of significant shifts in the outlook and orientation of the community toward assimilation and integration. Outward-looking orientations aside, it probably makes good business to expand its clientele base beyond Koreans with growing popularity of Korean food and culture.

SELECTIVE ASSIMILATION: BILINGUALISM AND BICULTURALISM

If the immigrant community seemed to be putting in more effort to assimilate than before, raising the prospects for integration, others like Chul Ho Choi, a forty-eight-year-old *Korea Central Daily* editorial staff member, argued that ethnic preservation and assimilation were not at odds with each other, positing that both could be pursued simultaneously. He said:

> Korean Americans are adapting to mainstream society but also maintaining a Korean identity. We can tell that Korean American interest in politics has increased from the fundraising events being held for the American presidential elections. Because America is a diverse society, it is desirable to hold on to

> one's identity while adapting to American society. It is possible to be a good Korean while being a model American. It is possible to keep one's identity, while complying with the rules that Americans follow well.

Here, Mr. Choi regards selective assimilation to be a better option than assimilation or ethnic preservation alone, advocating both for community integration.

In line with the above observations, a few countered the conventional wisdom of assimilation correlating with upward mobility, citing examples of success among those who retained the cultural traditions and identity. For example, Dae Sung Park, the self-employed man, said:

> I think that retaining things Korean is better. It may seem ironic, but although it is necessary to live in an American way having become a citizen, it is important to live without forgetting the fundamental principles. . . . It is possible I believe. Actually among some Koreans, there are many who have successfully entered the mainstream and assimilated, while maintaining Korean practices and culture.

In the quote above, although Mr. Park agrees with the need to acculturate, this did not mean that assimilation and ethnic retention had to be a zero sum game, namely that ethnic identities and culture have to be abandoned in order to achieve integration and success in the mainstream of American society.

This point was particularly salient when discussing identity expectations toward the U.S.-born/raised children. Although the inevitability of assimilation in the next generation was acknowledged, this did not mean that parents were uninterested in transmitting the ethnic culture and identity to the children. For example, Hong Jong Yoo, the forty-eight-year-old principal conductor of the Washington Youth Orchestra, said, "Personally, I think it's better to maintain and live a Koreanized lifestyle. It is easier and matches my identity better. But it may be better for the second generation to live an Americanized lifestyle and assimilate. Still, as a father I would wish that they hold on to their Korean background and roots." Here, Mr. Yoo is well aware that there will be generational differences in degrees of acculturation and assimilation between the more ethnically identified first generation and the more Americanized second generation. Yet, he hopes that the second generation will still preserve elements of the Korean culture and identity.

If the responses above concede the inevitability of assimilation in the next generation, others saw selective assimilation as an important safeguard against racism and marginalization. Fully aware of the continued salience of race and ethnicity, some parents sought to instill ethnic pride in the next generation since their status as immigrant minorities was certain to affect their acceptance and integration into American society. Wishing his children would embrace the Korean heritage instead of denying it, Ok Chae Kim, a forty-year-old WKTV producer said:

> If I were to live in America more permanently, my children will likely identify themselves as Korean Americans. And it will probably be impossible to be fully American given their racial backgrounds and the context of their upbringing. I would probably not want that either. I would wish that my child, even if they are not proud of their background, still acknowledge and accept their heritage and live as a Korean American.

In the quote above, knowing that race was likely to shape immigrant minorities' integration into American society, Mr. Kim, partly for this reason but also because of his daughter's Korean heritage, hopes his daughter would retain the Korean language and culture.

Others put emphasis on bilingualism and biculturalism in light of multicultural policies and expanding globalization. In other words, contrary to the past when the melting pot ideology had prioritized learning English over retaining the mother tongue, today's Korean parents were seeking to pass on the Korean language and culture to the children given the advantages of bilingualism in a globalizing world. For instance, Myung Suk Oh, the retired man, recalled that Korean parents in the past had derived greater satisfaction from the children's mastery of English than their bilingualism, which he deemed to be short-sided since most children came to resent the parents for not pressing them harder to retain the Korean language.

Hence, a Korean-only rule at home is what Jin Tae Kim, a sixty-year-old self-employed in construction, would have enforced to ensure strong bilingualism in the children. He said, "It is imperative that rules must be established within the Korean family. Korean should be taught. They should try to assimilate into American society by first having a strong Korean identity. At home, it should be a Korean way of life; at work, American. Even doctors would have to speak Korean if they wanted to treat Korean patients." Here, Mr. Kim argues that a strong ethnic identity and proficiency in Korean at home can go hand in hand with assimilation outside, which can be invaluable when looking for jobs in the mainstream as well as in the ethnic economy.

Others like Hye Jung Cho, the elementary school principal, advocated bilingualism and biculturalism in light of children's ability to code switch freely and effortlessly. She said:

> I have gone through this and when I see my child, when he is in school he acts American and when he comes home he acts Korean. Depending on whom they are talking to they tend to code switch into English or Korean. The children seem to be doing this very effortlessly. So it doesn't seem it is necessary to just pursue one but keep both. I have tried to raise my kids in a Korean way, but at the same time I have emphasized being independent at school.

As the quote illustrates, children had no difficulties in being bicultural and bilingual as they were able to act Korean at home and American in school. Code switching from Korean to English also did not take a lot of effort, but given the benefits, was worth pursuing.

Finally, instilling a sense of pride and identity through bilingualism and biculturalism was not solely about preserving ethnicity across generations and building human capital. It also had practical implications such as sustaining the ethnic church in light of generational shifts and the aging of the first generation. According to Mr. Ryu, during a seminar he attended at a Korean church in Los Angeles, he heard a pastor warn about the imminent decline of co-ethnic memberships in Korean, Chinese, and Vietnamese churches. With generational changes, many Korean churches were on the brink of losing members and facing closures as there were not enough first-generation Koreans members. The choice was either to attract larger numbers of 1.5 and later generations into the co-ethnic church, who were seen to be leaving the co-ethnic congregations in droves, by promoting a strong sense of pride and ethnic identity, or to become a multiethnic/racial church, which was already taking place across these churches in Los Angeles. This suggests that bilingualism and biculturalism are more than about building human capital and instilling pride, but have practical consequences in sustaining the ethnic church and the broader community.

In sum, while some faulted the Korean community for their unwillingness to blend in, others criticized the blaming-the-victim discourse popular in the wider society, taking a sympathetic view of the plight of first-generation immigrants who commonly struggle with language and cultural barriers. A few saw it as a matter of the institutional completeness of the immigrant community, which, along with growing tolerance of diversity and multiculturalism in the larger society, provides ample opportunities for ethnic identification and preservation. There was also recognition that assimilation can indeed be compatible with ethnic preservation (and transnationalism), positing that selective assimilation (bilingualism and biculturalism) makes more sense and can bring many benefits in a globalizing world.

COHORT AND GENERATIONAL CHANGES ON ASSIMILATION AND TRANSNATIONALISM

The previous section highlighted the views of community leaders and long-time residents on Korean Americans' prospects for assimilation. In this section, I consider the cohort and generational changes which impinge upon the assimilation as well as the ethnic preservation of the immigrant community in years to come. While based on demographic/socioeconomic data, which is limited, I argue, like Mr. Ryu, that cohort changes may accelerate the assimilation of the immigrant community, on the one hand, but also produce ethnic renewal/preservation, on the other, as transnational activities and ties exert pulls among recent cohorts in line with research findings on the compatibility of assimilation with transnationalism (Foner 2005, 74; Levitt 2001b, 5–6).

First and foremost, many Korean immigrants who immigrated to the United States during the 1960–1980 periods, like the looming aging and retirement of baby boomers in mainstream American society (Alba 2009), are about to retire or have retired. According to C. Kim (2017), the percentage of older Korean immigrants (aged sixty-five and older) jumped from less than 5% in 1990 to 17% in 2015.[3] Cross-tabulations of median age by time of arrival in the biggest three Korean communities in the United States (Los Angeles, New York, and Washington, D.C.) also find that the aging of Korean Americans is proceeding rapidly, especially among those who immigrated during the 1960–1980 period. For example, the median age among those who came before 1960s was early seventies, while those who arrived during the 1960–1970 period was late sixties and those who entered during the 1970–1980 period was mid-fifties.

In their place, a more educated and fluent first-generation cohort has been immigrating to the United States since the 1990s, fueling the growth of the adult, working-age Korean population. First, driven in part by the 1990 immigration law, which brought well-educated Asian immigrants and Asian international students, including Koreans, to the United States under the specialty occupational category, levels of education, which affect occupational choices, economic well-being, and prospects for upward mobility, have increased among the latest cohorts of Korean immigrants (Min 2013). For instance, the proportion with a BA or higher (twenty-five and older, not in school) among Korean Americans jumped from 33.3% in 1980 to 51.3% in 2012, while the proportion with high school or less declined over the thirty-year period (ACS 1980–2012).[4]

Second, with improved schooling among recent cohorts, Korean immigrants' self-employment rate (sixteen and older, not in school, working) declined to 25.1% in 2000 and 23.6% in 2012 from a high of 29.7% in 1990. This drop was even more visible among those with college degrees. According to Min's analysis of Korean self-employment in New York City, only 22% of Korean college graduates in 2005–2007 were self-employed compared to 36% of non-college Koreans (Min 2013, 60). Clearly, educational upgrading was a factor in the reduction of self-employment among recent cohorts, but greater English proficiency was an even bigger factor since despite immigrating with college degrees, earlier waves were highly concentrated in self-employment due to limited English proficiencies. For instance, while only 45.2% of Korean Americans spoke English only or very well (five and older) in 1980, the proportion speaking English only or very well increased to 54.3% in 2012 (ACS 1980–2012). Among the reasons for improvements in English for later cohorts, according to Min (2013, 59), have been the expansion of English education and emphasis on spoken English in South Korea since the 1980s. A number of recent cohorts have also been immigrating at an earlier age, enabling them to obtain their college degrees in the United States.[5]

Third, educational upgrading and improved English proficiencies widened the occupational and small business choices of later cohorts, enhancing their cultural and social integration into the mainstream of American society (Min 2013, 62). For example, in 1980, 61% of Korean-owned businesses in New York were in retail, while 10% were in wholesale and 7% in personal service. A decade later, 44% of Korean-owned businesses in New York were in retail, while 19% were in personal service. By 2000, personal-service businesses expanded to 32% and to 23% in 2005–2007, while retail trade fell to 30% in 2000 and 29% in 2005–2007 (Min 2013, 62).[6] Occupationally, whereas a quarter (24.7%) held professional and managerial specialty occupations (sixteen and older, not in school, working) in 1980, the proportion holding such occupations increased every decade, reaching a high of 44% in 2012 (ACS 1980–2012). A caveat with this figure, however, is the inclusion of 1.5- and second-generation Koreans, which raises the percentage of professional and managerial occupations.[7] Another way we can also observe the occupational upgrading is the decline of operators, fabricators, and laborers among recent cohorts, which fell from a high of 22.6% in 1980 to a low of 5.6% in 2012, suggesting shifts into more professional and service occupations among those arriving with more schooling and higher English proficiencies. It may also be the case that less educated cohorts in manual work have either retired or moved into better occupations with longer residence (and improved English proficiency) in the United States.

All in all, unlike the social and cultural isolation experienced by the earlier cohorts due to their concentration in the ethnic economy as well as affiliation and participation in co-ethnic churches and consumption of transnational media, which made Korean Americans the most segregated group among Asian immigrants, the assimilation of the community is growing apace as significant inroads bring the community closer to the mainstream of American society (Min 2013, 61). In sum, although small businesses continue to be the bread and butter of Korean immigrant adaptation, cohort changes are speeding up the professionalization of the community, and, in turn, their assimilation.

Cohort Changes and Transnationalism

Though earlier cohorts came to the United States with a more permanent orientation toward immigration, as discussed earlier, their greater cultural and social isolation also made them to rely far more on ethnicity and transnationalism to adapt in the United States, including attending mostly co-ethnic churches, practicing Korean cultural traditions, speaking Korean, befriending mostly Korean friends, and consuming transnational media, to name a few. It is without doubt for these reasons that the immigrant community has often been accused of not wanting to blend in. Furthermore, even if earlier cohorts sought to actively engage in transnational activities in the home country, which were beginning to take form during this period, the fact that ICTs were less developed in the 1960–1980s proved to be quite expensive and cumbersome for participating in activities in the home country.

By contrast, recent cohorts are not only immigrating with a more transnational orientation than earlier cohorts (Park 2009), but are also arriving at a time when rapid advances in ICTs are enabling a much easier, faster, and in many ways, effortless transnational engagement, which greatly reduce the transaction costs of transnational participation. In addition, the American society receiving these new cohorts in the late 1980s and onward has been undergoing dramatic shifts from the melting pot toward multiculturalism, resulting in greater tolerance toward ethnic and transnational activities and identities.[8]

Another important contextual change with rapid growth of the Korean population and ICT advances, which has been discussed in the Introduction, is the availability of numerous ethnic and transnational amenities. In other words, unlike earlier cohorts whose access to myriad ethnic and transnational amenities such as Korean groceries, restaurants, and transnational media was circumscribed during the 1960–1980 period, recent waves benefit from revolutions in ICT and a full-fledged ethnic enclave, which significantly lower the transaction costs of engaging in transnational activities with the home country. For example, in his interview with June Dawson, a former president of the Korean American Women's Foundation and the godmother of internationally married Korean women in the Washington-Baltimore region, Lee (2013b) noted that when Ms. Dawson first settled in Fort Belvoir with her husband around 1960, she was struck by the fact that there were separate seats on the bus for blacks and whites.[9] Today, however, she delights in the fact that the community has access to numerous ethnic and transnational amenities, including Korean supermarkets, restaurants, and spas, illustrating the contextual changes that receive the latest cohorts compared to earlier waves.[10] In addition, as Min and Kim (2013, 43) observe, these contextual changes that receive the newer cohorts are also present in not only traditional immigration gateways such as Los Angeles and New York, but also in medium-sized cities such as Atlanta and Dallas. Consequently, there has been sizable outmigration of Koreans from large areas of Korean settlement into medium-sized cities during the 1990–2010 period since they offer the same ethnic and transnational amenities found in big cities but with a lower cost of living. Furthermore, the ongoing Internet and smartphone revolutions that seep deeper into our lives, which enable an easier, faster, and wider interaction with the home country, are not something that earlier cohorts could have ever imagined, but which are taken for granted by later waves. Thus, cohort changes not only reflect shifts in the orientation of recent immigrants who arrive with more transnational goals, but also contextual changes which enable more trouble-free transnational engagement with the home country.

Generational Changes on Assimilation and Transnationalism

Cohort changes underscore both the assimilation of the immigrant community and ethnic preservation and transnationalism in the foreseeable future. By contrast, generational changes, from the first to the 1.5 and second generations, suggest the maturation and integration of the Korean community. Raised and schooled in America, the resulting linguistic and cultural assimilation, along with educational and occupational progress, of the second generation puts the community closer to the mainstream of American society although the continued significance of race and ethnicity raise doubts about the extension of full social citizenship to immigrant minorities. As shown in chapter 1, the adult children of Korean immigrants, exhibit many signs of rapid integration, including educational, occupational, income, linguistic, and marital assimilation.

Educationally, while 55.2% of first-generation Koreans (sixteen and older, not in school, working) had BA or higher degrees, three-fourths (74.3%) of 1.5-generation and 77.9% of U.S.-born counterparts did so (ACS 2009–2011).[11] Unlike the first generation (31.3%), only 14.5% of 1.5 and 7.5% of U.S.-born Koreans were involved in self-employment, rapidly exiting the ethnic economy of their immigrant parents and obtaining jobs in professional and managerial specialty occupations (D. Kim 2013). For instance, while 40.9% of first-generation Koreans held professional and managerial specialty occupations, 65.7% of 1.5-generation and 65.6% of U.S.-born Koreans were in these occupations.[12] Finally, marriage-wise, second-generation Koreans are marrying out in high numbers. For instance, over one-half (54%) of native-born Koreans in the United States married out in 2009, with 60.3% of native-born Korean women marrying out, suggesting rapid linguistic and cultural assimilation for the women and also their multiracial children (Min and Kim 2009, 452).

Hence, generational changes imply the decline of transnational participation in the second generation as much research on second-generation transnationalism has found. Nonetheless, there are signs that transnational influences may continue to affect the second generation in a number of ways.

First, as discussed earlier, the same contextual factors (ethnic enclaves, ICT, the *Hallyu*) that received the newer cohorts are also accessible to the second generation although it is unclear to what extent and how actively these will be pursued by the later generations. It is likely that a select group of the second generation will be involved in transnational activities with the home country depending on their levels of linguistic, cultural, and identity assimilation. (See Oh 2012, 2015.) More research is needed to assess which of these contextual factors captivate second-generation interest in and engagement with the home country.

Second, while the percentage of native-born Koreans marrying out was very high, interestingly among the in-married (46%) the proportion of native-born Korean men marrying first-generation Korean women stood at 18.2%, a figure which was slightly above those marrying 1.5-generation Korean women (12.4%) (Min and Kim 2009, 452). This suggests that ethnic preservation, including mother tongue use and transnational influences, will remain salient in these families, leading to both assimilation, on the one hand, and ethnic preservation and transnationalism, on the other. Thus, although the prospects of second-generation transnationalism are limited and temporary, contextual factors and in-marriage with first-generation co-ethnics, among others, suggest that transnational ties and identities will be sustained at least among a segment of the second generation.

SYNCHRONIZATION: PERSONAL BLOGS AND DISCUSSION THREADS

The consumption of home country cultural products and consumer goods and transnational communication, though it was also present and pursued by past immigrants, is occurring at a pace and volume that is qualitatively different from the past. In some ways, the significance of the growing convergence of the ethnic with the transnational via ICT and consumption of transnational media and homeland consumer goods lies in the ability to synchronize with events in the home country, which is what Aksoy and Robins (2000, 362) also found among Turkish immigrants who achieved synchronization with Turkish events through transnational media.

The facility with which immigrants can synchronize with home country events and the bifocality that gets produced was vividly captured by personal blogs and posts to discussion threads discussing the impact of the Internet and smartphones on transnational engagement with the home country. While personal blogs and web posts written by Korean immigrants themselves are self-selected, anecdotal, and few in number, they, nonetheless, illustrate the impact ICT and transnational media have had on sustaining transnational ties and identities. Using two key words in Korean—smartphones and immigration and Kakao Talk and immigration—I conducted searches on Google Korea, Naver (top Korean web portal), and MissyUSA.com to examine the scope of these discussions.[13] I discuss three of them below to illustrate the changes the Internet, smartphones, and Kakao Talk have brought to Korean immigrants.

One of these, entitled, "Life of an Immigrant in the Age of the Smartphone," written by Alice in Melb (12/3/2016), poignantly captures the impact of the Internet and smartphones on immigrant life.[14] Alice writes that smartphones have brought immigrants like her much closer to and in sync with the home country. She says that not only are immigrants able to watch Korean news in real time, but they can also shop on Korean Internet shopping malls and communicate regularly with friends back home, exchanging photos and video chatting with family and friends. In her case, she starts her day by reading the news on Naver (major Korean web portal), listens to a lecture on Chinese language instruction by opening Siwonschool app, talks to her friends using Kakao Talk, orders books from Yes24.com (Korean online bookstore) or GMarket (Korean Internet shopping mall), which has international delivery, uses an app to exchange money from Korea in real time, follows food trends in Korea by searching for best eateries and restaurants, cooks Korean meals following top recipes appearing on Facebook, and checks her ads for help on Korean community websites (she runs a restaurant in Australia) and responds to work inquiries via Kakao Talk.

By contrast, when she first arrived to Australia, she remembers going to a PCBang (Korean Internet café) to look for a place to rent and find work, made weekly stops at Korean supermarkets, even if there was no need to go there, to pick up free community newspapers to look for job ads, begged friends visiting Korea to bring her care packages, relied on currency-exchange firms to exchange money, used expensive international telephone cards to call Korea, and coordinated with her boyfriend in Seoul to make sure both of them were home to Skype with each other, which had a tendency to drop voice and video calls frequently. She notes that this was only eight years ago, but smartphones have completely transformed her life as well as those of other immigrants. Today, she can easily see and talk to her friends in Korea, can bring many consumer goods when necessary, and can follow the news at the same speed as those living in Korea, which gives her a sense of being close to Korea. She notes that life overseas has, indeed, become a lot easier, but she finds that the fun element has been eliminated. This means that unless she makes an effort to assimilate into Australia, she could lead the same lifestyle she had in Korea. She asks whether immigrants like her are able to make new friends in Australia, both Korean and non-Korean, when it is so convenient to talk to home country friends daily via Kakao Talk, which discourages them from breaking away from their comfort zone.

In my second key word search, which I conducted on MissyUSA.com, the search produced only one discussion thread discussing the impact of smartphones and Kakao Talk on immigrant life.[15] The question raised in this particular discussion thread (1/10/17) was about adapting to the United States as an immigrant before the arrival of the Internet and smartphones. Several postings mention writing letters, including waiting in line at the post office to send Christmas cards to Korea, while another posting mentions using fax machines, instead of letters, to communicate with family and friends. In one post, the author recalls spending her day writing letters to her mother in Korea, often getting teary eyed rereading the letters her mother had sent. Other postings describe spending hundreds of dollars on international telephone calls to Korea, while in another posting, the author recalls about the lack of ethnic amenities (Korean supermarkets) and the prohibitive cost of international calls unlike today when free calls can be made using Kakao Talk. The author also mentions making weekly trips to local video shops to borrow Korean dramas, which was one of the few perks the family enjoyed. Yet, the author notes that they were still able to adapt to the old technology by jotting down directions when they were driving or using the telephone booth when the beepers went off. Another posting acknowledges the comfort and connection the Internet and smartphones brought to immigrant life, but the author laments that the digital technology was preventing immigrants from breaking out of the ethnic mold, circumscribing their friendships to mostly Koreans.[16]

Finally, a blog (6/20/12) written by a Korean immigrant woman in Brazil captures again the role that the Internet and smartphones play in immigrant adaptation and retention of transnational ties and identities.[17] She writes that smartphones have brought more joy to her immigrant life since she was able to text message in real time with her friends in Korea and America via Kakao Talk. She was also able to check what her friends were up to by reading their Kakao Story. One of the things she liked most about smartphones was the ability to make free voice calls (via Kakao Talk) with friends in Korea anytime anywhere since in the past, international telephone calls were limited to landline connections. She notes that despite living in Brazil, she checks the weather in Korea and reads the Korean, rather than the Brazilian, news. The fact that she can voice and video call anytime has given her a sense of being very close to Korea despite the vast distance between Brazil and South Korea.

The blogs and the discussion thread above suggest growing synchronization of immigrant lives with their counterparts in the home country, enabling simultaneity despite residence abroad. As bifocality remains the mark and orientation of more recent immigrants, but even among long timers, the ubiquity, ease, and acceptance of cultural transnational activities may spur greater interest in them. The fact that there is very little lag time between immigrants and their home country counterparts means there is greater convergence between the ethnic and transnational, leading to greater uniformity in their cultural and consumer practices. In turn, as these practices become normative, bifocality may become an accepted practice among the first generation, and even gain traction with some 1.5- and second-generation immigrants.

CONCLUSION

A concern with synchronization and bifocality, as it binds migrants to both the home and host countries, is undoubtedly immigrants' commitment and loyalty toward their place of residence. Despite fears that bifocality could lead to divided loyalties, these should not be seen as producing dissimilation and reduced commitment to the host society with the latter. Instead, as most research has found, assimilation and transnationalism can be compatible, fulfilling an important void for first-generation immigrants during their transition and adaptation to the host society (Portes and Rumbaut 2014, 78–79, 183). As discussed earlier, immigrants' durable links with the home country persist because there is an acute desire to soothe separation from family and friends and to find a sense of continuity and purpose in a culturally unfamiliar environment (Cabanes and Acedera 2012; Madianou and Miller 2011; Metykova 2010; Parrenas 2005; Shi 2005; Uy-Tioco 2007; Yoon 2015). Furthermore, bifocality should also be seen as responses to exclusion and incomplete or imperfect belonging. As a result, immigrant bifocality or multiple sense of home and belonging represents typical phases of first-generation adaptation into the host society, but loses significance and influence in later generations. As Portes and Rumbaut (2014, 78–79) write:

> Transnationalism highlights the possibility that preserving ties to the home culture and language may be compatible with acculturation. . . . On the contrary, transnationalism offers a viable bridge and platform for successful integration. The fate of immigrant groups that have been unable to make use of the resources offered by this path stands in stark contrast, showing the dangers of premature assimilation without the means for educational and economic advancement.

In a world where ICT innovations continue to reduce the frictions of time and space, it remains to be seen to what extent and under what conditions this synchronization leads to a convergence between the ethnic and transnational, producing cultural uniformity and enabling a truly dual life.

NOTES

1. Unlike the 1925–65 period when European immigration came to a complete halt during the forty-year period, hastening the assimilation of Southern and Eastern European immigrants, the post-1960s period has seen uninterrupted immigration from Korea (and elsewhere), replenishing the first-generation population and in turn, delaying their assimilation (Alba and Foner 2015; Gjelten 2015).

2. Delegate Mark Keam, the first Korean American to serve in the Virginia Assembly and who represents parts of Oakton, Vienna, Dunn Loring, and Tysons Corner, makes similar observations about the self-segregation of Korean Americans coming from increased transnational ties and the ethnic institutional completeness of the immigrant community. According to Keam, "That mentality still pervades amongst a vast majority of Koreans who live in America. Look at Annandale or Korean town in L.A. and it's just like the Hermit Kingdom—everything is in Korean, they read Korean newspapers, they watch Korean TV, they shop in Korean stores, worship in Korean churches and go to Korean restaurants. So they're living in America, but in their little Korea Town it becomes like a Hermit Kingdom." (Quoted in Seminara 2011.)

3. As a result of the aging of this cohort, elderly welfare and care will become pressing social issues in the immigrant community in years to come.

4. I conducted an analysis of Korean American education, class of worker, English speaking ability, and occupation for 1980, 1990, 2000, and 2012 using the 1980–2012 ACS data. The results of these cross-tabulations inform the cohort discussions in this section.

5. While this is a plausible explanation, this figure needs to be examined more carefully as Min (2013) defines the first generation as those who were born abroad and came to the United States at the age of thirteen and older. By contrast, I define the first generation as those born abroad but having immigrated at the age of eighteen and older. I reserve the 1.25 generation category to classify those who immigrated between the ages of thirteen and seventeen.

6. A big reason for shifts from retail to personal services among Korean New Yorkers has been greater competition from big-box retailers/mega stores in the late 1990s as well as new competition from non-Korean merchants in minority neighborhoods (Min 2013, 63), which pushed Korean immigrants away from labor-intensive toward medium-size businesses. Leading the personal-service businesses in New York City have been nail salons and dry cleaners, which expanded threefold in the case of nail salons, while dry cleaners also grew rapidly over the fifteen-year period (Min 2013, 64).

7. Because the 1970, 1980, and 1990 decennial censuses from the IPUMS do not contain the disaggregated "years in the U.S." variable, which is needed to create the "generation" variable, I cannot examine if the occupational upgrading of Korean Americans has been due to the educational upgrading of recent cohorts or the greater influx of the 1.5 and second generation into the labor force. An analysis of the American Community Survey, 2009–2011, however, suggests that it is both.

8. Certainly, the election of Trump puts into question whether public and even private expressions of ethnicity and transnationalism will be tolerated in the near future. But at least prior to the current administration, the overall political climate of the country has been greater willingness toward expressions of ethnicity and transnationalism.

9. According to Lee (2013b), seeking to soothe nostalgia toward the homeland and establish social ties with other Koreans, June Dawson joined the Association of Korean American wives in the mid-1960s, an organization established in July of 1963 by Korean women in international marriages. Later she came to lead the organization, which eventually became the Korean American Women's Foundation. She explains that during the early period, the meetings were generally held at the members' homes since there were no Korean groceries and restaurants. The organization also played an important role in the immigrant community, providing services to its members as well as the larger community, including intervening on behalf of abused women and offering translation, finding places to live, obtaining driver's license, and locating jobs for newcomers, among other things. The organization also did other kinds of outreach work with the poor and senior citizens as well as spearheading the adoption of biracial Korean children.

10. Even county schools like Fairfax County Public Schools (FCPS) offer Korean language classes at four elementary schools and at Fairfax High School Academy, helping students to retain the Korean language (Seminara 2011).

11. The analysis of self-employment, education, and occupation is for Korean Americans (single race) in the Washington-Baltimore, New York-New Jersey, and Los Angeles-Long Beach metropolitan areas (all three areas combined).

12. The breakdown of professional and managerial specialty occupations was as follows: while 19.1% of first-generation Koreans held management, business, and financial operations occupations, 25.5% of 1.5- and 26.0% of 2.0+ generations did so. Similarly, while 21.8% of first-generation Koreans were in professional and related occupations, 40.2% of 1.5 and 39.6% of 2.0+ generations were in these occupations.

13. The vast majority of the search results, however, returned mostly blogs and ads focusing on firms advertising their immigration services, although a few blogs and news articles examining the impact of smartphones and Kakao Talk on their lives did turn up.

14. This blog, written by Alice in Melb, features many other articles regarding immigrant life in Australia. According to her, smartphones dominate our lives from morning till dawn, as we begin the day with the morning alarm bell from smartphones and close the day by checking emails, sending text messages, or following SNS before going to bed. She notes that we carry our smartphones everywhere every time to search for information, to complete tasks, and to communicate with others. But in the old days of back pack travel before the arrival of the Internet, she recalls having to find an Internet café in Vietnam to make international calls to Korea, where not only was it expensive to call internationally but also calls were dropping constantly. She also remembers carrying a heavy travel guide book with her, often taping together the maps that were about to fall apart with repeated use. Lodging reservations were

also made in person, and fellow backpackers had to be consulted on best places to eat. Today, as soon as we buy and insert a local SIM card, our smartphones (IPhone in her case,) do all the work for us. Alice points out that ten years ago, we were still able to carry our lives as we had in the past, but we can no longer imagine going back to daily life without smartphones (and the Internet). To her, all these changes are both comforting and discomforting because there is no way she would trade in the comfort and ease she gets from smartphones today, but at the same time, she also finds that her backpacking trip was not all that unbearable and miserable either.

15. Because MissyUSA.com restricts users to Korean women, I did not have access to the private sections of these discussion threads. I only came across this particular discussion thread on smartphones (and the Internet) when my wife, who is a regular user, happened to read the posting and alerted me to it. Although I am aware of the site, I do not have an account nor do I use my wife's user ID to access it. I underscore this point because Joon-Hwang Oh's recent book on Korean immigrant women's use of MissyUSA.com for exchanging information and building social capital was initially criticized after posts accusing him of logging in to the website and accessing the users-only section of the site were made (The *Korea Times* showcased the book in one of its news reports). According to my wife who read the postings on Oh's book, many women were furious that a man had illegitimately gained access to this women's only website, reading many personal and private postings they were sharing with each other. Though some later postings clarified that Oh's book had used the public section of the website, which did not require a user log in or password, for his analyses of information inquiry and exchange, many women were still fuming over what they perceived to be male transgressions over shared women's spaces among Korean women. I note this controversy to make it explicit that my key word search (smartphones and immigration and Kakao Talk and immigration), while producing many hits, did not grant me access to the links since I was not a member. In any event, my initial reason for the key word search was to check if there had, indeed, been many discussion threads on smartphones (and the Internet) and immigrant life like the posting my wife had alerted me to. But the key word search did not produce such discussion threads. I hope this will allay any concerns readers may have about accessing the private sections of this site, which were not viewed in any form.

16. Interestingly, a few hold on to idealistic views of establishing friendships across racial and ethnic boundaries, lamenting that the ease with which home country friendships can be maintained via the Internet and smartphones was preventing Korean immigrants from breaking out of the ethnic mold. Though there is some truth to this, was this ever a possibility even before the arrival of the Internet and smartphones? Here, many assume that immigrants can effortlessly cross racial and ethnic boundaries, especially with members of the dominant group, only if they had the initiative to leave their comfort zones, putting the blame on herself and other immigrants and especially the new technology for making it easier to retain co-ethnic friendships. What is forgotten is that it is not solely on initiatives alone that friendships can be established across racial boundaries given the salience of race and cultural and language differences in American society.

17. A fourth blog (1/9/15) written by a Korean immigrant in Australia also illustrates the far-reaching impact of the Internet and smartphones on immigrant lives. The author observes that she did not miss Korea that much because she was able to visit Korea regularly. During the first two years in Australia she missed Korean food a lot and had to improvise as best as she could, but since 2014 many Korean consumer goods were being imported to Australia with the exception of few dishes such as oysters, soy sauce-dipped crabs, and honey butter chips. She finds that the Internet and smartphones enhance the quality of their lives as immigrants, not only enabling them to watch Korean television but also making them even more aware of events in Korea than their friends back home. Also by using 070 Internet telephone, local calls can easily be made, reducing considerably the cost of international telephone calls. And because they are abroad, she finds she is calling her parents much more frequently than when she was living in Korea. This was also true with her friends, with whom she kept in touch more frequently abroad than when she was living in Korea.

Conclusion

Overview and Implications

This book has examined the transnational activities of Korean Americans, finding that cultural transnational activities, given their costless and effortless (and unconscious) quality, compared to those that require time, effort, and energy, will be most likely pursued by many. As discussions on personal blogs and postings to discussion threads in chapter 6 illustrated, immigrant lives in the smartphone age are marked by increasing synchronization with home country events and cultural trends, practices which not only underscore the compatibility of assimilation with ethnicity and transnationalism, but also the viability of bifocality at least at the cultural (and consumption) level.

But how will these transnational practices affect immigrants' commitment toward their place of residence as well as their sense of identity and belonging? Though data limitations make it difficult to draw reliable conclusions about the scope and intensity of bifocality versus belonging to host society among Korean immigrants, I offer some tentative observations about the direction of assimilation and transnationalism in years to come. The remarks are suggestive and more research needs to be conducted using larger and more diverse samples of immigrants. Nonetheless, the limited data suggest that there was, in fact, an effort and commitment to establishing deeper roots into the place of settlement, with many calling for greater community participation and engagement in local affairs. At least among long-time residents, the power of assimilation, namely long-term residence, seems to resonate unequivocally with the sense of home toward the host country. In some ways, these long-term residents' orientations and commitment toward their place of residence reinforce Carens's (2013) observations of long-term residence serving as principal criteria for granting rights to migrants in the host society.

Moreover, unlike immigrants from Central America and the Caribbean, who engaged more actively in economic and political transnationalism such as remittances, home visits, and homeland elections, these were not as prominent among Korean Americans. First, the practice of sending remittances has declined considerably among Korean Americans with the exception of occasional sums of money sent for various festivities. Though there was an increase in the size of remittances in the World Bank data, it probably represents investments by Korean Americans. Second, homeland visits, while far easier and regular than before, still required significant financial and time commitments, making them intermittent affairs for most Korean Americans. In short, the constraints of distance, despite living in the age of jet travel, do matter for immigrants coming from countries far away from the United States (Waldinger 2015). Third, political transnationalism, especially voting in home country elections, while becoming more institutionalized as home country parties and politicians seek campaign contributions and their vote, was not met with much enthusiasm and support as many remained generally apathetic toward politics in general, and homeland politics in particular. Still, given the benefits of remittances, investments, and lobbying on behalf of the home country, the Korean state will continue to engage in transnationalism from above, providing funding for cultural and educational programs, courting emigrant voters, and intervening in community affairs. Though some members of the community will respond to these efforts, political apathy seems to characterize a large segment of the immigrant community despite calls for community empowerment and engagement from community leaders. Even if dual citizenship is granted, which seems unlikely due to concerns about dodging compulsory military service, political transnationalism among Korean Americans will be more selective and occasional, given that most were more interested in the instrumental aspects of citizenship such as ease of travel and health and other social benefits than their duties as citizens.[1]

Finally, though a fair number of interviewees express a general sentiment of going back to retire in the home country, almost none of them, in fact, were making actual preparations to go back to live. Furthermore, the prospects of separating from loved ones, such as older retirees wanting to help raise the grandchildren, or having to start from scratch, including finding a place to live, landing well-paying jobs, rebuilding social networks, and readjusting to a changed homeland, was sharply at odds with a general wishful thinking of going back. To be sure, return migration is more likely among those who are recent immigrants and who hold instrumental views of immigration as they seek to hedge against an unsuccessful immigration by holding on to homes and other assets in the home country. Temporary migrants and visitors are also more likely to entertain going back since they have no other choice but to return if they are unable to change their immigration status. But at least among long-timers, going back to live was not an easy choice having established long-term roots in the host country, hinting at the power of long-term residence on the sense of home.

This suggests that Korean immigrants' involvement in economic and political transnationalism, which is occasional, is less likely to produce a strong bifocal orientation. Instead, given the ubiquity of ICT, transnational media, and homeland consumer goods, Korean Americans' bifocality is likely to stem from their participation in cultural transnational activities, which is more regular (Itzigsohn et al. 1999, 333) and better suits immigrants coming from geographically distant places.

TRANSNATIONAL ACTIVITIES IN THE FUTURE

Portes and Rumbaut (2014; 183) observe that immigrants' transnational connections and identities represent phases of first-generation adaptation in their attempts to reconcile old loyalties with newfound attachment and commitment toward the host country. Moreover, as long as there is uninterrupted immigration, states continue to court emigrants, newcomers experience exclusion from full social membership in the host country, and immigrants gain a sense of purpose and meaning through transnational participation, transnational activities are likely to continue in the foreseeable future (Levitt 2001b, 19–20). In fact, one of the reasons why Korean immigrant women engaged in transnational activities was to reduce their devalorization and marginalization in American society (Park 2009, 140). Noh et al. (2013, 131–132) also observe that transnational informal ties may be helpful in integrating recent arrivals to a new and unfamiliar environment. For instance, regular transnational contacts with family members, relatives, and friends among Korean immigrants in Toronto were associated with less acculturative stress, higher self-esteem, and lower depressive symptoms (Noh et al. 2013, 132).

To this list, we should probably add the role played by ICT and transnational media as they not only facilitate transnational communication and consumption of home country cultural products but also fulfill a deep emotional need for intimacy, nostalgia, information, and entertainment within the immigrant community (Cabanes and Acedera 2012; Y. Kim 2011; Lee 2004; Metykova 2010; Nedelcu 2012; Parrenas 2005; Wilding 2006; Yoon 2015). As noted throughout the book, the ease, speed, and volume with which homeland media and consumer products can be consumed today differentiates the context of reception for immigrants whose lives are in greater sync with their counterparts in the home country. Won Sang Lee, the seventy-three-year-old former senior pastor, aptly describes the hallmarks of transnational life, which was much more difficult to sustain in the past because of the practical constraints of space and time. He summed it up:

> I had not visited Korea for the first 19 years. At that time, I felt Korea was far away from me. Now, I read *Hankook Ilbo* (*The Korea Times*), *Joong-Ang Ilbo* (*The Korean Central Daily*), *Dong-A Ilbo* every day through the Internet. I feel Korea is very close to me. I experience Korea directly. Rather than feeling Korea as a homeland which I have left from, I feel it as if I am currently living in Korea. I have a sense of reality from Korea as much as from America.

Here, Mr. Lee observes that through active consumption of transnational media, one can experience more intense emotional attachments to and feelings of simultaneity with the home country than ever before.

In addition to ICT and home country media and consumer goods, as Min (2012, 77) observes, the role played by Korean ethnic associations and Korean government agencies/cultural organizations should be noted since Korean immigrants' individual transnational cultural activities are closely intertwined with those pursued by the Korean state and ethnic organizations. For instance, in his content analysis of Korean dailies in New York, Min (2012, 56, 57) found 105 transnational cultural events taking place in 2010, out of which 47 were Korean performing arts (music, dances, plays, and movies), 24 were fine arts, calligraphy, ceramic arts, and photography, 19 were food and food festivals, 12 were literature and language, and 8 were others. Out of these, music and dance performances by popular Korean singers and dance groups during cultural/holiday festivals and other cultural events organized by Korean ethnic associations and Korean government agencies, according to Min (2012, 60, 63, 75), were likely to have had the most impact on the community as they occurred more frequently and drew larger Korean audiences compared to exhibitions of artistic or literary work by Korean painters, photographers, or writers, which drew a smaller, well-educated Korean American crowd.

Transnational cultural events involving food also had the most visible imprint of the state as both the Korean government agencies and Korean conglomerates sought to globalize Korean food. For example, the Korean Food Foundation, a semi-government organization, working together with both Korean restaurants in the New York area and Korean government agencies, including the Korea Agro-Fisheries Trade Corporation, the Ministry of Food, Agriculture, Forestry and Fisheries, and the Korean Cultural Service of New York, were instrumental in promoting Korean food to New Yorkers (Min 2012, 64, 68). Food-producing companies from Korean provinces as well as top chefs from large Korean cities were also active in many food-related cultural events, showcasing and selling their agricultural and food items during cultural/holiday festivals and promoting their products and regional dishes to Korean and non-Korean attendees (Min 2012, 65). The Seoul City government and Seoul Tourism Organization also helped to organize a

Korean food festival at the United Nations Plaza restaurant, bringing famous chefs from Korea to prepare a wide range of Korean dishes (Min 2012, 66). Finally, South Korean franchises such as Paris Baguette (bakery business) and Kyochon and Bonchon (fried chicken business) have made inroads in New York and in other large metropolitan areas, including the Washington-Baltimore region, bringing the latest homeland food trends to both Korean and non-Korean customers.

These developments suggest that cultural transnational engagement by the first- and select 1.5- and second-generations will persist in the years to come as the state, Korean conglomerates, and ethnic associations continue to promote durable connections with the home country. Though not as conspicuous and contentious as other forms of transnational activities, these practices, precisely for their overlooked and mundane nature, will be longer lasting and perhaps serve as a backbone for maintaining transnational ties and identities in the foreseeable future.

NOTE

1. Although regular political transnationalism may be less common, there were a number of homeland events that did trigger greater participation from the Korean immigrant community. One of these was the Sewol ferry tragedy in which more than three hundred people, mostly high school students, died on April 16, 2014. The botched rescue effort from the Park Geun-Hye administration prompted massive protests not only from South Koreans but also from Korean immigrant women who participated on MissyUSA and other forums to raise funds calling for a special independent investigation of the accident through a full-page ad on the *New York Times*. Through crowdfunding on indiegogo.com, the campaign was able to raise more than $66,000 in a matter of days, highlighting effective use of social media and crowdfunding to mobilize the immigrant community. Additionally, the corruption scandal which led to the successful impeachment of Park Geun-Hye from the presidency also raised Korean Americans' interest in the May 2017 presidential elections, which brought a much higher percentage of Korean Americans to the polling booths than in previous homeland elections.

References

Abbott, Carl. *Political Terrain: Washington, D.C., From Tidewater Town to Global Metropolis*. Chapel Hill: The University of North Carolina Press, 1999.

Abelmann, Nancy, and John Lie. *Blue Dreams: Korean Americans and the L.A. Riots*. Cambridge: Harvard University Press, 1995.

Abelmann, Nancy, So Jin Park, and Hyunhee Kim. "College Rank and Neo-Liberal Subjectivity in South Korea: The Burden of Self-Development." *Inter-Asia Cultural Studies* 10 (2009): 229–247.

Adler, Rachel. *Yucatecans in Dallas, Texas: Breaching the Border, Bridging the Distance*. New York: Pearson Education, Inc, 2004.

Aksoy, Asu, and Kevin Robins. "Thinking Across Spaces: Transnational Television from Turkey." *European Journal of Cultural Studies* 3 (2000): 343–365.

Alba, Richard. *Blurring the Color Line: The New Chance for a More Integrated America*. Cambridge: Harvard University Press, 2009.

Alba, Richard, and Nancy Foner. *Strangers No More: Immigration and the Challenges of Integration in North America and Western Europe*. Princeton: Princeton University Press, 2015.

Alba, Richard, and Victor Nee. "Rethinking Assimilation Theory for a New Era of Immigration." *International Migration Review* 31 (1997): 826–867.

Alba, Richard, and Victor Nee. *Remaking the American Mainstream: Assimilation and Contemporary Immigration*. Cambridge: Harvard University Press, 2003.

Alonso, Andoni, and Pedro J. Oiarzabal. *Diasporas in the New Media Age: Identity, Politics, and Community*. Las Vegas: University of Nevada Press, 2008.

Anderson, Benedict. *Imagined Communities: Reflection on the Origin and Spread of Nationalism*. London: Verso, 1991.

Bacigalupe, Gonzalo, and Susan Lambe. "Virtualizing Intimacy: Information Communication Technologies and Transnational Families in Therapy." *Family Process* 50 (2011): 12–26.

Bahk, C. M., and Fred E. Jandt. "Korean Immigrants' Use of Ethnic and Host Media in the United States." *Asian Communication Research* 1 (2004): 68–92.

Bailey, Olga G., Myria Georgiou, and R. Harindranath. *Transnational Lives and the Media: Re-Imagining Diasporas*. New York: Palgrave Macmillan, 2007.

Baily, Samuel. *Immigrants in the Lands of Promise: Italians in Buenos Aires and New York City, 1870–1914*. Ithaca: Cornell University Press, 1999.

Barrera, Vivian, and Denise Bielby. "Places, Faces, and Other Familiar Things: The Cultural Experience of Telenovela Viewing among Latinos in the United States." *The Journal of Popular Culture* 34 (2001): 1–18.

Basch, Linda, Nina Glick-Schiller, and Cristina Szanton Blanc. *Nations Unbound: Transnational Projects, Postcolonial Predicaments, and Deterritorialized Nation-States*. Langhorne: Gordon and Breach, 1994.

Bates, Timothy. *Race, Self-Employment, and Upward Mobility: An Illusive American Dream*. Baltimore: The Johns Hopkins University Press, 1997.

Beck, Ulrich. "Rooted Cosmopolitanism: Emerging from a Rivalry of Distinctions," in *Global America? The Cultural Consequences of Globalization*, edited by Ulrich Beck et al., 15–29. Liverpool: Liverpool University Press, 2003.

Belluck, Pam. "Healthy Korean Economy Draws Immigrants Home." *The New York Times*, August 22, 1995.

Benitez, Jose Luis. "Transnational Dimensions of the Digital Divide among Salvadoran Immigrants in the Washington, D.C. Metropolitan Area." *Global Networks* 6 (2006): 181–199.

Benítez, José Luis. "Salvadoran Transnational Families: ICTs and Communication Practices in the Network Society." *Journal of Ethnic and Migration Studies* 38 (2012): 1439–1449.

Bernal, Victoria. "Diaspora, Cyberspace and Political Imagination: The Eritrean Diaspora Online." *Global Networks* 6 (2006): 161–179.

Bonacich, Edna, and Ivan Light. *Immigrant Entrepreneurs: Koreans in Los Angeles, 1965–1982*. Berkeley: University of California Press, 1988.

Boyd, Danah. "Participation in the Always on Lifestyle," in *The Social Media Reader*, edited by M. Mandiberg, 71–76. New York: New York University Press, 2012.

Brandon, Peter. "The Child Care Arrangements of Preschool-Age Children in Immigrant Families in the United States." *International Migration* 42 (2004): 65–85.

Brouwer, Lenie. "Dutch Moroccan Websites: A Transnational Imagery?" *Journal of Ethnic and Migration Studies* 32 (2006): 1153–1168.

Burrell, Jenna, and Ken Anderson. "'I Have Great Desires to Look beyond My World': Trajectories of Information and Communication Technology Use among Ghanaians Living Abroad." *New Media and Society* 10 (2008): 203–224.

Butcher, Melissa. "From 'Fish Out of Water' to 'Fitting In': The Challenge of Re-placing Home in a Mobile World." *Population, Space and Place* 16 (2010): 23–36.

Cabanes, Jason, and Kristel Acedera. "Of Mobile Phones and Mother-Fathers: Calls, Text Messages, and Conjugal Power Relations in Mother-Away Filipino Families." *New Media and Society* 14 (2012): 916–930.

Carens, Joseph. *The Ethics of Immigration*. London: Oxford University Press, 2013.

Carstens, Sharon. "Constructing Transnational Identities? Mass Media and the Malaysian Chinese Audience." *Ethnic and Racial Studies* 26 (2003): 321–344.

Chan, Sucheng. *Asian Americans: An Interpretive History*. Boston: Twayne Publishers, 1991.

Chanda, Nayan. *Bound Together: How Traders, Preachers, Adventurers, and Warriors Shaped Globalization*. New Haven: Yale University Press, 2008.

Chee, Maria WL. "Migrating for the Children: Taiwanese American Women in Transnational Families," in *Wife or Worker? Asian Women and Migration*, edited by Nicola Piper and Mina Roces, 137–156. Lanham: Rowman & Littlefield Publishers, INC., 2003.

Chen, Brian. *Always On: How the iPhone Unlocked the Anything-Anytime-Anywhere Future—and Locked Us In*. Cambridge: Da Capo Press, 2011.

Cheng, Chung-Tai. "Floating Workers and Mobile QQ: The Struggle in the Search for Roots," in *Migration, Diaspora and Information Technology in Global Societies*, edited by Leopoldina Fortunati, Raul Pertierra, and Jane Vincent. New York: Routledge, 2012.

Chiang, Lan-Yung Nora. "Astronaut Families': Transnational Lives of Middle-Class Taiwanese Married Women in Canada." *Social and Cultural Geography* 9 (2008): 505–518.

Chib, Arul, Holley Wilkin, Sri Ranjini, and Mei Hua. "International Migrant Workers' Use of Mobile Phones to Seek Social Support in Singapore." *Information Technologies and International Development* 9 (2013): 19–34.

Chib, Arul, Shelly Malik, Rajiv George Aricat, and Siti Zubeidah Kadir. "Migrant Mothering and Mobile Phones: Negotiations of Transnational Identity." *Mobile Media and Communication* 2 (2014): 73–93.

Chin, Ku-Sup, In-Jin Yoon, and David Smith. "Immigrant Small Business and International Economic Linkage: A Case of the Korean Wig Business in Los Angeles, 1968–1977." *International Migration Review* 30 (1996): 485–510.

Chinchilla, Norma, and Nora Hamilton. "Changing networks and alliances in a transnational context: Salvadoran and Guatemalan immigrants in Southern California." *Social Justice* 26 (1999): 4–26.

Chohan, Hyejung. "Reading the 'Korean Wave' as a Sign of Global Shift," *Korean Journal* 45 (2005): 147–182.

Choi, Eunjeong. "Kakao Talk, a Mobile Social Platform Pioneer," *SERI Quarterly* (2013): 63–70.

Choy, Bong-Youn. *Koreans in America*. Chicago: Nelson Hall, 1979.

Chung, Angie. "From Caregivers to Caretakers: The Impact of Family Roles on Ethnicity among Children of Korean and Chinese Immigrant Families." *Qualitative Sociology* 36 (2013): 279–302.

Clark, Juliet. "Nation-State Belonging among Asian Australians and the Question of Transnationalism." *Current Sociology* 57 (2009): 27–46.

Collins, Francis Leo. "Connecting 'Home' with 'Here': Personal Homepages in Everyday Transnational Lives." *Journal of Ethnic and Migration Studies* 35 (2009): 839–859.

Cornell, Stephen, and Douglas Hartmann. *Ethnicity and Race: Making Identities in a Changing World*. Thousand Oaks: Pine Forge Press, 1998.

Covert, Adrian. "Facebook Buys WhatsApp for $19 Billion." *CNN*, February 19, 2014. Retrieved from http://money.cnn.com/2014/02/19/technology/social/facebook-whatsapp/index.html

Dahan, Michael, and Gabriel Sheffer. "Ethnic Groups and Distance Shrinking Communication Technologies." *Nationalism and Ethnic Politics* 7 (2001): 85–107.

Danico, Mary Yu. *The 1.5 Generation: Becoming Korean American in Hawaii*. Honolulu: University of Hawaii Press, 2004.

Denison, Tom, and Graeme Johanson. "Community Connections and ICTs: The Chinese Community in Prato, Italy and Melbourne, Australia—Networks, ICTs and Chinese Diasporas," in *Migration, Diaspora and Information Technology in Global Societies*, edited by Leopoldina Fortunati, Raul Pertierra, and Jane Vincent. New York: Routledge, 2012.

Department of Homeland Security (DHS). Washington, DC: DHS, 2015. Retrieved from https://www.dhs.gov/

DeWind, Josh, and Philip Kasinitz. "Everything Old is New Again? Processes and Theories of Immigrant Incorporation." *International Migration Review* 31 (1997): 1096–1111.

Dhingra, Pawan. *Life Behind the Lobby: Indian American Motel Owners and the American Dream*. Stanford: Stanford University Press, 2012.

Dicken, Peter. *Global Shift: Transforming the World Economy*, 3rd Edition. New York: The Guilford Press, 1998.

Diminescu, Dana. "The Connected Migrant: An Epistemological Manifesto." *Social Science Information* 47 (2008): 565–579.

Duany, Jorge. *Blurred Borders: Transnational Migration between the Hispanic Caribbean and the United States*. Chapel Hill: The University of North Carolina Press, 2011.

Dunn, Kevin. "Embodied Transnationalism: Bodies in Transnational Spaces." *Population, Space and Place* 16 (2010): 1–9.

Elias, Nelly. *Coming Home: Media and Returning Diaspora in Israel and Germany*. Albany: SUNY Press, 2008.

Elias, Nelly, and Dafna Lemish. "Media Uses in Immigrant Families: Torn between 'Inward' and 'Outward' Paths of Integration." *The International Communication Gazette* 70 (2008): 21–40.

Elias, Nelly, and Dafna Lemish. "Between Three Worlds: Host, Homeland, and Global Media in the Lives of Russian Immigrant Families in Israel and Germany." *Journal of Family Issues* 32 (2011): 1245–1274.

Espiritu, Yen Le, and Thom Tran. "'Viet Nam, Nuoc Toi' (Vietnam, My Country): Vietnamese Americans and Transnationalism," in *The Changing Face of Home: The Transnational Lives of the Second Generation*, edited by Peggy Levitt and Mary C. Waters, 367–398. New York: The Russell Sage Foundation, 2002.

Evers, Clifton, and Gerard Goggin. "Mobiles, Men and Migration: Mobile Communication and Everyday Multiculturalism in Australia," in *Migration, Diaspora and Information Technology in Global Societies*, edited by Leopoldina Fortunati, Raul Pertierra, and Jane Vincent. New York: Routledge, 2012.

Faist, Thomas. "Transnationalization in International Migration: Implications for the Study of Citizenship and Culture." *Ethnic and Racial Studies* 23 (2000): 189–222.

Finch, John, and Seung-Kyung Kim. "Kirŏgi Families in the US: Transnational Migration and Education." *Journal of Ethnic and Migration Studies* 38 (2012): 485–506.

Fitzgerald, David. "Negotiating Extra-Territorial Citizenship: Mexican Migration and the Transnational Politics of Community." San Diego: Center for Comparative Immigration Studies, University of California, San Diego, 2000.

Foner, Nancy. "What's New about Transnationalism? New York Immigrants Today and at the Turn of the Century." *Diaspora* 6 (1997): 355–376.

Foner, Nancy. "Transnationalism Then and Now: New York Immigrants Today and at the Turn of the Twentieth Century," in *Migration, Transnationalization and Race in a Changing New York*, edited by Hector Cordero-Guzman, Robert C. Smith, and Ramon Grosfoguel, 35–57. Philadelphia: Temple University Press, 2001.

Foner, Nancy. *In a New Land: A Comparative View of Immigration*. New York: New York University Press, 2005.

Fortunati, Leopoldina, Raul Pertierra, and Jane Vincent, ed. *Migration, Diaspora and Information Technology in Global Societies*. New York: Routledge, 2012.

Friedman, Thomas. *The World is Flat: A Brief History of the Twenty-First Century*. New York: Farrar, Straus and Giroux, 2005.

Frith, Simon. "Anglo-America and its Discontents." *Cultural Studies* 5 (1991): 263–269.

Frith, Simon, and Lee Marshall, ed. *Music and Copyright*. New York: Routledge, 2004.

Georgiou, Myria. *Diaspora, Identity and the Media: Diasporic Transnationalism and Mediated Spatialities*. Cresskill: Hampton Press, 2006.

Georgiou, Myria. "Seeking Ontological Security beyond the Nation: The Role of Transnational Television." *Television & New Media* XX (2012a): 1–18.

Georgiou, Myria. "Watching Soap Opera in the Diaspora: Cultural Proximity or Critical Proximity?" *Ethnic and Racial Studies* 35 (2012b): 868–887.

Gjelten, Tom. *A Nation of Nations: A Great American Immigration Story*. New York: Simon and Schuster, 2016. (Ebook)

Glenn, Evelyn Nakano. *Issei, Nisei, War Bride: Three Generations of Japanese American Women in Domestic Service*. Philadelphia: Temple University Press, 1986.

Glick–Schiller, Nina, Linda Basch, and Christina Blanc–Szanton. "Transnationalism: A New Framework for Understanding Migration." *Annals of the New York Academy of Sciences* 645 (1992): 1–24.

Goggin, Gerard. "Ubiquitous apps: Politics of Openness in Global Mobile Cultures." *Digital Creativity* 22 (2011): 148–159.

Goggin, Gerard. "Google Phone Rising: The Android and the Politics of Open Source." *Continuum* 26 (2012): 741–752.

Goldring, Luin. "The Mexican State and Transmigrant Organizations: Negotiating the Boundaries of Membership and Participation." *Latin American Research Review* 37 (2002): 55–99.

Gordon, Milton. *Assimilation in American Life: The Role of Race, Religions, and National Origins*. New York: Oxford University Press, 1964.

Grasmuck, Sherri, and Patricia Pessar. *Between Two Islands: Dominican International Migration*. Berkeley: University of California Press, 1991.

Greschke, Heike M. "Make Yourself at Home in civervalle.com: Meanings of Proximity and Togetherness in the Era of 'Broadband Society,'" in *Migration, Diaspora and Information Technology in Global Societies*, edited by Leopoldina Fortunati, Raul Pertierra, and Jane Vincent. New York: Routledge, 2012.

Guarnizo, Luis E. "The Economics of Transnational Living." *International Migration Review* 37 (2003): 666–699.

Guarnizo, Luis, and Michael Peter Smith. "The Locations of Transnationalism," in *Transnationalism from Below*, edited by Michael Peter Smith and Luis Guarnizo, 3–34. New Brunswick: Transaction Publishers, 1998.

Guarnizo, Luis, Alejandro Portes, and William Haller. "Assimilation and Transnationalism: Determinants of Transnational Political Action among Contemporary Migrants." *American Journal of Sociology* 108 (2003): 1211–1248.

Hamel, Jean-Yves. "Information and Communication Technologies and Migration." United Nations Development Programme, Human Development Reports Research Paper, 1–46, 2009.

Hamilton, Norma, and Nora Hamilton. "Changing Networks and Alliances in a Transnational Context: Salvadoran and Guatemalan Immigrants in Southern California." *Social Justice* 26 (1999): 4–26.

Han, Jane. "Emotional Voters' Overseas to Rush to Polls." *The Korea Times*, March 27, 2017.

Harvey, David. *The Condition of Postmodernity: An Inquiry into the Origins of Cultural Change*. Oxford: Blackwell, 1989.

Held, David, Anthony McGrew, David Goldblatt, and Jonathan Perraton. "Global Transformations." *ReVision* 22 (1999): 7–7.

Hepp, Andreas, Cigdem Bozdag, and Laura Suna. "Mediatized Migrants: Media Cultures and Communicative Networking in the Diaspora," in *Migration, Diaspora and Information Technology in Global Societies*, edited by Leopoldina Fortunati, Raul Pertierra, and Jane Vincent. New York: Routledge, 2012.

Hiebert, Daniel, and David Ley. "Characteristics of Immigrant Transnationalism in Vancouver," in *Transnational Identities and Practices in Canada*, edited by Vic Satzewich and Lloyd Wong, 71–90. Vancouver: University of British Columbia Press, 2006.

Hiller, H. and F. Tara. "New Ties, Old Ties, and Lost Ties: The Use of the Internet in Diaspora." *New Media and Society* 6 (2004): 731–752.

Hong, Euny. *The Birth of Korean Cool: How One Nation is Conquering the World Through Pop Culture*. New York: Picador, 2014.

Horst, Heather A. "The Blessings and Burdens of Communication: Cell Phones in Jamaican Transnational Social Fields." *Global Networks* 6 (2006): 143–159.

Horst, Heather, and Daniel Miller. *The Cell Phone: An Anthropology of Communication*. Oxford: Berg, 2006.

Hsu, Madeline Y. *Dreaming of Gold, Dreaming of Home: Transnationalism and Migration between the United States and South China, 1882–1943*. Stanford: Stanford University Press, 2000.

Huang, Shuling. "Nation-Branding and Transnational Consumption: Japan-Mania and the Korean Wave in Taiwan." *Media, Culture and Society* 33 (2011): 3–18.

Huat, Chua Beng, and Koichi Iwabuchi. *East Asian Pop Culture: Analyzing the Korean Wave*. Hong Kong: Hong Kong University Press, 2008.

Hurh, Won Moo. *The Korean Americans*. Westport: Greenwood Press, 1998.

Hurh, Won Moo, and Kwang Chung Kim. *Korean Immigrants in America: A Structural Analysis of Ethnic Confinement and Adhesive Adaptation*. Madison: Fairleigh Dickinson University Press, 1984.

Hurh, Won Moo, and Kwang Chung Kim. "Religious Participation of Korean Immigrants in the United States." *Journal of the Scientific Study of Religion* 29 (1990): 19–34.

Ignacio, Emily. *Building Diaspora: Filipino Community Formation on the Internet*. New Brunswick: Rutgers University Press, 2005.

Irving, Jacqueline, Sanket Mohapatra, and Dilip Ratha. *Migrant Remittance Flows*. Washington DC: The World Bank, 2010.

Itzigsohn, Jose. "Migrant Remittances, Labor Markets, and Household Strategies: A Comparative Analysis of Low-Income Household Strategies in the Caribbean Basin." *Social Forces* 74 (1995): 633–655.

Itzigsohn, Jose, and Silvia Giorguli Saucedo. "Immigrant Incorporation and Sociocultural Transnationalism." *International Migration Review* 36 (2002): 766–798.

Itzigsohn, Jose, Carlos Cabral, Esther Hernandez Medina, and Obed Vazquez. "Mapping Dominican Transnationalism: Narrow and Broad Transnational Practices." *Ethnic and Racial Studies* 22 (1999): 316–339.

Iwabuchi, Koichi. "Becoming 'Culturally Proximate': The A/scent of Japanese Idol Dramas in Taiwan," in *Asian Media Productions*, edited by Brian Moeran, 54–74. Richmond: Curzon, 2001.

Iwabuchi, Koichi. "'Soft' Nationalism and Narcissism: Japanese Popular Culture Goes Global." *Asian Studies Review* 26 (2002): 447–469.

Iwabuchi, Koichi, ed. *Feeling Asian Modernities*. Hong Kong: Hong Kong University Press, 2004.

Jiménez, Tomás R. *Replenished Ethnicity: Mexican Americans, Immigration, and Identity*. Berkeley: University of California Press, 2010.

Johnson, Melissa. "Latinas and Television in the United States: Relationships among Genre Identification, Acculturation, and Acculturation Stress." *The Howard Journal of Communications* 7 (1996): 289–313.

Johnson, Valerie C. *Black Power in the Suburbs: The Myth or Reality of African-American Suburban Political Incorporation*. Albany: SUNY Press, 2002.

Jones-Correa, Michael. *Between Two Nations: The Political Predicament of Latinos in New York City*. Ithaca: Cornell University Press, 1998.

Jung, Sun. *Korean Masculinities and Transcultural Consumption: Yonsama, Rain, Oldboy, K-Pop Idols*. Hong Kong: Hong Kong University Press, 2011.

Jung, Young A. "Emplacing Parenting: Migration and Belonging among Korean *Gireogi* Families." PhD diss., George Mason University, 2015.

Kama, Amit, and Vered Malka. "Identity Prosthesis: Roles of Homeland Media in Sustaining Native Identity." *Howard Journal of Communications* 24 (2013): 370–388.

Kang, Miliann. *The Managed Hand: Race, Gender, and the Body in Beauty Service Work*. Berkeley: University of California Press, 2010.

Kang, Sun-Ae. "Demonstration for Extending K-Pop Concert in Paris." *My Daily News*, May 2, 2011. Retrieved from http://www.mydaily.co.kr/news/read.html?newsid=201105022031171132

Kang, Yoonhee. "Any One Parent Will Do: Negotiations of Fatherhood among South Korean 'Wild Geese' Fathers in Singapore." *Journal of Korean Studies* 17 (2012): 269–297.

Karim, Karim H. "From Ethnic Media to Global Media: Transnational Communication Networks among Diasporic Communities," WPTC (1998): 99–02.

Karim, Karim. H. *The Media of Diaspora*. London and New York: Routledge, 2003.

Kasinitz, Philip, John H. Mollenkopf, Mary C. Waters, ed. *Becoming New Yorkers: Ethnographies of the New Second Generation*. New York: Russell Sage Foundation, 2004.

Kasinitz, Philip, John H. Mollenkopf, Mary C. Waters, and Jennifer Holdaway. *Inheriting the City: The Children of Immigrants Come of Age*. Cambridge: Harvard University Press, 2008.

Katz, Vikki S. "How Children of Immigrants Use Media to Connect Their Families to the Community: The Case of Latinos in South Los Angeles." *Journal of Children and Media* 4 (2010): 298–315.

Kearney, Michael. "Borders and Boundaries of State and Self at the End of Empire." *Journal of Historical Sociology* 4 (1991): 52–74.

Kearney, Michael. "The Local and the Global: The Anthropology of Globalization and Transnationalism." *Annual Review of Anthropology* 24 (1995): 547–565.

Kelly, Philip. "Canadian-Asian Transnationalism." *The Canadian Geographer* 47 (2003): 209–218.

Kibria, Nazli. "The Construction of 'Asian American': Reflections on Intermarriage and Ethnic Identity among Second-generation Chinese and Korean Americans." *Ethnic and Racial Studies* 20 (1997): 523–544.

Kibria, Nazli. *Becoming Asian American: Second-Generation Chinese and Korean American Identities*. Baltimore: The Johns Hopkins University Press, 2002.

Kibria, Nazli. "Of Blood, Belonging, and Homeland Trips: Transnationalism and Identity among Second-Generation Chinese and Korean Americans," in *The Changing Face of Home: The Transnational Lives of the Second Generation*, edited by Peggy Levitt and Mary Waters, 295–311. New York: Russell Sage Foundation, 2002.

Kim, Chigon. "The Economic Value of Bilingualism among 1.5- and Second-Generation Korean Americans." *Development and Society* 42 (2013): 89–112.

Kim, Chigon. "The Aging Korean Immigrant Population in the United States: Living Arrangements, Health Conditions, and Socio-economic Status of Older Korean

Immigrants." Paper presented to the Research Center for Korean Community (RCKC), Bayside, New York, June 9, 2017.
Kim, Chigon, and Pyong Gap Min. "Marital Patterns and Use of Mother Tongue at Home among Native-Born Asian Americans." *Social Forces* 89 (2010): 233–256.
Kim, Dae Young. *Second-Generation Korean Americans: Their Struggle for Full Inclusion*. El Paso: LFB Scholarly Publishing, 2013.
Kim, Ill Soo. *New Urban Immigrants: The Korean Community in New York*. Princeton: Princeton University Press, 1981.
Kim, Ill Soo. "The Koreans: Small Business in an Urban Frontier," in *New Immigrants in New York*, edited by Nancy Foner. New York: Columbia University Press, 1987.
Kim, Jinwon. "Branding Korea or Marketing Ethnicity?: Manhattan's Koreatown as a Transclave in the Global Economy." PhD diss., CUNY Academic Works, 2016. Retrieved from http://academicworks.cuny.edu/gc_etds/1268
Kim, Kwang Chung, and Won Moo Hurh. "Asian Americans and the 'Success' Image: A Critique." *Amerasia Journal* 10 (1986): 3–21.
Kim, Nadia Y. *Imperial Citizens: Koreans and Race from Seoul to LA*. Stanford: Stanford University Press, 2008.
Kim, Soochul. "Sociocultural Analysis of the Commodification of Ethnic Media and Asian Consumers in Canada." *International Journal of Communication* 5 (2011): 19.
Kim, Youna. *Transnational Migration, Media and Identity of Asian Women: Diasporic Daughters*. London: Routledge, 2011.
Kivisto, Peter. "Theorizing Transnational Migration: A Critical Review of Current Efforts." *Ethnic and Racial Studies* 24 (2001): 549–577.
Kluzer, Stefano, and Cristiano Codagnone. "ICT Adoption by Immigrants and Ethnic Minorities in Europe: Overview of Quantitative Evidence and Discussion of Drivers," in *Migration, Diaspora and Information Technology in Global Societies*, edited by Leopoldina Fortunati, Raul Pertierra, and Jane Vincent, 189–203. New York: Routledge, 2012.
Korea Immigration Service. Gwacheon-si: Ministry of Justice, June 17, 2017. Retrieved from http://www.immigration.go.kr
Korea Times, Washington, D.C. "The Shining of 'Dynamic Korea.'"(in Korean) *The Korea Times, Washington, D.C.*, October 24, 2011.
Korea Times, Washington, D.C. "More Koreans Enter the U.S. without Visas." (in Korean) *The Korea Times, Washington, D.C.*, November 19. 2012.
Korea Times. "44,000 Naturalized Korean Americans Reside in Korea." *The Korea Times*, April 20, 2013. (Dae Yong Chung).
Korea Times, Washington, D.C. "Immigrant Community and Religion." (in Korean) *The Korea Times, Washington, D.C.*, November 1, 2013.
Korea Times, Washington, D.C. "Gains and Losses, Korean Community in Hawaii." (in Korean) *The Korea Times, Washington, D.C.*, December 18, 2013.
Korean American Foundation-Greater Washington (KAFGW). *워싱턴 지역 한인사: 1883–2005*. Fairfax: CNC Printing, 2006. (History of Korean Americans in the Washington Area: 1883–2005).

Korean American Foundation-Greater Washington (KAFGW). *History of Korean Americans in the Washington Area 1883–2005*. Seoul: C&C Media, 2009.

Korean Association of Washington, D.C. (KAW). *워싱턴 한인사: 1883–1993*. Seoul: Baeksan Printing, 1994. (History of Korean Americans in the Washington Area: 1883–1993).

Koreanclick. Nielsen Koreanclick, 2011. Retrieved from http://www.koreanclick.com/index.html

Kwak, Minjung, and Daniel Hiebert. "Globalizing Canadian Education from Below: A Case Study of Transnational Immigrant Entrepreneurship between Seoul, Korea and Vancouver, Canada." *Journal of International Migration and Integration* 11 (2010): 131–153.

Kwon, Okyun. *Buddhist and Protestant Korean Immigrants: Religious Beliefs and Socioeconomic Aspects of Life*. El Paso: LFB Scholarly Publishing, 2003.

Kyle, David. *Transnational Peasants: Migrations, Networks, and Ethnicity in Andean Ecuador*. Baltimore: Johns Hopkins University Press, 2000.

Law, Pui-Lam. "Migrant Workers, New Media Technologies, and Decontextualization: a Preliminary Observation in Southern China," in *Migration, Diaspora and Information Technology in Global Societies*, edited by Leopoldina Fortunati, Raul Pertierra, and Jane Vincent, 207–217. New York: Routledge, 2012.

Lee, Byong Han. "Korean-Owned Drycleaners, 216 Close within 10 Years." (in Korean) *The Korea Times, Washington, D.C.*, September 14, 2012.

Lee, Changho. "Korean Immigrants' Viewing Patterns of Korean Satellite Television and its Role in Their Lives." *Asian Journal of Communication* 14 (2004): 68–80.

Lee, Francis. "Cultural Discount and Cross-Culture Predictability: Examining the Box Office Performance of American Movies in Hong Kong." *Journal of Media Economics* 19 (2006): 259–278.

Lee, Gyu Tag. "De-Nationalization and Re-Nationalization of Culture: The Globalization of K-Pop." PhD diss., George Mason University, 2013.

Lee, Jinah, and Kwangho Lee. "Multilingual Experiences, Media Consumption, and Transnational Identity in a Double Diasporic Context: The Case of Korean-Chinese in Japan." *Keio Communication Review* 37 (2015): 27–39.

Lee, Jong-guk. "Shadows of the Economic Recession Overtaken." (in Korean) *The Korea Times, Washington, D.C.*, 2008.

Lee, Jong-guk. "110 Years of Immigration, The Korean Community in Washington, D.C., Part One." (in Korean) *The Korea Times, Washington, D.C.*, March 11, 2013a.

Lee, Jong-guk. "110 Years of Immigration, The Korean Community in Washington, D.C., Part Two." (in Korean) *The Korea Times, Washington, D.C.*, March 11, 2013b.

Lee, Jong-guk. "The State of the Economy of the Korean Community." (in Korean) *The Korea Times, Washington, D.C.*, 2014a.

Lee, Jong-guk. "The Era of Centreville: The Beginnings of a New Koreatown, Part One." (in Korean) *The Korea Times, Washington, D.C.*, 2014b.

Lee, Jong-guk. "New Koreatown: Centreville, Part Two." (in Korean) *The Korea Times, Washington, D.C.*, April 4, 2015a.

Lee, Jong-guk. "The Korean Community in Washington, D.C. Achieving No Economic Growth." (in Korean) *The Korea Times, Washington, D.C.*, 2015b.

Lee, Sun Kyong, and James E. Katz. "Bounded Solidarity Confirmed? How Korean Immigrants' Mobile Communication Configures Their Social Networks." *Journal of Computer Mediated Communication* 20 (2015): 615–631.

Lee, Wei-Na, and David K. Tse. "Changing Media Consumption in a New Home: Acculturation Patterns among Hong Kong Immigrants to Canada." *Journal of Advertising* 23 (1994): 57–70.

Levitt, Peggy. "Social Remittances: Migration Driven Local-Level Forms of Cultural Diffusion." *The International Migration Review* 32 (1998): 926–948.

Levitt, Peggy. "Transnational Migration: Taking Stock and Future Directions." *Global Networks* 1 (2001a): 195–216.

Levitt, Peggy. *The Transnational Villagers*. Berkeley: University of California Press, 2001b.

Levitt, Peggy, and Mary Waters, ed. *The Changing Face of Home: The Transnational Lives of the Second Generation*. New York: Russell Sage Foundation, 2002.

Levitt, Peggy, and Nina Glick Schiller. "Conceptualizing Simultaneity: A Transnational Social Field Perspective on Society." *International Migration Review* 38 (2004): 1002–1039.

Li, Wei. *Ethnoburb: The New Ethnic Community in Urban America*. Honolulu: University of Hawaii Press, 2009.

Louie, Andrea. "Creating Histories for the Present: Second-Generation (Re)definitions of Chinese American Culture," in *The Changing Face of Home: The Transnational Lives of the Second Generation*, edited by Peggy Levitt and Mary Waters, 312–340. New York: Russell Sage Foundation, 2002.

Madianou, Mirca. "Contested Communicative Spaces: Rethinking Identities, Boundaries and the Role of the Media among Turkish Speakers in Greece." *Journal of Ethnic and Migration Studies* 31 (2005): 521–541.

Madianou, Mirca. "Smartphones as Polymedia." *Journal of Computer-Mediated Communication* 19 (2014): 667–680.

Madianou, Mirca, and Daniel Miller. "Mobile Phone Parenting: Reconfiguring Relationships Between Filipina Migrant Mothers and Their Left-Behind Children." *New Media & Society* 13 (2011): 457–470.

Madianou, Mirca, and Daniel Miller. "Introduction," in *Migration and New Media: Transnational Families and Polymedia*, edited by Mirca Madianou and Daniel Miller. London: Routledge, 2012.

Mahler, Sarah J. "Engendering Transnational Migration A Case Study of Salvadorans." *American Behavioral Scientist* 42 (1999): 690–719.

Mahler, Sarah J. "Transnational Relationships: The Struggle to Communicate across Borders." *Identities Global Studies in Culture and Power* 7 (2001): 583–619.

Mankekar, Purnima. "India Shopping': Indian Grocery Stores and Transnational Configurations of Belonging." *Ethnos* 67 (2002): 75–97.

Manning, Robert. "Multicultural Washington, DC: The Changing Social and Economic Landscape of a Post-industrial Metropolis." *Ethnic and Racial Studies* 21 (1998): 328–355.

Mansumitrchai, Somkiat, Choo-Hui Park, and Candy Lim Chiu. "Factors Underlying the Adoption of Social Network: A Study of Facebook Users in South Korea." *Intern* 7 (2012): 138.

Massey, Douglas S., and Emilio Parrado. "Migradollars: The Remittances and Savings of Mexican Migrants to the USA." *Population Research and Policy Review* 13 (1994): 3–30.

Matsaganis, Matthew D., Sandra J. Ball-Rokeach, and Vikki S Katz. *Understanding Ethnic Media: Producers, Consumers, and Societies*. Thousand Oaks: Sage, 2011.

Matthaei, Julie, and Teresa Amott. "Race, Gender, Work: The History of Asian and Asian-American Women." *Race and Class* 31 (1990): 61–79.

Mayer, Vicki. "Living Telenovelas/Telenovelizing Life: Mexican American Girls' Identities and Transnational Telenovelas." *Journal of Communication* 53 (2003): 479–495.

McCart, Melissa. "A World of Bargains: Asian Supermarkets Attract Chefs and the Budget-Minded." *The Washington Post*, January 7, 2009. Retrieved from http://www.washingtonpost.com/wp-dyn/content/article/2009/01/06/AR2009010600531.html

Menjivar, Cecilia. "Remittance Behavior among Salvadoran and Filipino Immigrants in Los Angeles." *International Migration Review* 32 (1998): 97–126.

Metykova, Monika. "Only a Mouse Click Away from Home: Transnational Practices of Eastern European Migrants in the United Kingdom." *Social Identities* 16 (2010): 325–338.

Miller, Daniel, and Don Slater. *The Internet: An Ethnographic Approach*. Berg, 2000.

Min, Pyong Gap. "The Structure and Social Functions of Korean Immigrant Churches in the United States." *International Migration Review* 26 (1992): 1370–1395.

Min, Pyong Gap. *Asian Americans: Contemporary Trends and Issues*. Newbury Park: Sage Publications, 1995.

Min, Pyong Gap. *Caught in the Middle: Korean Communities in New York and Los Angeles*. Berkeley: University of California Press, 1996.

Min, Pyong Gap. *Changes and Conflicts: Korean Immigrant Families in New York*. Needham Heights: Allyn and Bacon, 1998.

Min, Pyong Gap. *Preserving Ethnicity through Religion in America: Korean Protestants and Indian Hindus across Generations*. New York: New York University Press, 2010.

Min, Pyong Gap. *Ethnic Solidarity for Economic Survival: Korean Greengrocers in New York City*. New York: Russell Sage Foundation, 2011.

Min, Pyong Gap. "Transnational Cultural Activities among Korean Immigrants in the New York-New Jersey Area: A Content Analysis." *재외한인연구 제28호* (2012): 49–83.

Min, Pyong Gap. "Changes in Korean Immigrants' Business Patterns," in *Koreans in North America: Their Twenty-First Century Experiences*, edited by Pyong Gap Min, 57–73. Lanham: Lexington Books, 2013.

Min, Pyong Gap, and Chigon Kim. "Patterns of Intermarriages and Cross-Generational In-Marriages among Native-Born Asian Americans." *The International Migration Review* 43 (2009): 447–470.

Min, Pyong Gap, and Chigon Kim. "Growth and Settlement Patterns of Korean Americans," in *Koreans in North America: Their Twenty-First Century Experiences*, edited by Pyong Gap Min, 35–56. Lanham: Lexington Books, 2013.

Min, Pyong Gap, and Sou Hyun Jang. "The Concentration of Asian Americans in STEM and Health-Care Occupations: An Intergenerational Comparison," *Ethnic and Racial Studies* 38 (2015a): 841–859.

Min, Pyong Gap, and Sou Hyun Jang. "The Diversity of Asian Immigrants' Participation in Religious Institutions in the United States." *Sociology of Religion* 76 (2015b): 253–274.

Min, Pyong Gap, and Young Oak Kim. "Ethnic and Sub-Ethnic Attachments among Chinese, Korean, and Indian Immigrants in New York City." *Ethnic and Racial Studies* 32 (2009): 758–780.

Morello, Carol and Dan Keating. "Va.'s Numbers of Hispanics and Asians Skyrocket as White Population Dwindles." *The Washington Post*, February 4, 2011.

Mōri, Yoshitaka. "Reconsidering Cultural Hybridities: Transnational Exchanges of Popular Music in Between Korea and Japan," in *Cultural Studies and Cultural Industries in Northeastern Asia: What a Difference a Region Makes*, edited by Jonathan D. Mackintosh et al., 213–230. Hong Kong: Hong Kong University Press, 2009.

Mui, Ylan Q. "Tastes from Home: Immigration Feeds Rhee Bros.' Growth." *The Washington Post*, October 16, 2006. Retrieved from https://www.washingtonpost.com/archive/business/2006/10/16/tastes-from-home-span-classbank-headimmigration-feeds-rhee-bros-growth-span/fd5a35a3–375d-46d3–8f77–4a4a33d1f7d9/?utm_term=.65d5ea3750e5

National Retail Federation (NRF). "Hot 100 Chart 2014." National Retail Federation, 2014. Retrieved from https://nrf.com/2014/hot100-table

Nedelcu, Mihaela. "Migrants' New Transnational Habitus: Rethinking Migration through a Cosmopolitan Lens in the Digital Age." *Journal of Ethnic and Migration Studies* 38 (2012): 1339–1356.

Noh, Samuel, Min-Jung Kwak and Joe J. H. Han. "Transnational Interactions among Korean Immigrants in Toronto," in *Koreans in North America: Their Twenty-First Century Experiences*, edited by Pyong Gap Min, 121–134. Lanham: Lexington Books, 2013.

O'Brien, Eileen. *The Racial Middle: Latinos and Asian Americans Living Beyond the Racial Divide*. New York: New York University Press, 2008.

Oghuma, Apollos, Younghoon Chang, Christian Libaque-Saenz, Myeong-Cheol Park, and Jae Jeung Rho. "Benefit-Confirmation Model for Post-Adoption Behavior of Mobile Instant Messaging Applications: A Comparative Analysis of Kakaotalk and Joyn in Korea." *Telecommunications Policy* 39 (2015): 658–677.

Oh, David C. "Mediating the Boundaries Second-Generation Korean American Adolescents' Use of Transnational Korean Media as Markers of Social Boundaries." *International Communication Gazette* 74 (2012): 258–276.

Oh, David C. *Second-Generation Korean Americans and Transnational Media: Diasporic Identifications*. Lanham: Lexington Books, 2015.

Oh, Joong-Hwan. "Immigration and Social Capital in a Korean-American Women's Online Community: Supporting Acculturation, Cultural Pluralism, and Transnationalism." *New Media & Society* 18 (2016): 2224–2241.

Oh, Joong-Hwan. *Immigration and Social Capital in the Age of Social Media*. Lanham: Lexington Books, 2016.

Oh, Sookhee, and Pyong Gap Min. "Generation and Earnings Patterns among Chinese, Filipino, and Korean Americans in New York." *The International Migration Review* 45 (2011): 852–871.

Ong, Aiwha. *Flexible Citizenship: The Cultural Logics of Transnationality*, 2nd *Edition*. Durham: Duke University Press, 1999.

Panagakos, Anastasia. "Downloading New Identities: Ethnicity, Technology, and Media in the Global Greek Village." *Identities: Global Studies in Culture and Power* 10 (2003): 201–219.

Panagakos, Anastasia, and Heather Horst. "Return to Cyberia: Technology and the Social Worlds of Transnational Migrants." *Global Networks* 6 (2006): 109–124.

Paragas Fernando. "Migrant Workers and Mobile Phones: Technological, Temporal, and Spatial Simultaneity," in *The Reconstruction of Space and Time: Mobile Communication Practices*, edited by Rich Ling and Scott Campbell, 39–66. New Brunswick: Transaction, 2009.

Park, Jung-Sun. "Korean American Youth and Transnational Flows of Popular Culture across the Pacific." *Amerasia Journal* 30 (2004): 147–169.

Park, Keumjae. "Constructing Transnational Identities without Leaving Home: Korean Immigrant Women's Cognitive Border-Crossing." *Sociological Forum* 22 (2007): 200–218.

Park, Keumjae. *Korean Immigrant Women and the Renegotiation of Identity: Class, Gender, and the Politics of Identity*. El Paso: LFB Scholarly Publishing, 2009.

Park, Kyeyoung. *The Korean American Dream: Immigrants and Small Business in New York City*. Ithaca: Cornell University Press, 1997.

Park, So Jin, and Nancy Abelmann. "Class and Cosmopolitan Striving: Mothers' Management of English Education in South Korea." *Anthropological Quarterly* 77 (2004): 645–672.

Parreñas, Rhacel Salazar. "Mothering from a Distance: Emotions, Gender, and Intergenerational Relations in Filipino Transnational Families." *Feminist Studies* 27 (2001): 361–390.

Parrenas, Rhacel. "Transgressing the Nation-State: The Partial Citizenship and 'Imagined (Global) Community' of Migrant Filipina Domestic Workers." *Signs* 26 (2001): 1129–1154.

Parreñas, Rhacel. "Long Distance Intimacy: Class, Gender and Intergenerational Relations between Mothers and Children in Filipino Transnational Families." *Global Networks* 5 (2005): 317–336.

Parreñas, Rhacel. "Transnational Fathering: Gendered Conflicts, Distant Disciplining and Emotional Gaps." *Journal of Ethnic and Migration Studies* 34 (2008): 1057–1072.

Patterson, Wayne. *The Korean Frontier in America: Immigration to Hawaii*, 1896–1910. Honolulu: University of Hawaii Press, 1988.

Pease, Rowan. "Korean Pop Music in China: Nationalism, Authenticity, and Gender," in *Cultural Studies and Cultural Industries in Northeastern Asia: What a Difference a Region Makes*, edited by Jonathan D. Mackintosh et al., 151–167. Hong Kong: Hong Kong University Press, 2009.

Pew Research Center. *The Rise of Asian Americans*. Washington, DC: Pew Social and Demographic Trends, 2012.

Portes, Alejandro. "Introduction: The Debates and Significance of Immigrant Transnationalism." *Global Networks* 1 (2001): 181–193.

Portes, Alejandro. "Conclusion: Theoretical Convergencies and Empirical Evidence in the Study of Immigrant Transnationalism." *International Migration Review* 37 (2003): 874–892.

Portes, Alejandro, and Ruben Rumbaut. *Immigrant America: A Portrait*. 4th Edition. Berkeley: University of California Press, 2014.

Portes, Alejandro, Cristina Escobar, and Renelinda Arana. "Bridging the Gap: Transnational and Ethnic Organizations in the Political Incorporation of Immigrants in the United States." *Ethnic and Racial Studies* 31 (2008): 1056–1090.

Portes, Alejandro, Luis Guarnizo, and Patricia Landolt. "The Study of Transnationalism: Pitfalls and Promise of an Emergent Research Field." *Ethnic and Racial Studies* 22 (1999): 217–237.

Portes, Alejandro, Luis Guarnizo, and William Haller. "Transnational Entrepreneurs: An Alternative Form of Immigrant Economic Adaptation." *American Sociological Review*, 67 (2002): 278–298.

Price, Marie, and Audrey Singer. "Edge gateways: Suburbs, Immigrants and the Politics of Reception in Metropolitan Washington," in *Twenty-First Century Immigrant Gateways*, edited by Henry G. Cisneros, Audrey Singer, Susan W. Hardwick, and Caroline B. Brettell, 137–168. Washington, DC: Brookings Institution Press, 2008.

Repak, Terry. *Waiting on Washington: Central American Workers in the Nation's Capital*. Philadelphia: Temple University Press, 1995.

Ritzer, George. *Globalization: The Essentials*. West Sussex: Wiley-Blackwell, 2011.

Ros, Adela. "Interconnected Immigrants in the Information Society," in *Diasporas in the New Media Age: Identity, Politics, and Community*, edited by Andoni Alonso and Pedro J. Oiarzabal, 19–38. Las Vegas: University of Nevada Press, 2008.

Ruggles, Steven, Matthew Sobek, Trent Alexander, Catherine A. Fitch, Ronald Goeken, Patricia Kelly Hall, Miriam King, and Chad Ronnander. *Integrated Public Use Microdata Series: Version 3.0* [Machine-readable database]. Minneapolis: Minnesota Population Center, 2004. [producer and distributor].

Rusinovic, Katja. *Dynamic Entrepreneurship: First and Second-Generation Immigrant Entrepreneurs in Dutch Cities*. Amsterdam: Amsterdam University Press, 2006.

Ryu, Jung Il. "South Korean Capital Also 'Call for Buy' American Real Estate." (in Korean) *The Korea Times*, October 2, 2015.

Seminara, Dave. "Koreans Make Their Mark in Fairfax." *Fairfax Times*. October 5, 2011.

Shi, Yu. "Identity Construction of the Chinese Diaspora, Ethnic Media Use, Community Formation, and the Possibility of Social Activism." *Continuum* 19 (2005): 55–72.

Shim, Doobo. "The Growth of Korean Cultural Industries and the Korean Wave," in *East Asian Pop Culture: Analyzing the Korean Wave*, edited by Chua Beng Huat and Koichi Iwabuchi, 15–32. Hong Kong: Hong Kong University Press, 2008.

Shim, J. P., Sasha Dekleva, Aaron M. French, and Chengqi Guo. "Social Networking and Social Media in the United States, South Korea, and China." *Communications of the Association for Information Systems* 33 (2013): 485–496.

Shutika, Debra Lattanzi. *Beyond the Borderlands: Migration and Belonging in the United States and Mexico*. Berkeley: University of California Press, 2011.

Silverstone, Roger. "Television, Ontological Security and the Transitional Object." *Media, Culture & Society* 15 (1993): 573–598.

Silverstone, Roger. *Television and Everyday Life*. London: Routledge, 1994.

Sklair, Leslie. *The Transnational Capitalist Class*. Oxford: Wiley-Blackwell, 2001.

Skop, Emily, and Paul C. Adams. "Creating and Inhabiting Virtual Places: Indian Immigrants in Cyberspace." *National Identities* 11 (2009): 127–147.

Smith, Michael Peter, and Luis Guarnizo, ed. *Transnationalism from Below*. New Brunswick: Transaction Publishers, 1998.

Smith, Robert C. *Mexican New York: Transnational Lives of New Immigrants*. Berkeley: University of California Press, 2006.

Solorzano, Daniel, Miguel Ceja, and Tara Yosso. "Critical Race Theory, Racial Microaggressions, and Campus Racial Climate: The Experiences of African American College Students." *The Journal of Negro Education* 69 (2000): 60–73.

Son, Juyeon. "Immigrant Incorporation, Technology, and Transnationalism among Korean American Women." *Journal of International Migration and Integration* 16 (2015): 377–395.

Steger, Manfred B. *Globalization: A Short Introduction*. London: Oxford University Press, 2009.

Sung, Sang-Yeon. "The *Hanliu* Phenomenon in Taiwan: TV Dramas and Teenage Pop," in *Korean Pop Music: Riding the Wave*, edited by Keith Howard, 168–175. Folkestone: Global Oriental, 2006.

Taylor, J. Edward. "The New Economics of Labour Migration and the Role of Remittances in the Migration Process." *International Migration* 37 (1999): 63–86.

The World Bank. "Migration and Remittances Data." Washington, DC: The World Bank, 2011.

Thompson, Kenneth. "Border Crossings and Diasporic Identities: Media Use and Leisure Practices of an Ethnic Minority." *Qualitative Sociology* 25 (2002): 409–418.

Tsuda, Takeyuki. *Strangers in the Ethnic Homeland: Japanese Brazilian Return Migration in Transnational Perspective*. New York: Columbia University Press, 2003.

Ugaya, Hiromichi. *What is J-pop* (in Japanese). Tokyo: Iwamura Shoten, 2005.

Urry, John. *The Tourist Gaze*. Thousand Oaks: Sage, 2002.

Uy-Tioco. C. "Overseas Filipino Workers and Text Messaging: Reinventing Transnational Mothering." *Continuum* 21 (2007): 253–265.

Vasquez, Jessica M. *Mexican Americans across Generations: Immigrant Families, Racial Realities*. New York: New York University Press, 2011.

Vertovec, Steven. "Cheap Calls: The Social Glue of Migrant Transnationalism." *Global Networks* 4 (2004): 219–224.

Vertovec, Steven. *Transnationalism (Key Ideas)*. London: Routledge, 2007.

Vickerman, Milton. "Second-Generation West Indian Transnationalism," in *The Changing Face of Home: The Transnational Lives of the Second Generation*, edited by Peggy Levitt and Mary Waters, 341–366. New York: Russell Sage Foundation, 2002.

Vu, Hong Tien, and Tien-Tsung Lee. "Soap Operas as a Matchmaker a Cultivation Analysis of the Effects of South Korean TV Dramas on Vietnamese Women's Marital Intentions." *Journalism & Mass Communication Quarterly* 90 (2013): 308–330.

Waldinger, Roger. "Between Here and There: How Attached Are Latino Immigrants to Their Native Country?" *Pew Hispanic Center Report* (2007): 1–23.

Waldinger, Roger. "Between 'Here' and 'There': Immigrant Cross-Border Activities and Loyalties." *International Migration Review* 42 (2008): 3–29.

Waldinger, Roger. *The Cross-Border Connection: Immigrants, Emigrants, and Their Homelands*. Cambridge: Harvard University Press, 2015.

Waldinger, Roger, and David Fitzgerald. "Transnationalism in Question." *American Journal of Sociology* 109 (2004): 1177–1195.

Waldinger, Roger, Thomas Soehl, and Nelson Lim. "Emigrants and the Body Politic Left Behind: Results from the Latino National Survey." *Journal of Ethnic and Migration Studies* 38 (2012): 711–736.

Waters, Johanna L. "Flexible Families? 'Astronaut' Households and the Experiences of Lone Mothers in Vancouver, British Columbia," *Social & Cultural Geography* 3 (2002): 117–134.

Waters, Johanna. "Transnational Family Strategies and Education in the Contemporary Chinese Diaspora." *Global Networks* 5 (2005): 359–377.

Waters, Johanna. "Geographies of Cultural Capital: Education, International Migration and Family Strategies between Hong Kong and Canada." *Transactions of the Institute of British Geographers, New Series* 31 (2006): 179–192.

Waters, Johanna, and Rachel Brooks. "Accidental Achievers? International Higher Education, Class Reproduction and Privilege in the Experiences of UK Students Overseas." *British Journal of Sociology of Education* 31 (2010): 217–228.

Wayland, Sarah. "The Politics of Transnationalism: Comparative Perspectives," in *Transnational Identities and Practices in Canada*, edited by Vic Satzewich and Lloyd Wong, 18–34. Vancouver: University of British Columbia Press, 2006.

Wilding, Raelene. "'Virtual' Intimacies? Families Communicating across Transnational Contexts." *Global Networks* 6 (2006): 125–142.

Wolf, Diane. "There's No Place Like 'Home': Emotional Transnationalism and the Struggles of Second-Generation Filipinos," in *The Changing Face of Home: The Transnational Lives of the Second Generation*, edited by Peggy Levitt and Mary Waters. New York: Russell Sage Foundation, 2002.

Wong, Lloyd and Vic Satzewich. "Introduction: The Meaning and Significance of Transnationalism," in *Transnational Identities and Practices in Canada*, edited by

Vic Satzewich and Lloyd Wong, 1–17. Vancouver: University of British Columbia Press, 2006.

Yin, Hang. "Chinese-Language Cyberspace, Homeland Media and Ethnic Media: A Contested Space for Being Chinese." *New Media & Society* 17 (2015): 556–572.

Yoon, In-Jin. *On My Own: Korean Businesses and Race Relations in America*. Chicago: University of Chicago Press, 1997.

Yoon, Kyong. "The Cultural Appropriation of Smartphones in Korean Transnational Families," in *Mobile Communication and the Family—Asian Experiences in Technology Domestication*, edited by Sun Sun Lim. Springer Netherlands, 2016a.

Yoon, Kyong. "Korean Migrants' Use of the Internet in Canada." *Journal of International Migration and Integration* (2016b): 1–16.

Yoon, Sung-won. "Koreans Use Smartphones for Over 3 Hours a Day." *The Korea Times*, December 2014.

Yoon, Won K. *Global Pulls on the Korean Communities in Sao Paulo and Buenos Aires*. Lanham: Lexington Books, 2015.

Yu, Eui Young. "Korean Communities in America: Past, Present, and Future," *Amerasia Journal* 10 (1983): 23–51.

Zhou, Min, and Guoxuan Cai. "Chinese language media in the United States: Immigration and assimilation in American life." *Qualitative Sociology* 25 (2002): 419–441.

Index

About the Author

Dae Young Kim is associate professor of sociology in the Department of Sociology and Anthropology at George Mason University.

www.ingramcontent.com/pod-product-compliance
Ingram Content Group UK Ltd.
Pitfield, Milton Keynes, MK11 3LW, UK
UKHW040154091026
15587UKWH00018B/223

9 781498 541756